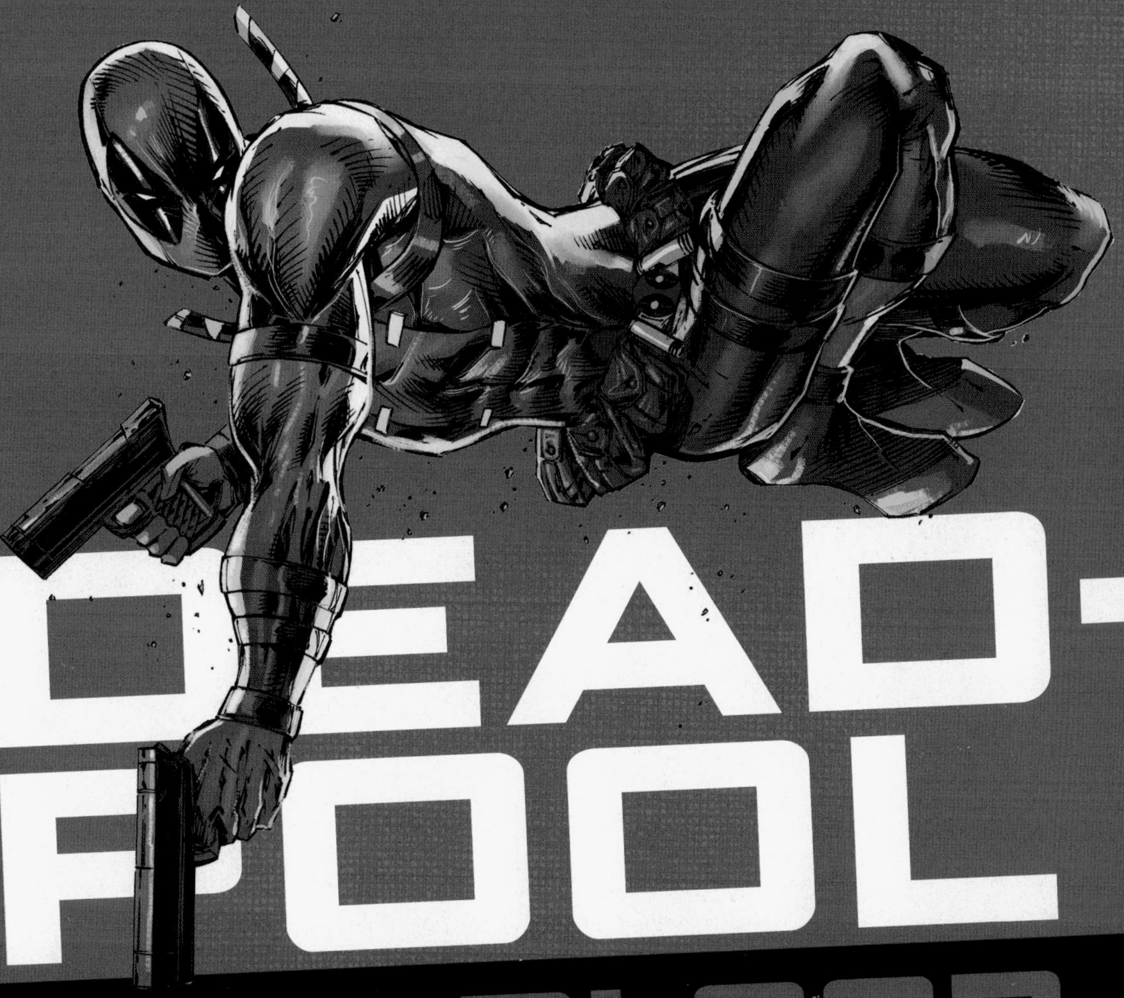

DEAD-POOL

BAD BLOOD

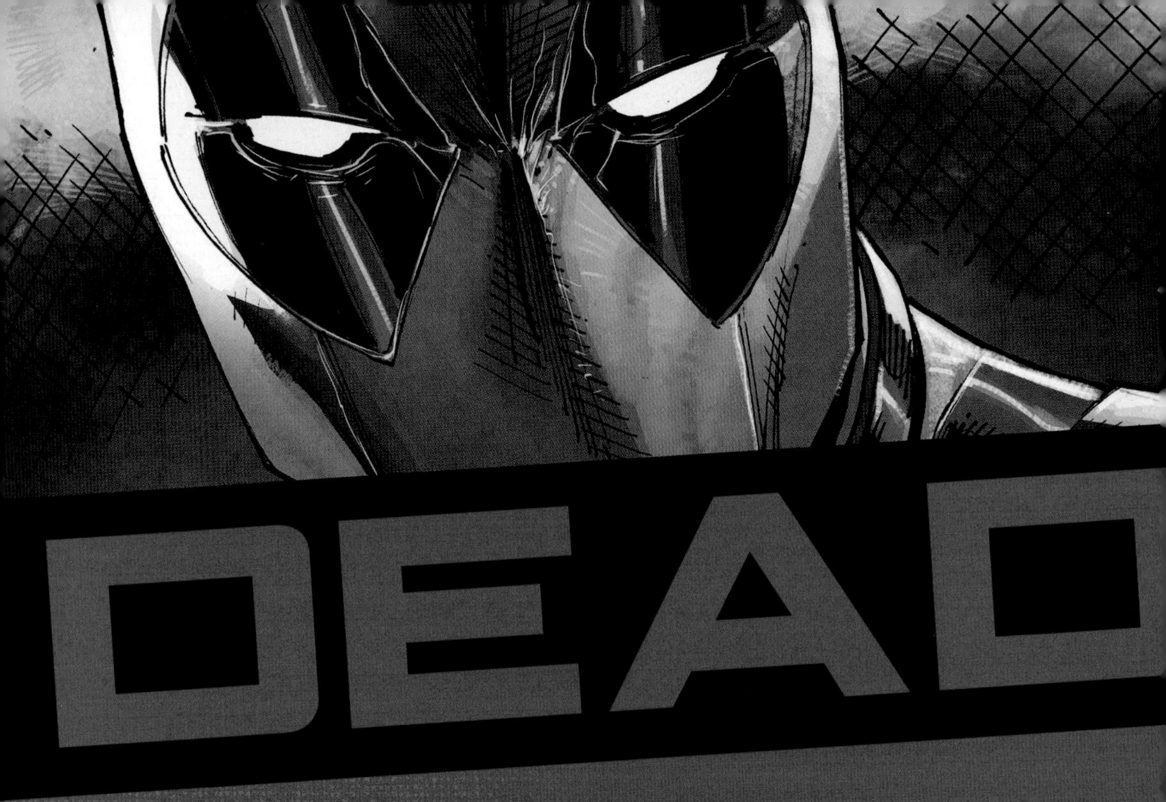
DEAD

COLLECTION EDITOR JENNIFER GRÜNWALD • ASSISTANT EDITOR CAITLIN O'CONNELL
ASSOCIATE MANAGING EDITOR KATERI WOODY • EDITOR, SPECIAL PROJECTS MARK D. BEAZLEY
VP PRODUCTION & SPECIAL PROJECTS JEFF YOUNGQUIST • SVP PRINT, SALES & MARKETING DAVID GABRIEL
BOOK DESIGNER JAY BOWEN

EDITOR IN CHIEF AXEL ALONSO • CHIEF CREATIVE OFFICER JOE QUESADA
PRESIDENT DAN BUCKLEY • EXECUTIVE PRODUCER ALAN FINE

BAD BLOOD
POOL

STORY
ROB LIEFELD

SCRIPT
CHRIS SIMS & CHAD BOWERS

PENCILER
ROB LIEFELD

INKERS
ROB LIEFELD, SHELBY ROBERTSON, ADELSO CORONA & MARAT MYCHAELS

COLOR ARTIST
ROMULO FAJARDO JR.

LETTERER
VC's JOE SABINO

ASSISTANT EDITOR
HEATHER ANTOS

EDITOR
JORDAN D. WHITE

DEADPOOL CREATED BY
ROB LIEFELD & FABIAN NICIEZA

DEADPOOL: BAD BLOOD. First printing 2017. ISBN# 978-1-302-90153-0. Published by MARVEL WORLDWIDE, INC., a subsidiary of MARVEL ENTERTAINMENT, LLC. OFFICE OF PUBLICATION: 135 West 50th Street, N
York, NY 10020. Copyright © 2017 MARVEL No similarity between any of the names, characters, persons, and/or institutions in this magazine with those of any living or dead person or institution is intended, and
such similarity which may exist is purely coincidental. **Printed in the U.S.A.** DAN BUCKLEY, President, Marvel Entertainment; JOE QUESADA, Chief Creative Officer; TOM BREVOORT, SVP of Publishing; DAVID BOGART, N
of Business Affairs & Operations, Publishing & Partnership; C.B. CEBULSKI, VP of Brand Management & Development, Asia; DAVID GABRIEL, SVP of Sales & Marketing, Publishing; JEFF YOUNGQUIST, VP of Productic
Special Projects; DAN CARR, Executive Director of Publishing Technology; ALEX MORALES, Director of Publishing Operations; SUSAN CRESPI, Production Manager; STAN LEE, Chairman Emeritus. For information regard
advertising in Marvel Comics or on Marvel.com, please contact Vit DeBellis, Integrated Sales Manager, at vdebellis@marvel.com. For Marvel subscription inquiries, please call 888-511-5480. **Manufactured betw**
3/10/2017 and 4/11/2017 by WORZALLA PUBLISHING CO., STEVENS POINT, WI, USA.

10 9 8 7 6 5 4 3 2 1

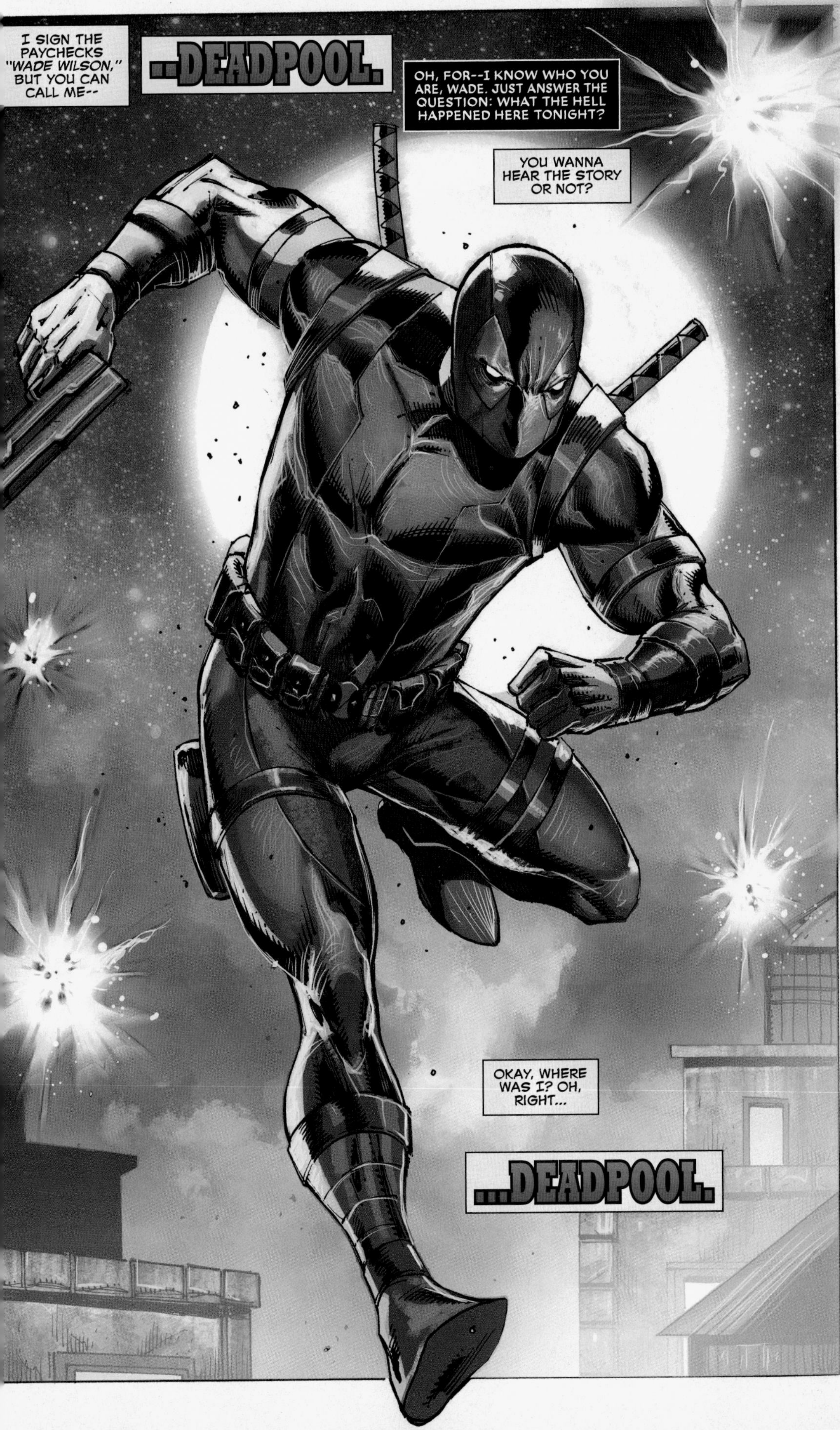
I SIGN THE PAYCHECKS "WADE WILSON," BUT YOU CAN CALL ME--
...DEADPOOL.
OH, FOR--I KNOW WHO YOU ARE, WADE. JUST ANSWER THE QUESTION: WHAT THE HELL HAPPENED HERE TONIGHT?
YOU WANNA HEAR THE STORY OR NOT?
OKAY, WHERE WAS I? OH, RIGHT...
...DEADPOOL.

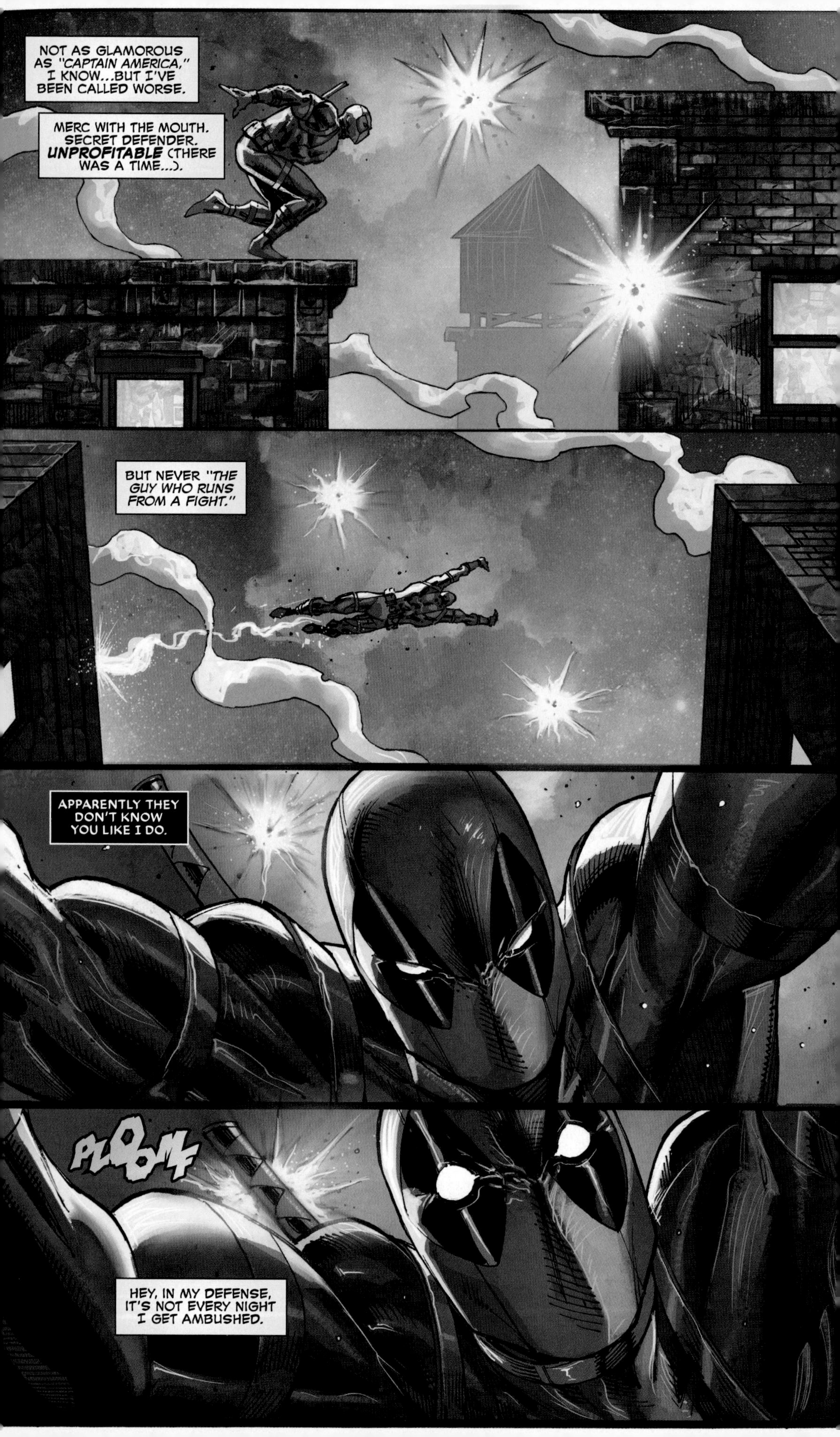
NOT AS GLAMOROUS AS "CAPTAIN AMERICA," I KNOW...BUT I'VE BEEN CALLED WORSE.
MERC WITH THE MOUTH. SECRET DEFENDER. UNPROFITABLE (THERE WAS A TIME...).
BUT NEVER "THE GUY WHO RUNS FROM A FIGHT."
APPARENTLY THEY DON'T KNOW YOU LIKE I DO.
PLOOMF
HEY, IN MY DEFENSE, IT'S NOT EVERY NIGHT I GET AMBUSHED.

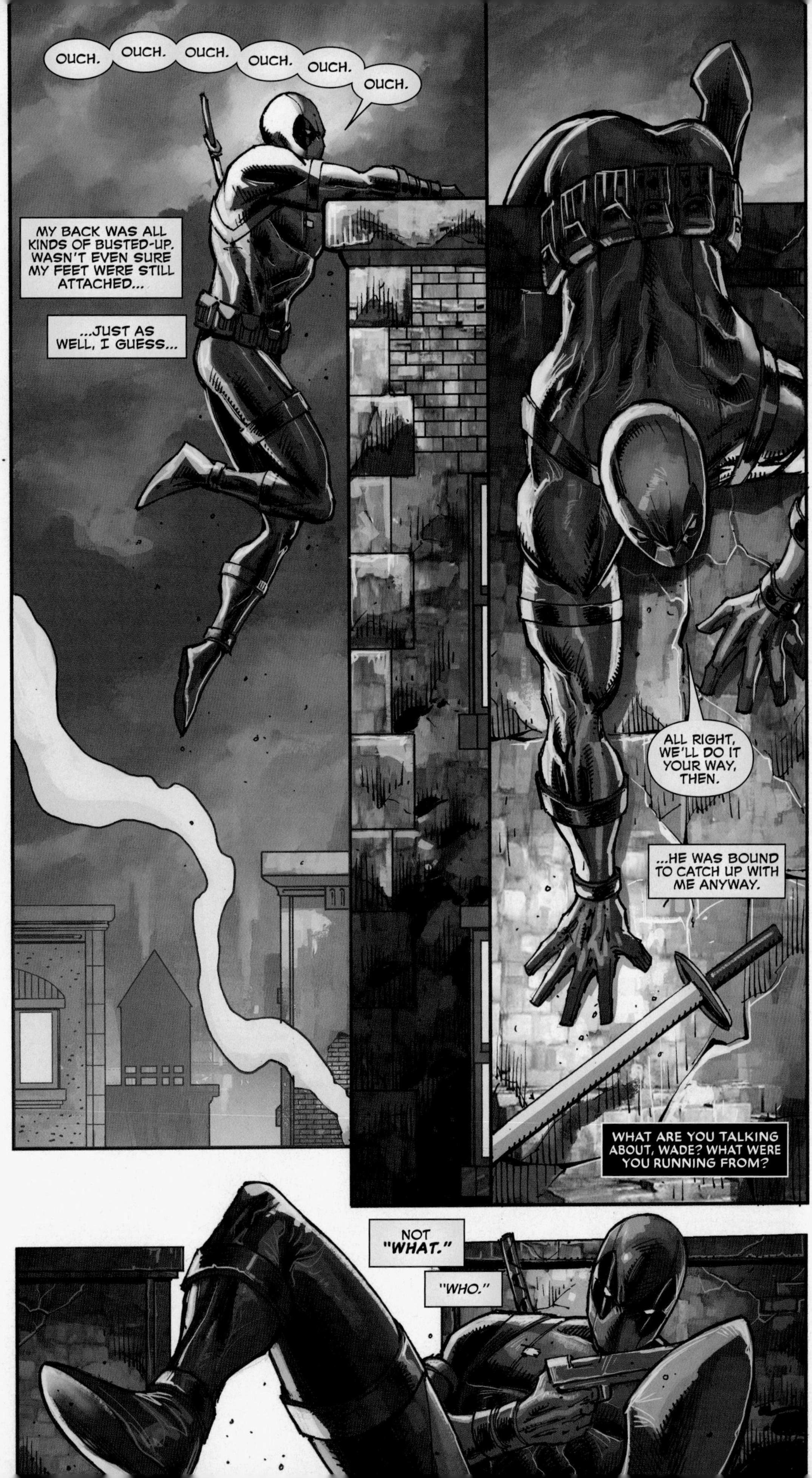
OUCH.
OUCH.
OUCH.
OUCH.
OUCH.
OUCH.
MY BACK WAS ALL KINDS OF BUSTED-UP. WASN'T EVEN SURE MY FEET WERE STILL ATTACHED...
...JUST AS WELL, I GUESS...
ALL RIGHT, WE'LL DO IT YOUR WAY, THEN.
...HE WAS BOUND TO CATCH UP WITH ME ANYWAY.
WHAT ARE YOU TALKING ABOUT, WADE? WHAT WERE YOU RUNNING FROM?
NOT "WHAT."
"WHO."

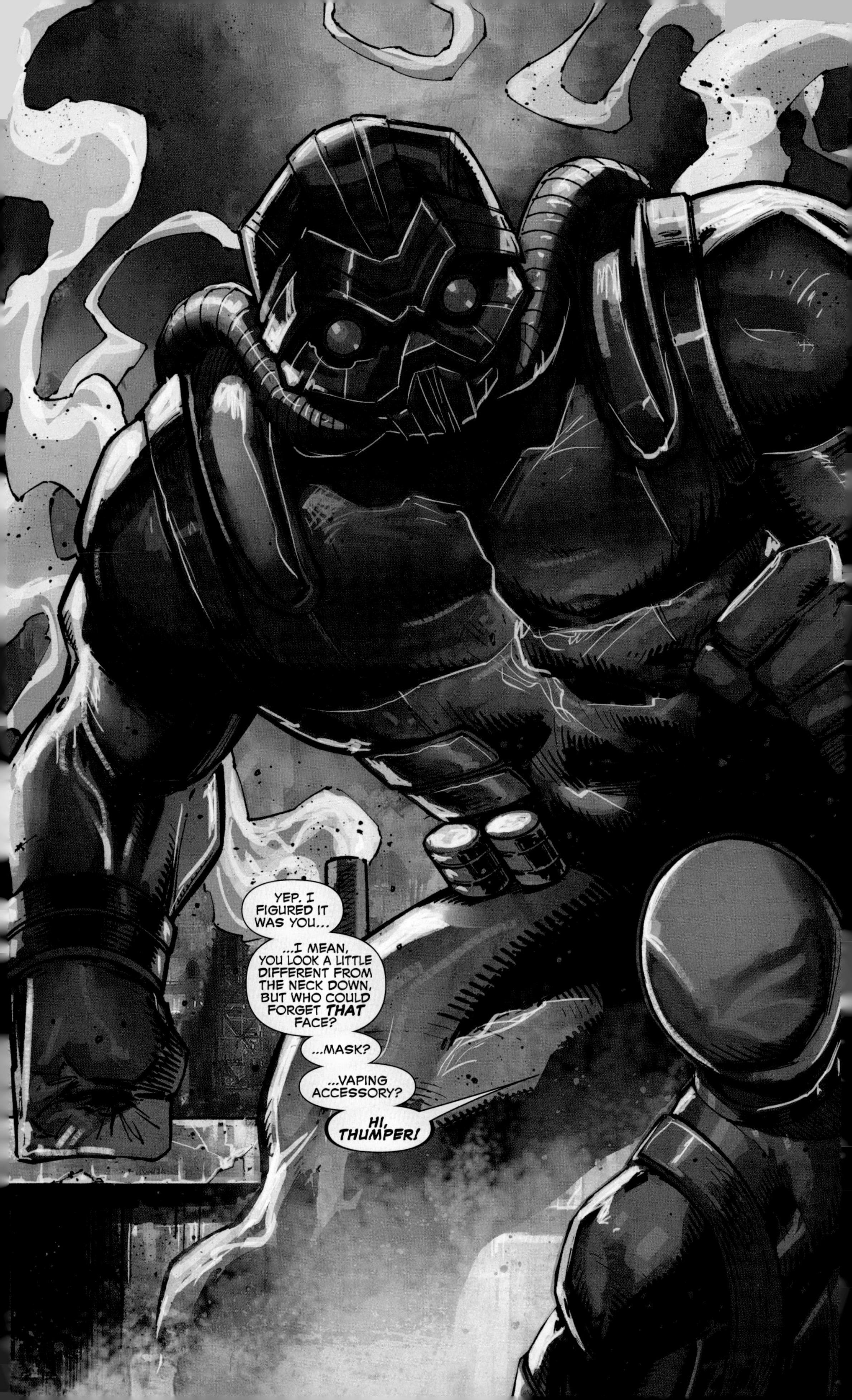
YEP. I FIGURED IT WAS YOU...
...I MEAN, YOU LOOK A LITTLE DIFFERENT FROM THE NECK DOWN, BUT WHO COULD FORGET *THAT* FACE?
...MASK?
...VAPING ACCESSORY?
HI, THUMPER!

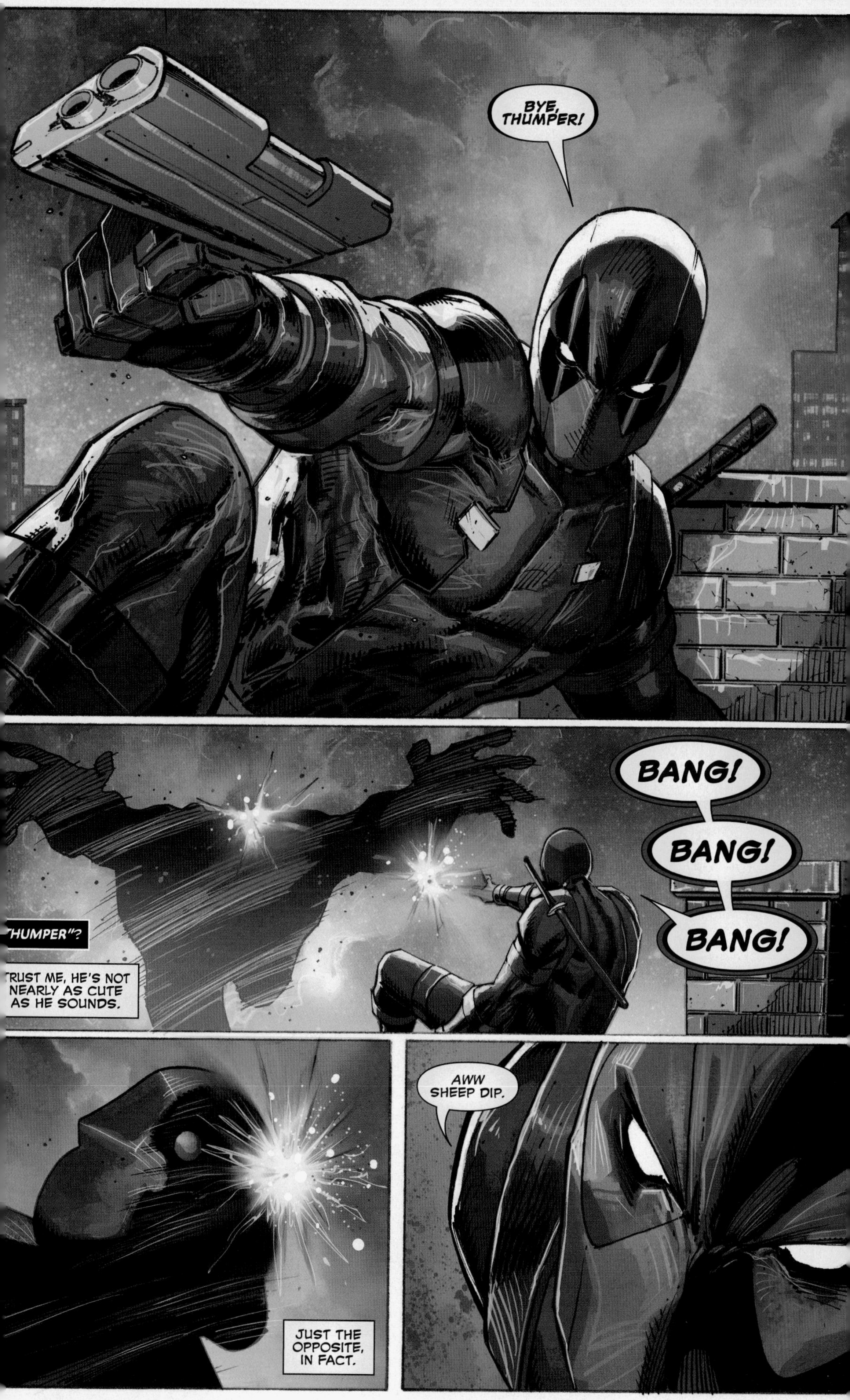
BYE, THUMPER!
BANG!
BANG!
BANG!
"THUMPER"?
TRUST ME, HE'S NOT NEARLY AS CUTE AS HE SOUNDS.
JUST THE OPPOSITE, IN FACT.
AWW SHEEP DIP.

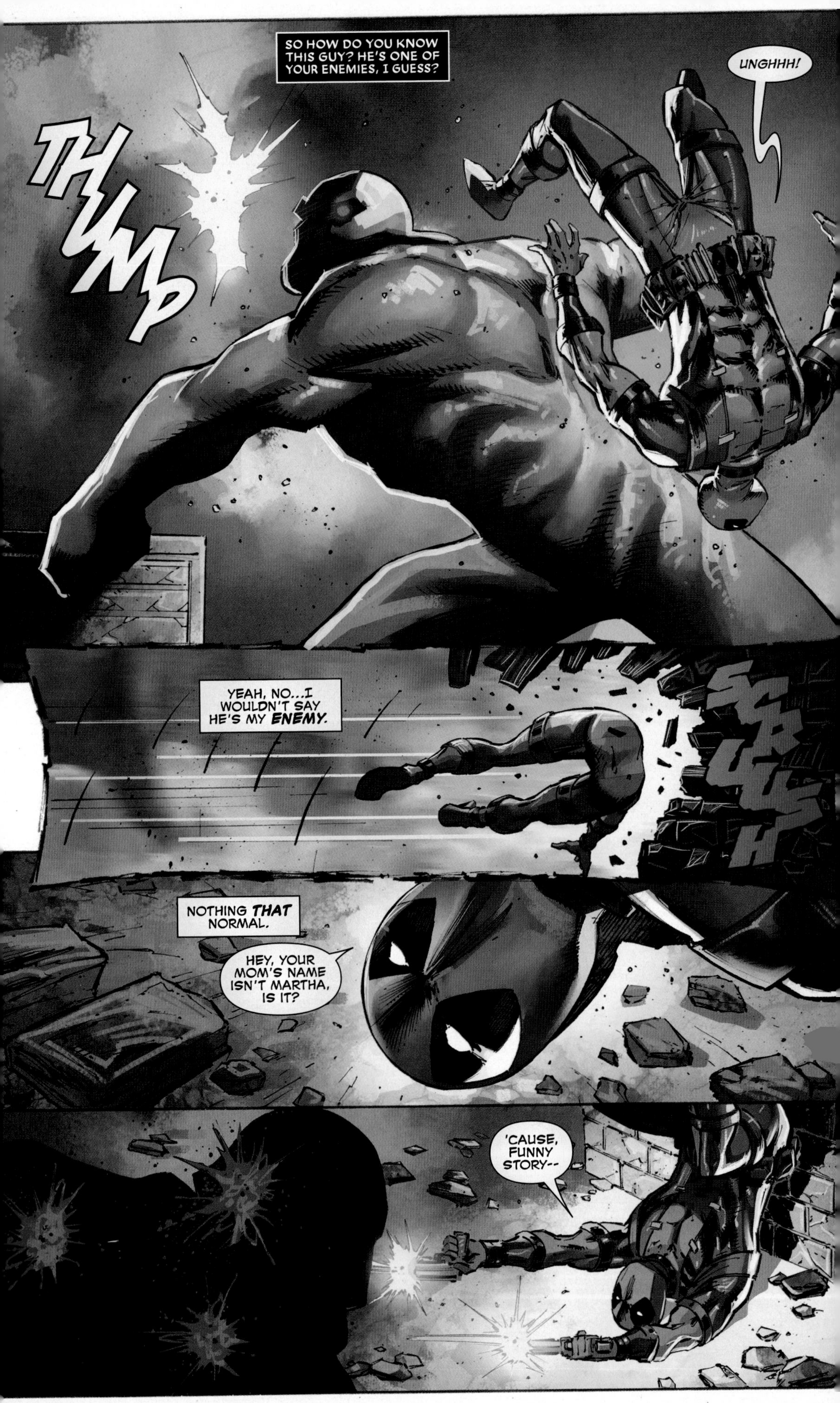
SO HOW DO YOU KNOW THIS GUY? HE'S ONE OF YOUR ENEMIES, I GUESS?
UNGHHH!
THUMP
YEAH, NO...I WOULDN'T SAY HE'S MY ENEMY.
SCRUNSH
NOTHING THAT NORMAL.
HEY, YOUR MOM'S NAME ISN'T MARTHA, IS IT?
'CAUSE, FUNNY STORY--

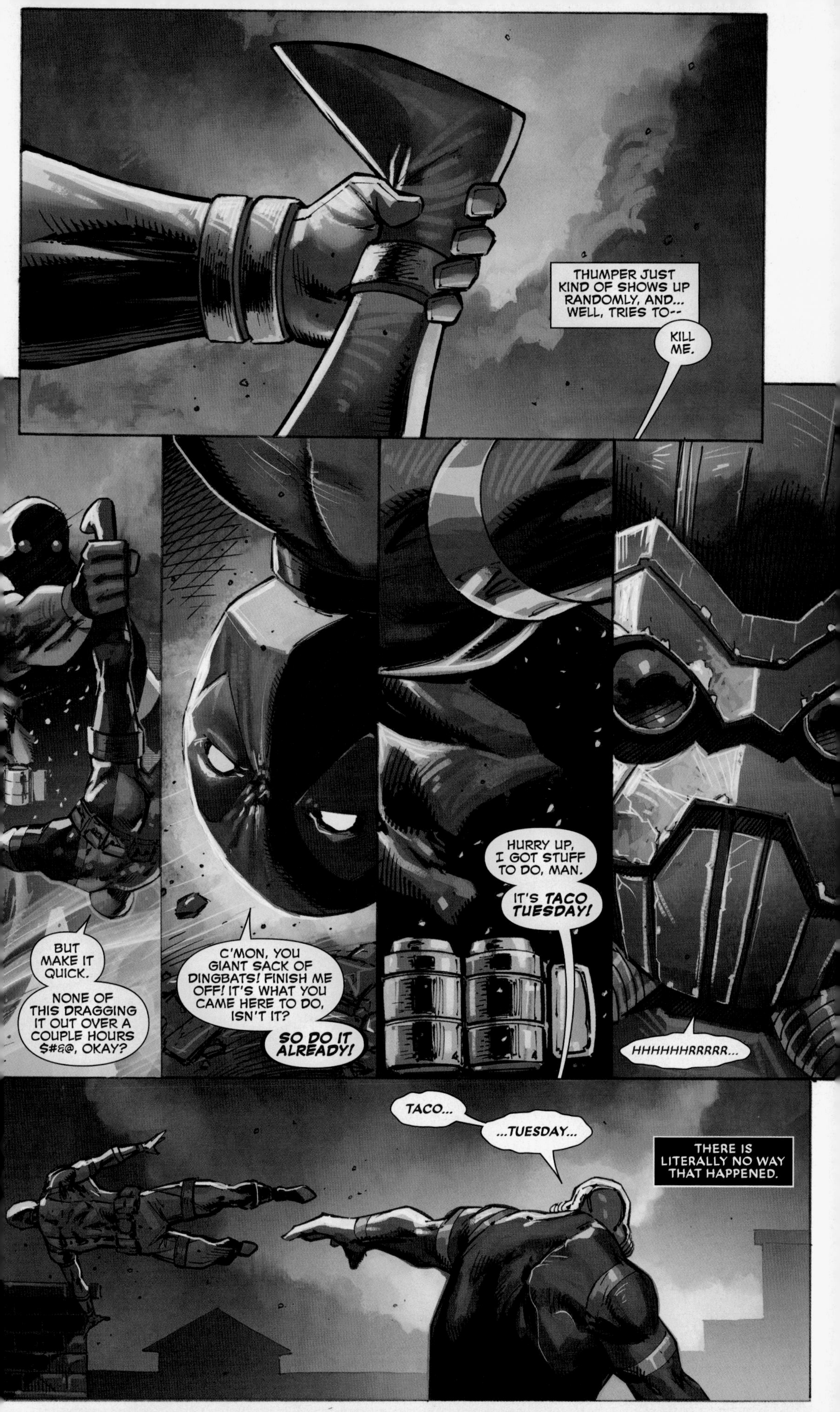
THUMPER JUST KIND OF SHOWS UP RANDOMLY, AND... WELL, TRIES TO--
KILL ME.
BUT MAKE IT QUICK.
NONE OF THIS DRAGGING IT OUT OVER A COUPLE HOURS $#&@, OKAY?
C'MON, YOU GIANT SACK OF DINGBATS! FINISH ME OFF! IT'S WHAT YOU CAME HERE TO DO, ISN'T IT?
SO DO IT ALREADY!
HURRY UP, I GOT STUFF TO DO, MAN.
IT'S TACO TUESDAY!
HHHHHHRRRRR...
TACO...
...TUESDAY...
THERE IS LITERALLY NO WAY THAT HAPPENED.

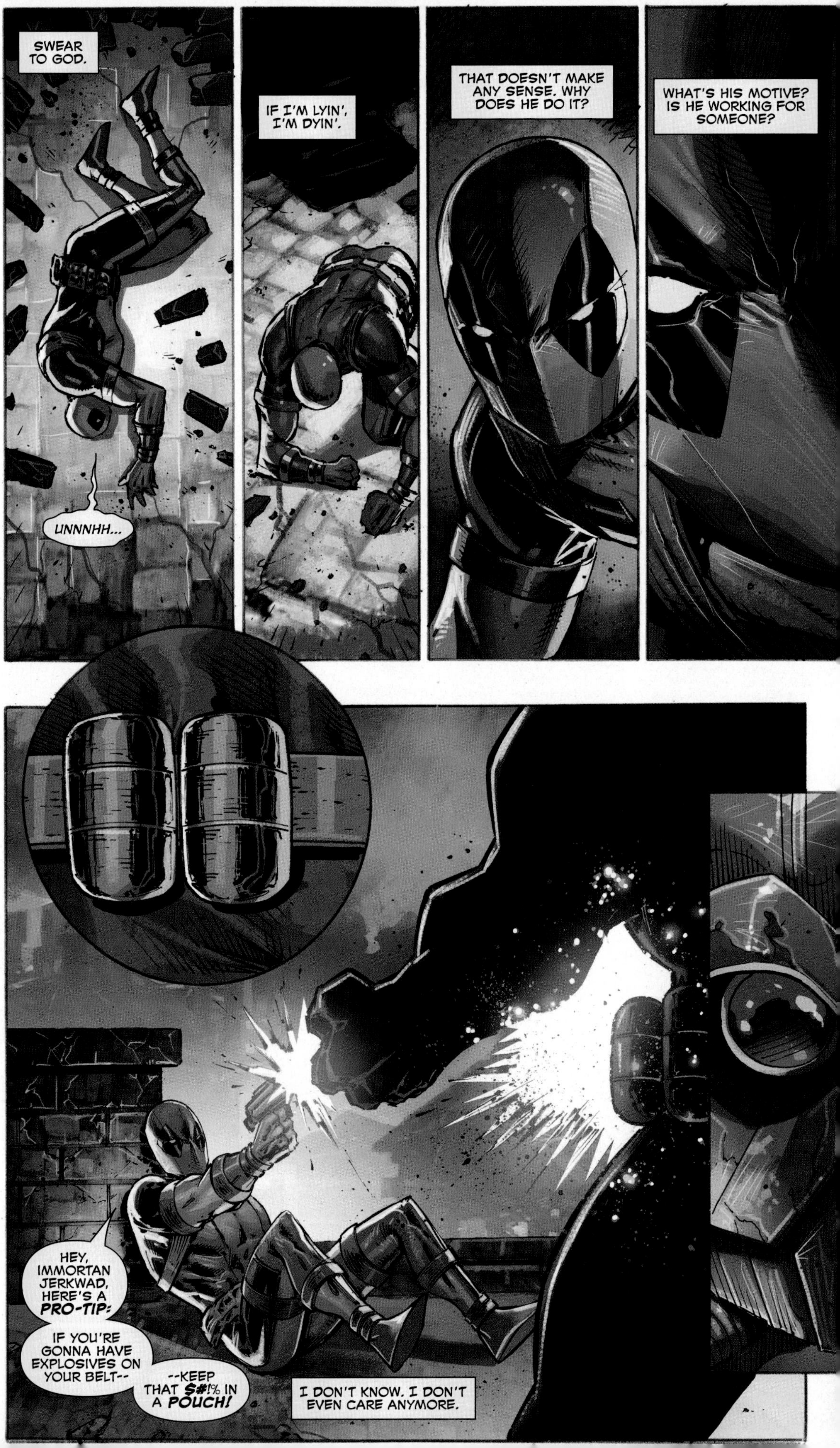
SWEAR TO GOD.
UNNNHH...
IF I'M LYIN', I'M DYIN'.
THAT DOESN'T MAKE ANY SENSE. WHY DOES HE DO IT?
WHAT'S HIS MOTIVE? IS HE WORKING FOR SOMEONE?
HEY, IMMORTAN JERKWAD, HERE'S A PRO-TIP:
IF YOU'RE GONNA HAVE EXPLOSIVES ON YOUR BELT--
--KEEP THAT $#!% IN A POUCH!
I DON'T KNOW. I DON'T EVEN CARE ANYMORE.

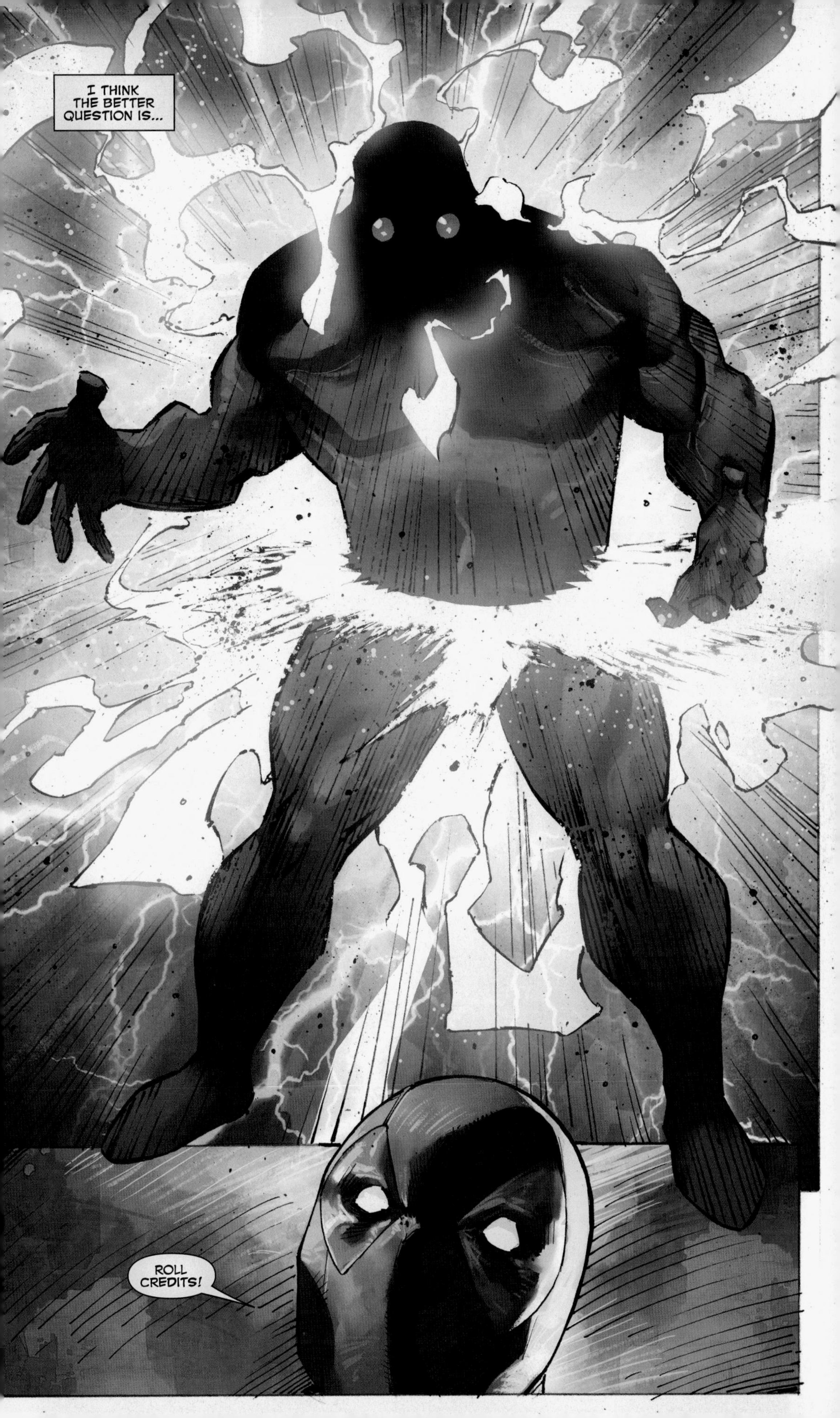
I THINK THE BETTER QUESTION IS...
ROLL CREDITS!

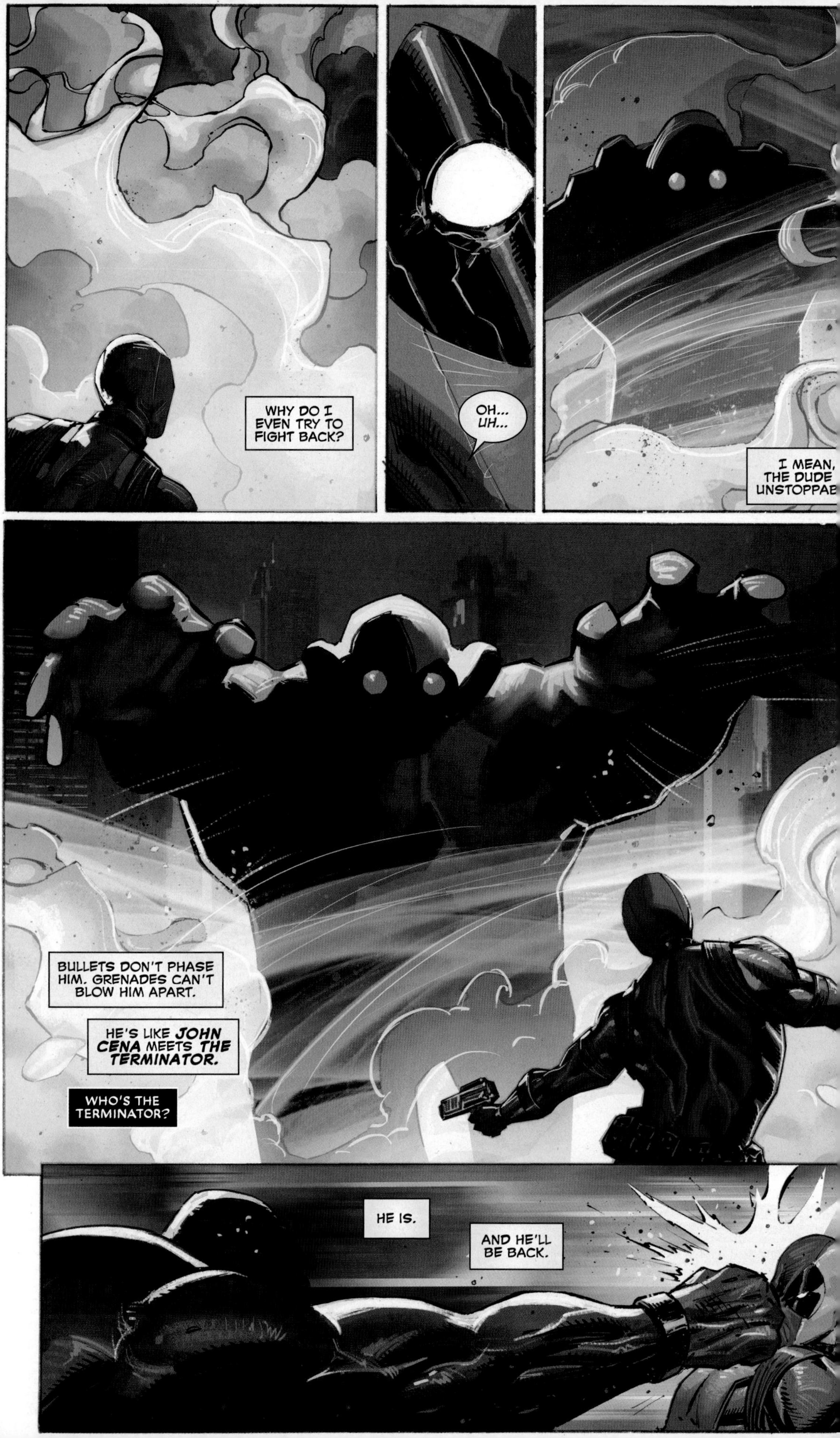
WHY DO I EVEN TRY TO FIGHT BACK?
OH... UH...
I MEAN, THE DUDE UNSTOPPAB
BULLETS DON'T PHASE HIM. GRENADES CAN'T BLOW HIM APART.
HE'S LIKE JOHN CENA MEETS THE TERMINATOR.
WHO'S THE TERMINATOR?
HE IS.
AND HE'LL BE BACK.

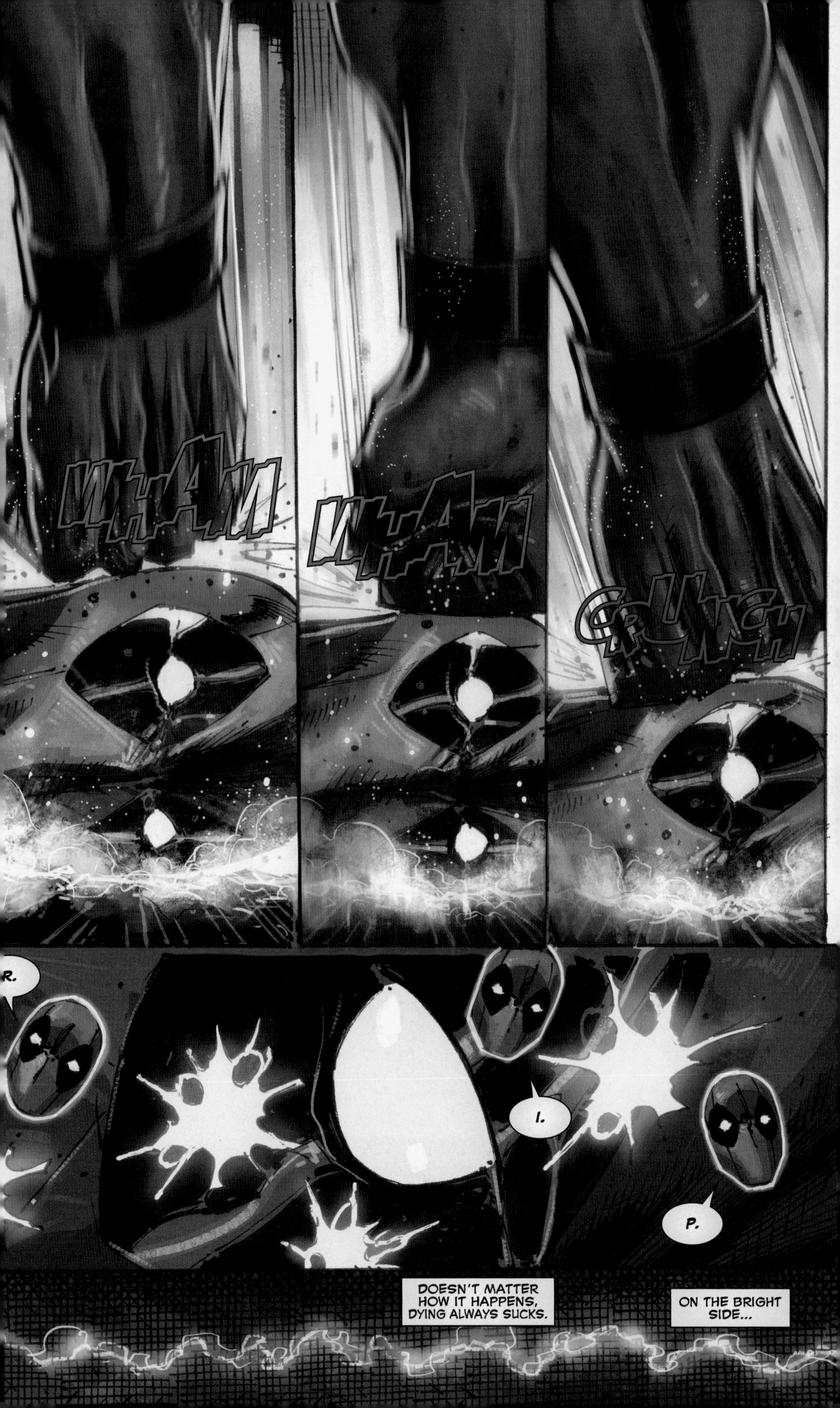
WHAM
WHAM
CRUNCH
R.
I.
P.
DOESN'T MATTER HOW IT HAPPENS, DYING ALWAYS SUCKS.
ON THE BRIGHT SIDE...

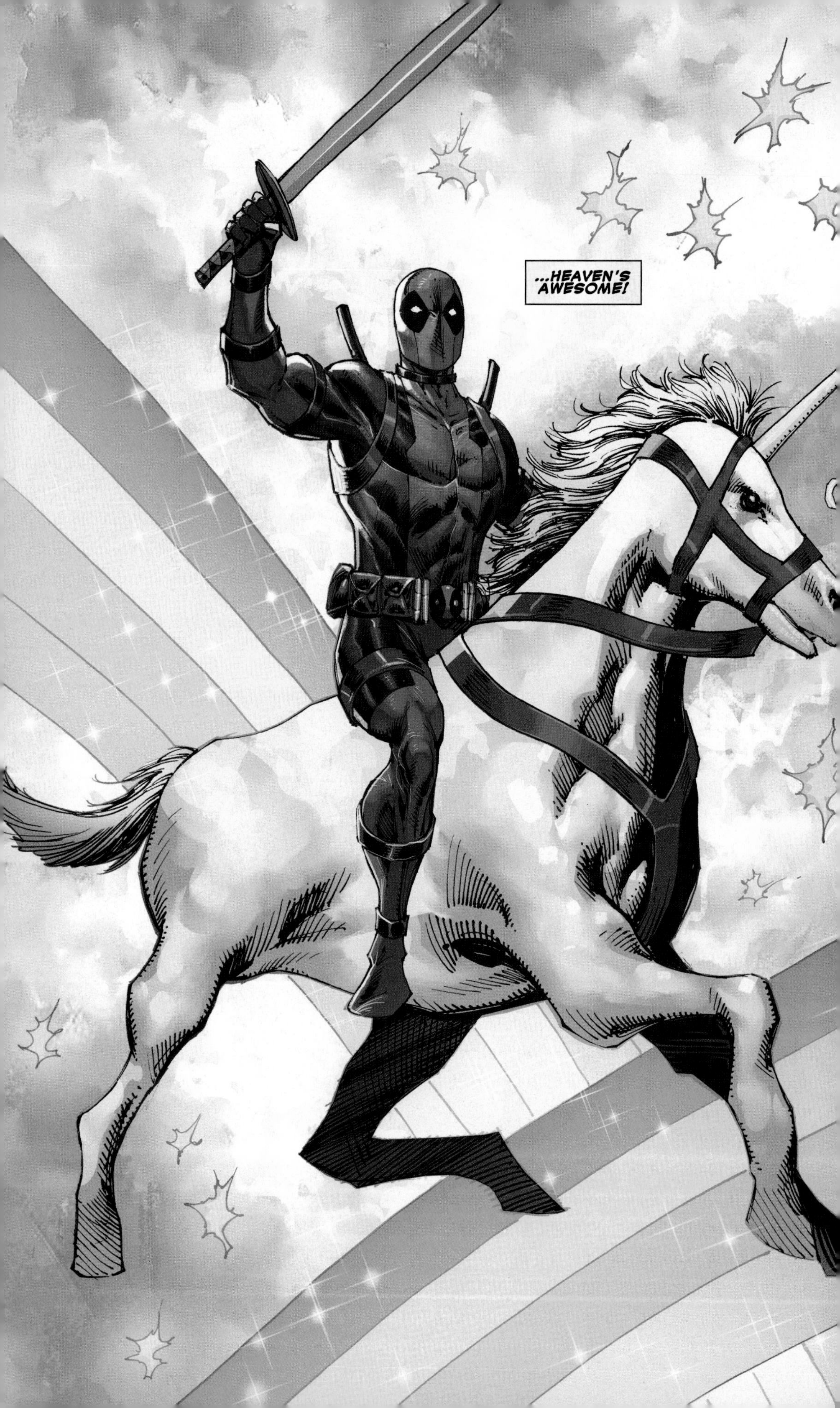
...HEAVEN'S AWESOME!

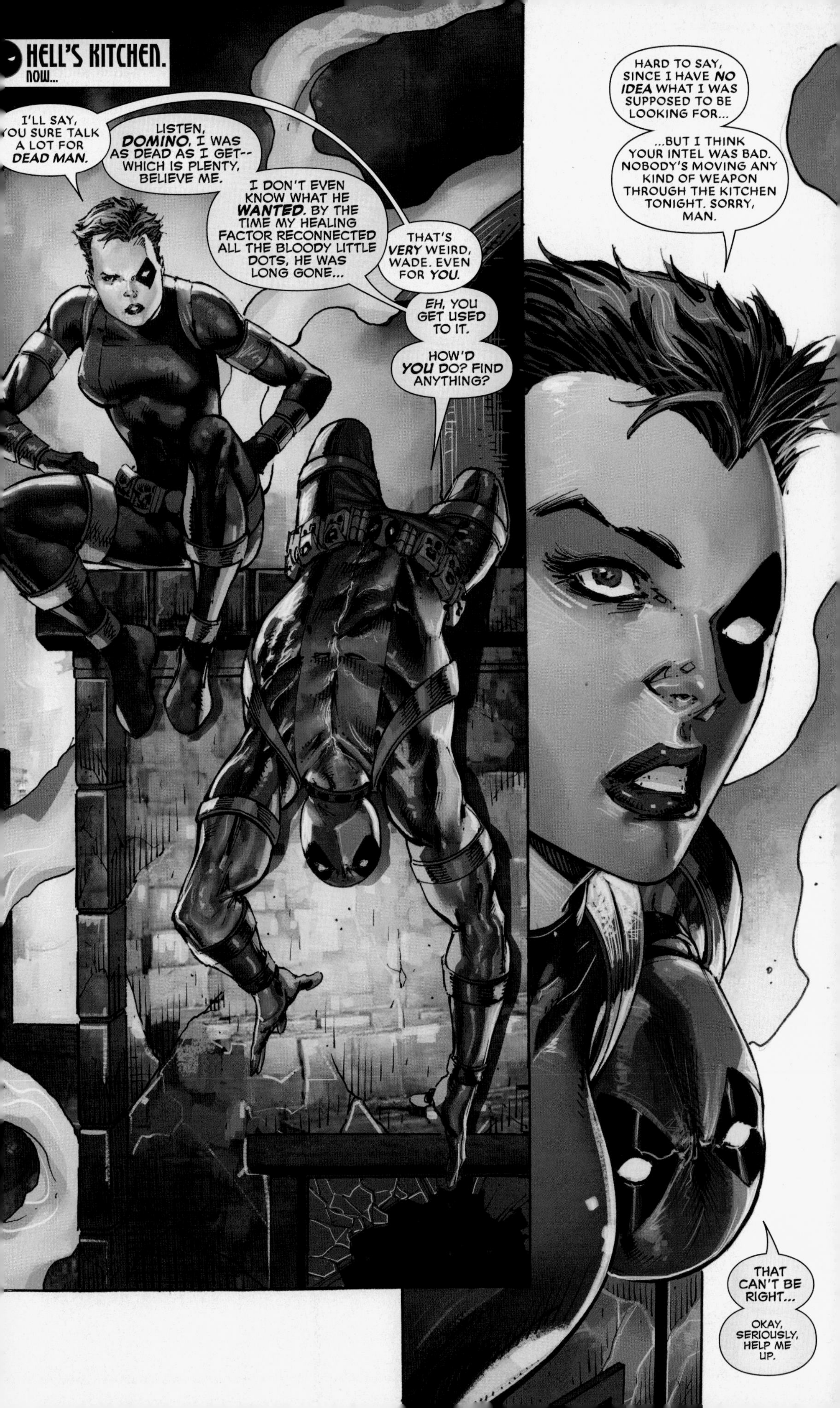

HELL'S KITCHEN. NOW...
I'LL SAY, YOU SURE TALK A LOT FOR DEAD MAN.
LISTEN, DOMINO, I WAS AS DEAD AS I GET-- WHICH IS PLENTY, BELIEVE ME.
I DON'T EVEN KNOW WHAT HE WANTED. BY THE TIME MY HEALING FACTOR RECONNECTED ALL THE BLOODY LITTLE DOTS, HE WAS LONG GONE...
THAT'S VERY WEIRD, WADE. EVEN FOR YOU.
EH, YOU GET USED TO IT.
HOW'D YOU DO? FIND ANYTHING?
HARD TO SAY, SINCE I HAVE NO IDEA WHAT I WAS SUPPOSED TO BE LOOKING FOR...
...BUT I THINK YOUR INTEL WAS BAD. NOBODY'S MOVING ANY KIND OF WEAPON THROUGH THE KITCHEN TONIGHT. SORRY, MAN.
THAT CAN'T BE RIGHT...
OKAY, SERIOUSLY, HELP ME UP.

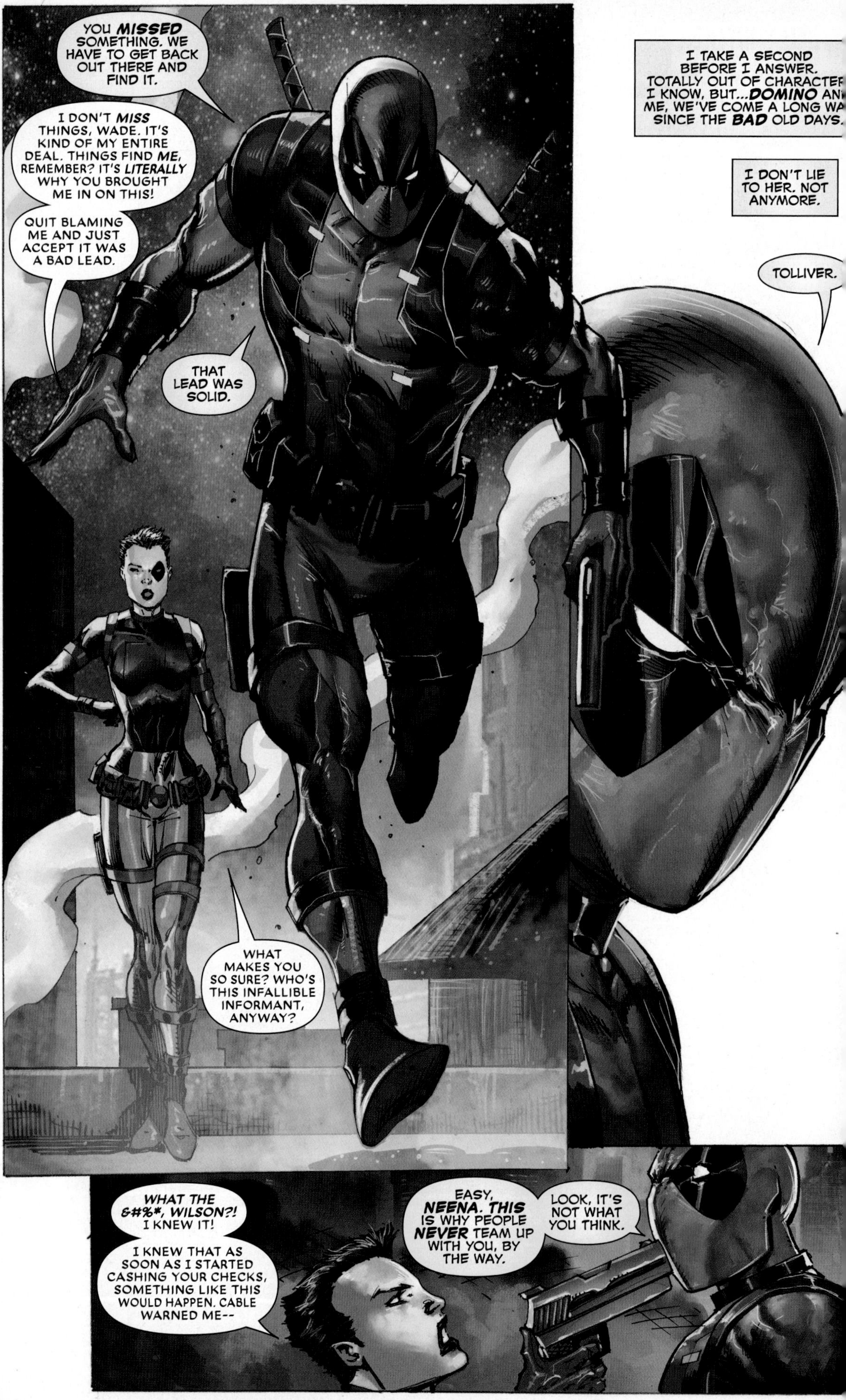
YOU MISSED SOMETHING. WE HAVE TO GET BACK OUT THERE AND FIND IT.
I DON'T MISS THINGS, WADE. IT'S KIND OF MY ENTIRE DEAL. THINGS FIND ME, REMEMBER? IT'S LITERALLY WHY YOU BROUGHT ME IN ON THIS!
QUIT BLAMING ME AND JUST ACCEPT IT WAS A BAD LEAD.
THAT LEAD WAS SOLID.
WHAT MAKES YOU SO SURE? WHO'S THIS INFALLIBLE INFORMANT, ANYWAY?
I TAKE A SECOND BEFORE I ANSWER. TOTALLY OUT OF CHARACTEF I KNOW, BUT...DOMINO AN ME, WE'VE COME A LONG WA SINCE THE BAD OLD DAYS.
I DON'T LIE TO HER. NOT ANYMORE.
TOLLIVER.
WHAT THE &#%*, WILSON?! I KNEW IT!
I KNEW THAT AS SOON AS I STARTED CASHING YOUR CHECKS, SOMETHING LIKE THIS WOULD HAPPEN. CABLE WARNED ME--
EASY, NEENA. THIS IS WHY PEOPLE NEVER TEAM UP WITH YOU, BY THE WAY.
LOOK, IT'S NOT WHAT YOU THINK.

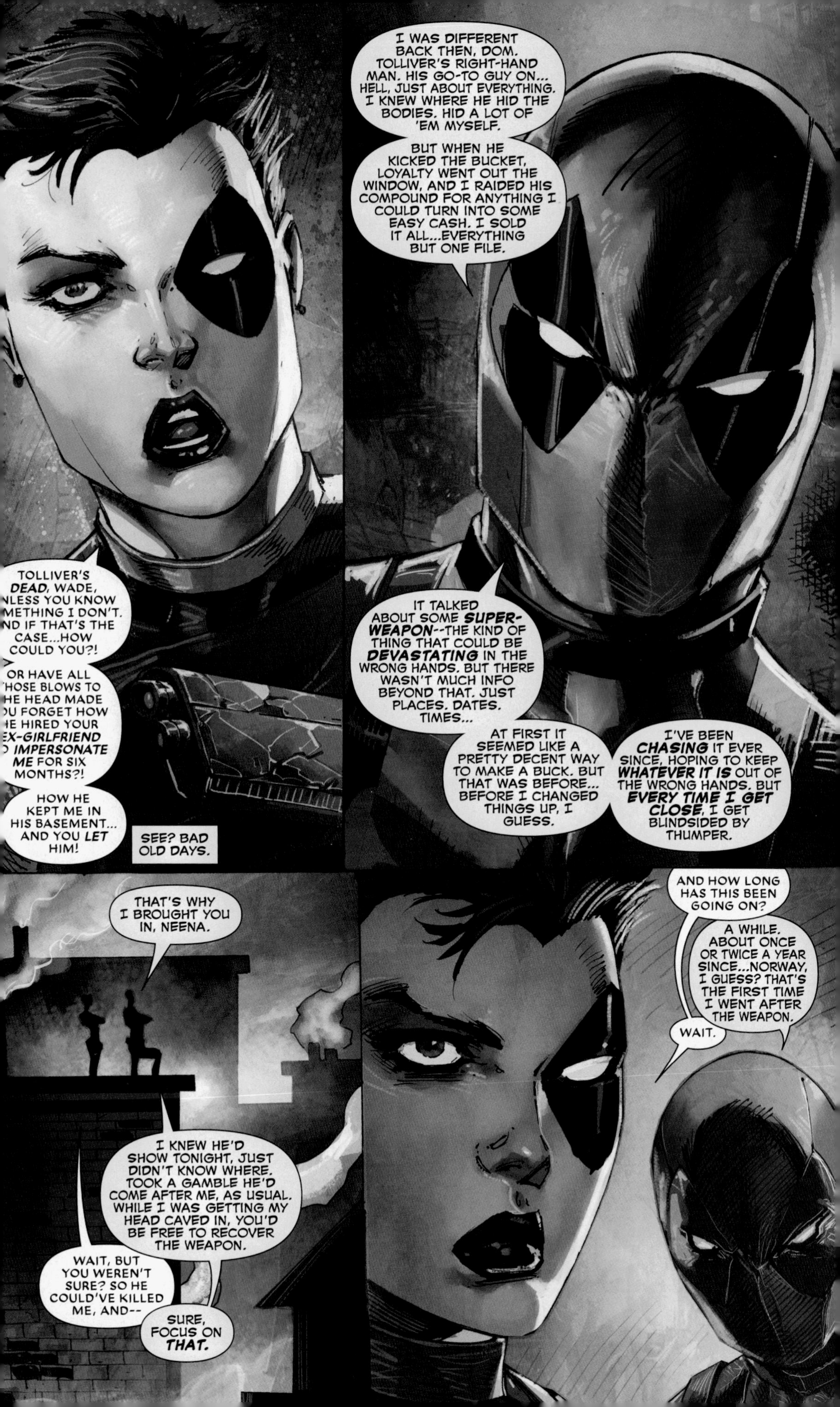

TOLLIVER'S DEAD, WADE, NLESS YOU KNOW METHING I DON'T. ND IF THAT'S THE CASE...HOW COULD YOU?!
OR HAVE ALL HOSE BLOWS TO HE HEAD MADE U FORGET HOW E HIRED YOUR EX-GIRLFRIEND O IMPERSONATE ME FOR SIX MONTHS?!
HOW HE KEPT ME IN HIS BASEMENT... AND YOU LET HIM!
SEE? BAD OLD DAYS.
I WAS DIFFERENT BACK THEN, DOM. TOLLIVER'S RIGHT-HAND MAN. HIS GO-TO GUY ON... HELL, JUST ABOUT EVERYTHING. I KNEW WHERE HE HID THE BODIES. HID A LOT OF 'EM MYSELF.
BUT WHEN HE KICKED THE BUCKET, LOYALTY WENT OUT THE WINDOW, AND I RAIDED HIS COMPOUND FOR ANYTHING I COULD TURN INTO SOME EASY CASH. I SOLD IT ALL...EVERYTHING BUT ONE FILE.
IT TALKED ABOUT SOME SUPER-WEAPON--THE KIND OF THING THAT COULD BE DEVASTATING IN THE WRONG HANDS. BUT THERE WASN'T MUCH INFO BEYOND THAT. JUST PLACES. DATES. TIMES...
AT FIRST IT SEEMED LIKE A PRETTY DECENT WAY TO MAKE A BUCK. BUT THAT WAS BEFORE... BEFORE I CHANGED THINGS UP, I GUESS.
I'VE BEEN CHASING IT EVER SINCE, HOPING TO KEEP WHATEVER IT IS OUT OF THE WRONG HANDS. BUT EVERY TIME I GET CLOSE, I GET BLINDSIDED BY THUMPER.
THAT'S WHY I BROUGHT YOU IN, NEENA.
I KNEW HE'D SHOW TONIGHT, JUST DIDN'T KNOW WHERE. TOOK A GAMBLE HE'D COME AFTER ME, AS USUAL. WHILE I WAS GETTING MY HEAD CAVED IN, YOU'D BE FREE TO RECOVER THE WEAPON.
WAIT, BUT YOU WEREN'T SURE? SO HE COULD'VE KILLED ME, AND--
SURE, FOCUS ON THAT.
AND HOW LONG HAS THIS BEEN GOING ON?
A WHILE. ABOUT ONCE OR TWICE A YEAR SINCE...NORWAY, I GUESS? THAT'S THE FIRST TIME I WENT AFTER THE WEAPON.
WAIT.

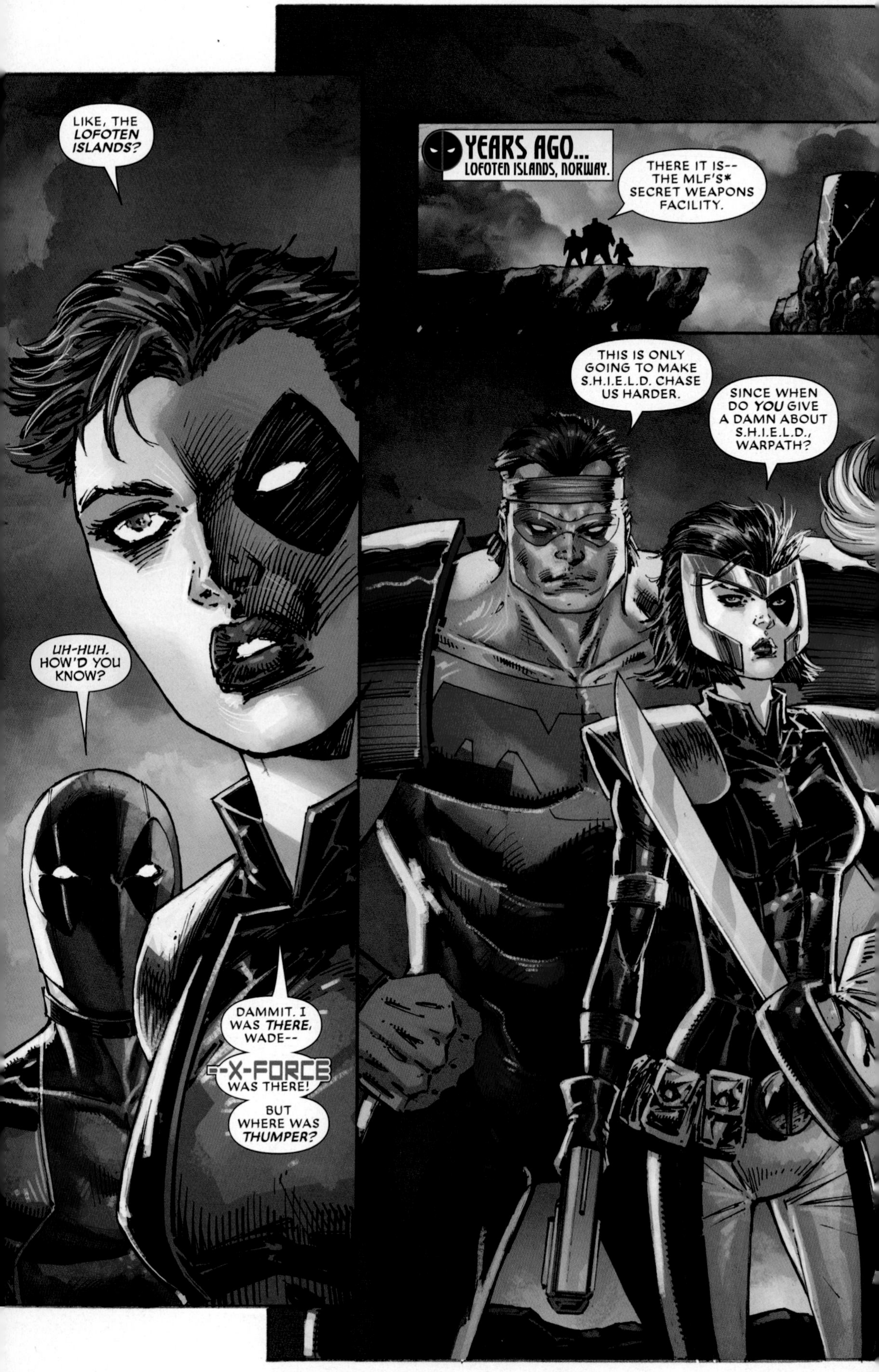

LIKE, THE LOFOTEN ISLANDS?
UH-HUH. HOW'D YOU KNOW?
DAMMIT. I WAS THERE, WADE--
--X-FORCE WAS THERE!
BUT WHERE WAS THUMPER?
YEARS AGO...
LOFOTEN ISLANDS, NORWAY.
THERE IT IS-- THE MLF'S* SECRET WEAPONS FACILITY.
THIS IS ONLY GOING TO MAKE S.H.I.E.L.D. CHASE US HARDER.
SINCE WHEN DO YOU GIVE A DAMN ABOUT S.H.I.E.L.D., WARPATH?

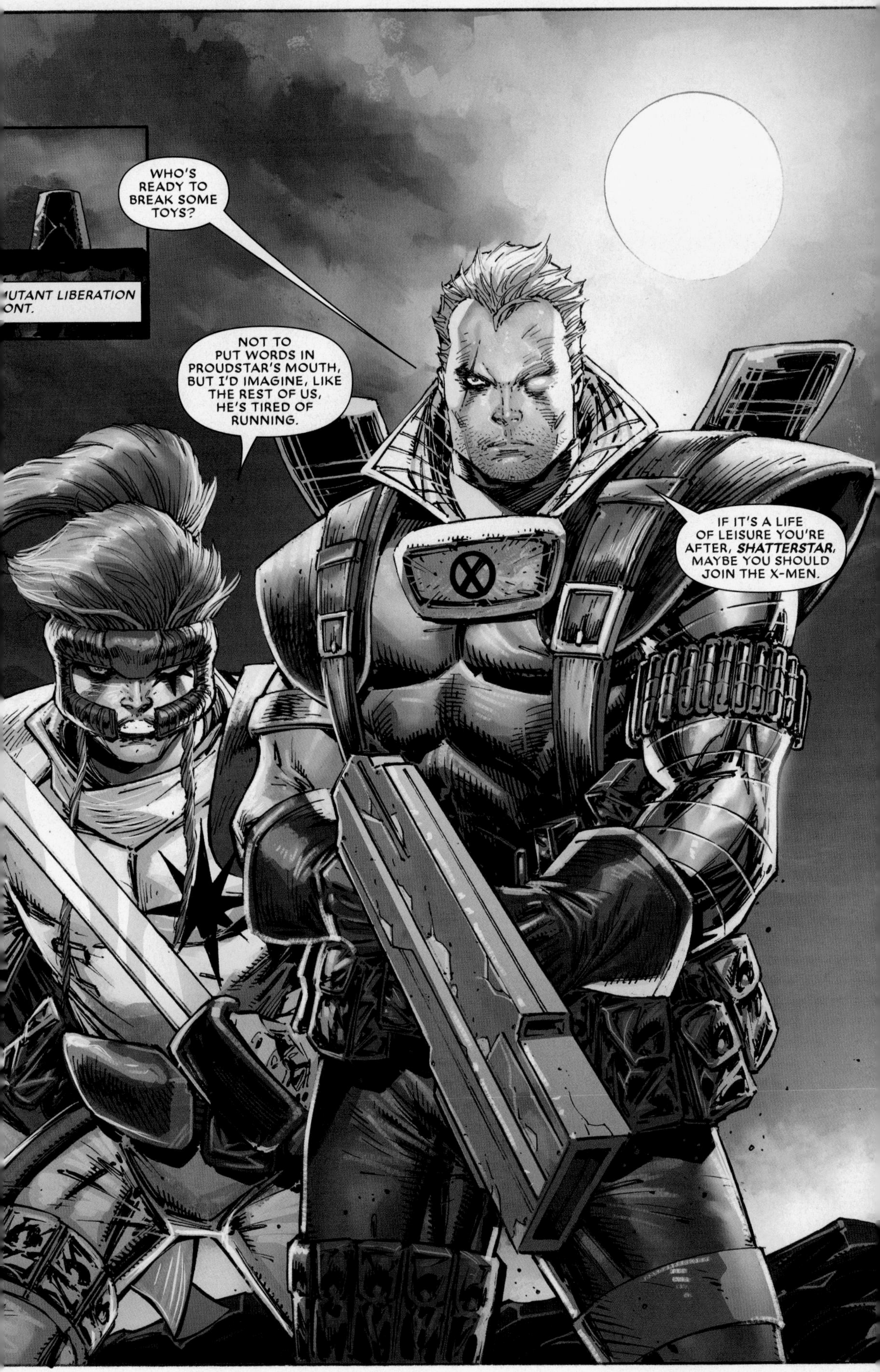
UTANT LIBERATION
ONT.
WHO'S READY TO BREAK SOME TOYS?
NOT TO PUT WORDS IN PROUDSTAR'S MOUTH, BUT I'D IMAGINE, LIKE THE REST OF US, HE'S TIRED OF RUNNING.
IF IT'S A LIFE OF LEISURE YOU'RE AFTER, SHATTERSTAR, MAYBE YOU SHOULD JOIN THE X-MEN.

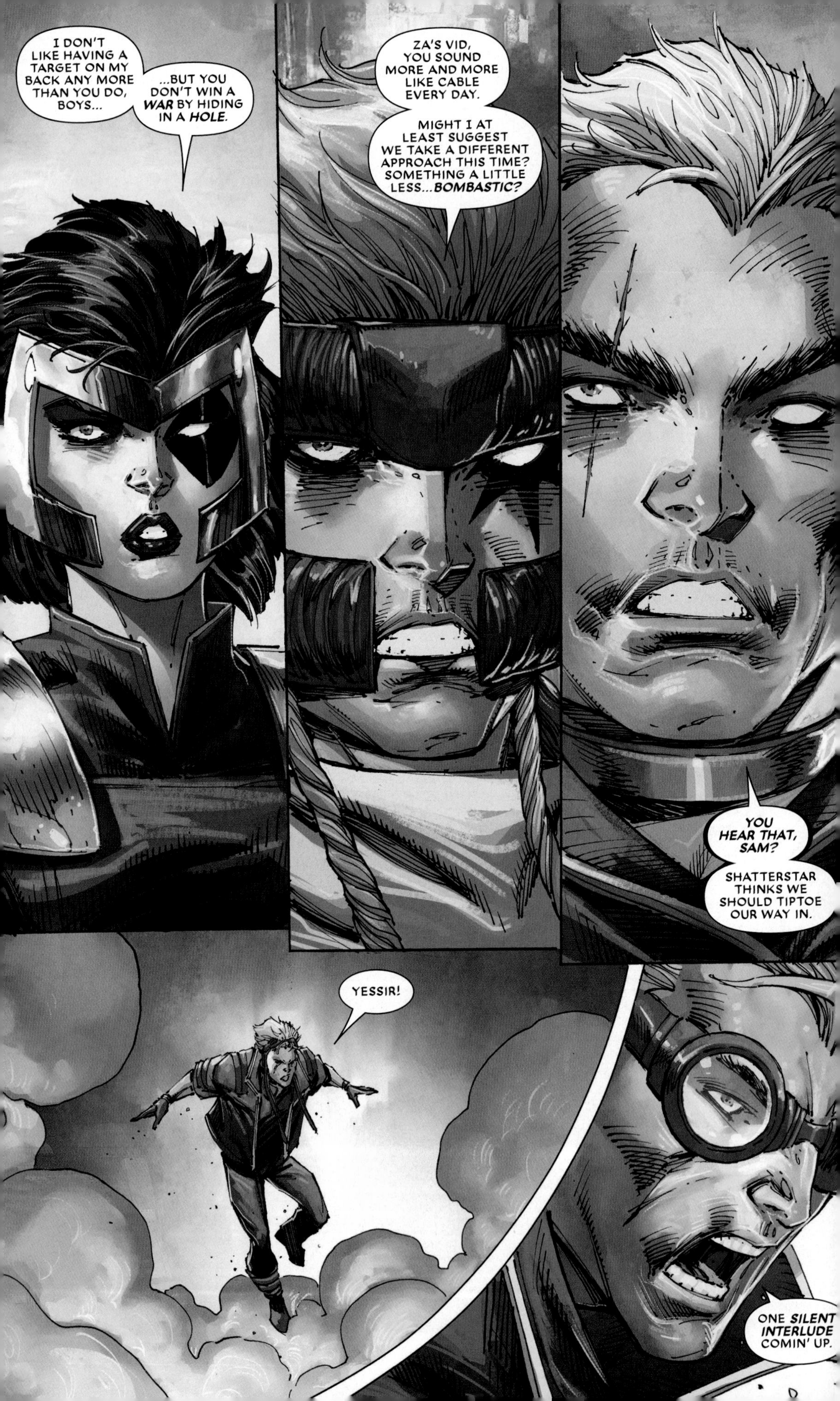

I DON'T LIKE HAVING A TARGET ON MY BACK ANY MORE THAN YOU DO, BOYS...
...BUT YOU DON'T WIN A *WAR* BY HIDING IN A *HOLE*.
ZA'S VID, YOU SOUND MORE AND MORE LIKE CABLE EVERY DAY.
MIGHT I AT LEAST SUGGEST WE TAKE A DIFFERENT APPROACH THIS TIME? SOMETHING A LITTLE LESS...*BOMBASTIC?*
YOU HEAR THAT, SAM?
SHATTERSTAR THINKS WE SHOULD TIPTOE OUR WAY IN.
YESSIR!
ONE *SILENT INTERLUDE* COMIN' UP.

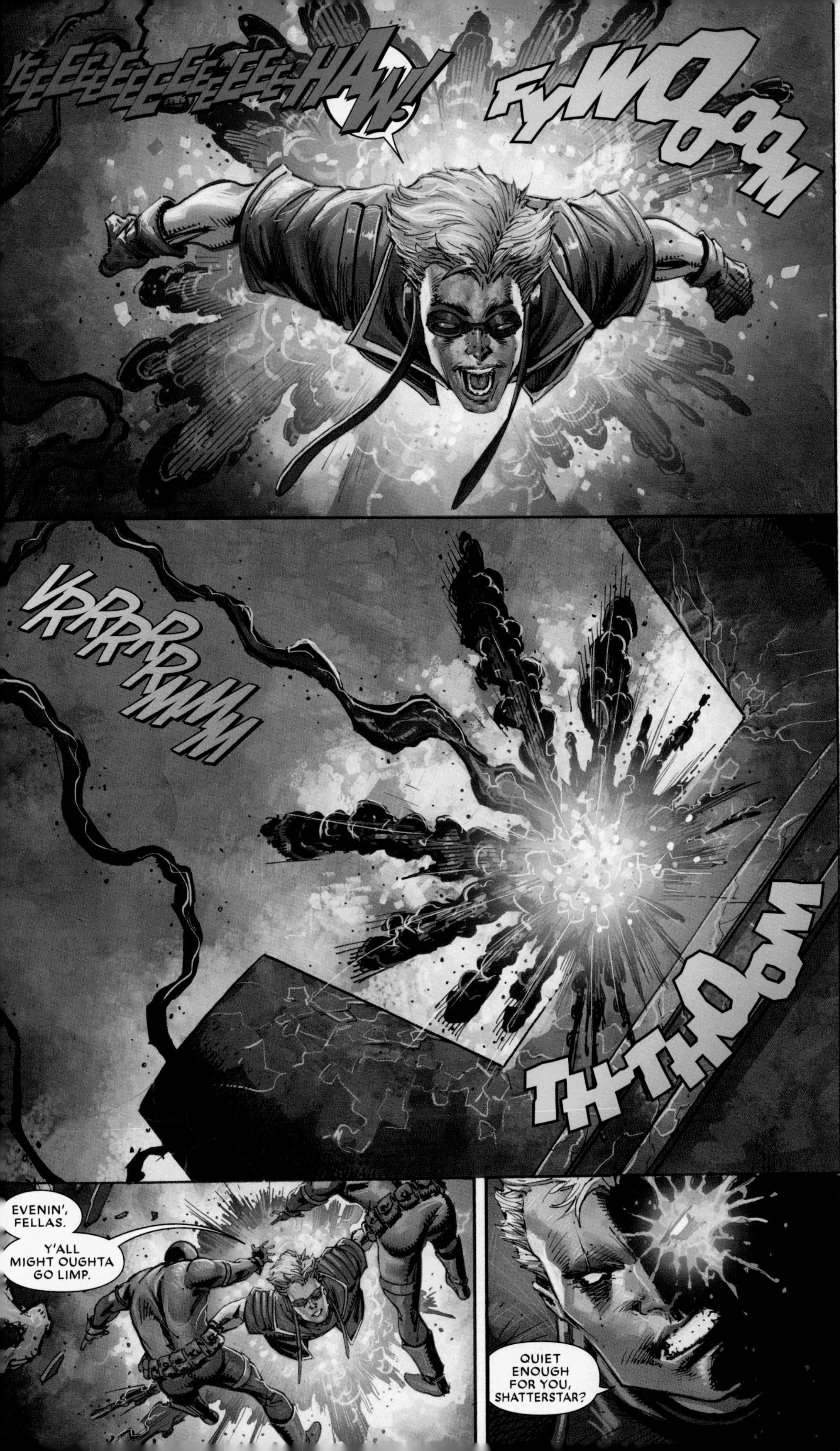
YEEEEEEEEEEEEEEEEE-HAW!
FVWOOOOM
VRRRRRMMMM
THTHOOOM
EVENIN', FELLAS.
Y'ALL MIGHT OUGHTA GO LIMP.
QUIET ENOUGH FOR YOU, SHATTERSTAR?

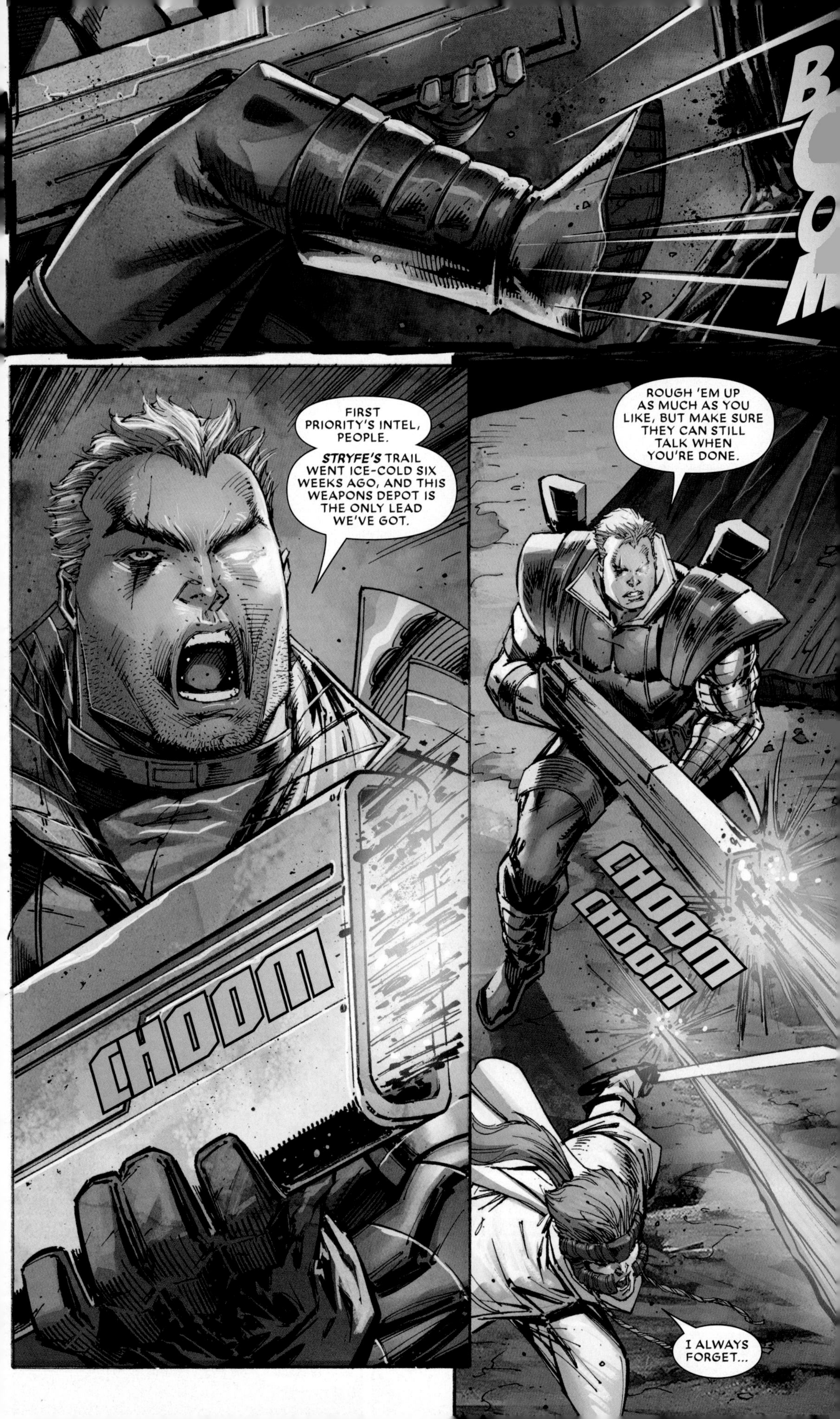
BOOM
FIRST PRIORITY'S INTEL, PEOPLE.
STRYFE'S TRAIL WENT ICE-COLD SIX WEEKS AGO, AND THIS WEAPONS DEPOT IS THE ONLY LEAD WE'VE GOT.
CHOOM
ROUGH 'EM UP AS MUCH AS YOU LIKE, BUT MAKE SURE THEY CAN STILL TALK WHEN YOU'RE DONE.
CHOOM CHOOM
I ALWAYS FORGET...

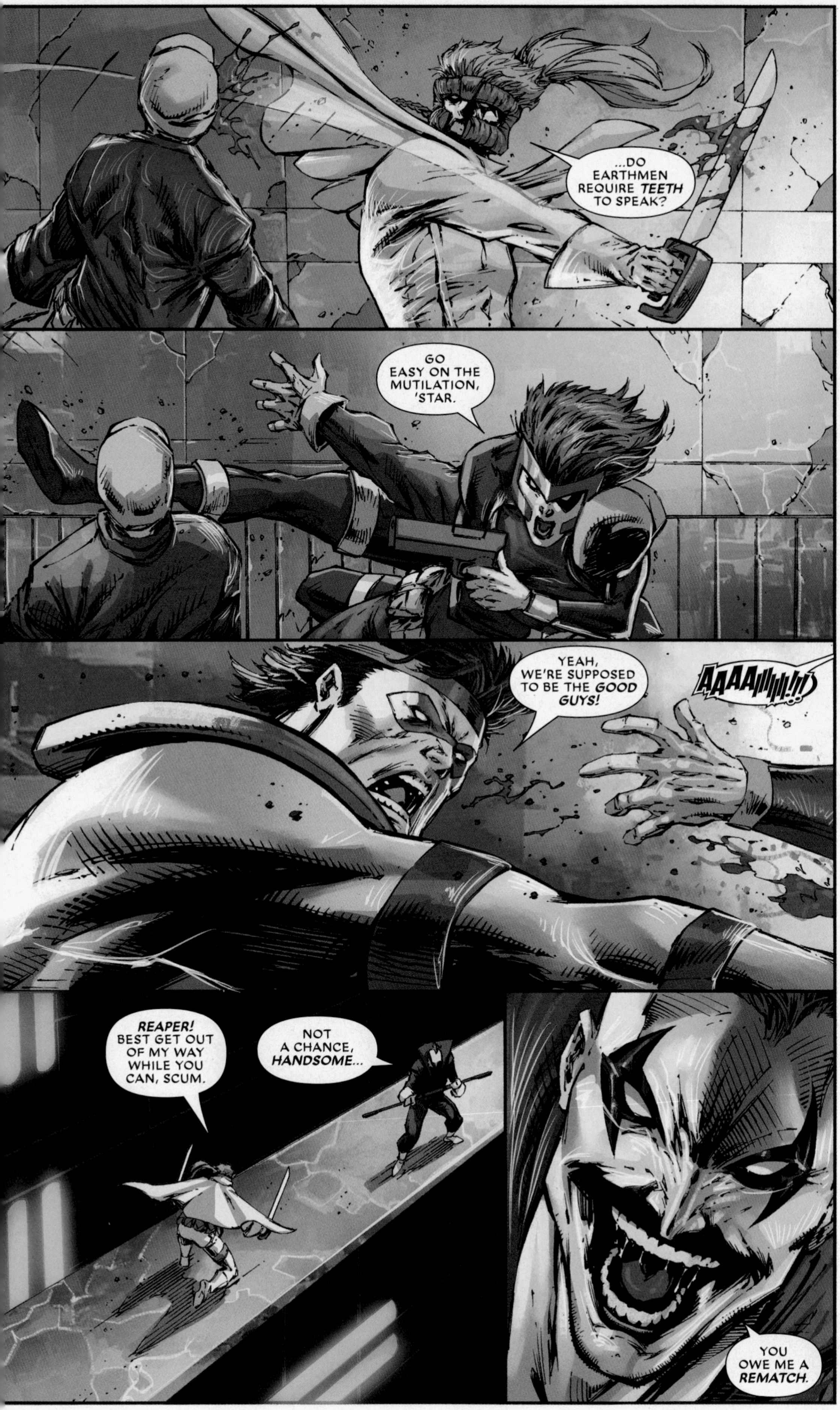

...DO EARTHMEN REQUIRE *TEETH* TO SPEAK?
GO EASY ON THE MUTILATION, 'STAR.
YEAH, WE'RE SUPPOSED TO BE THE *GOOD GUYS!*
AAAIIIIIII!!!
REAPER! BEST GET OUT OF MY WAY WHILE YOU CAN, SCUM.
NOT A CHANCE, *HANDSOME*...
YOU OWE ME A *REMATCH*.

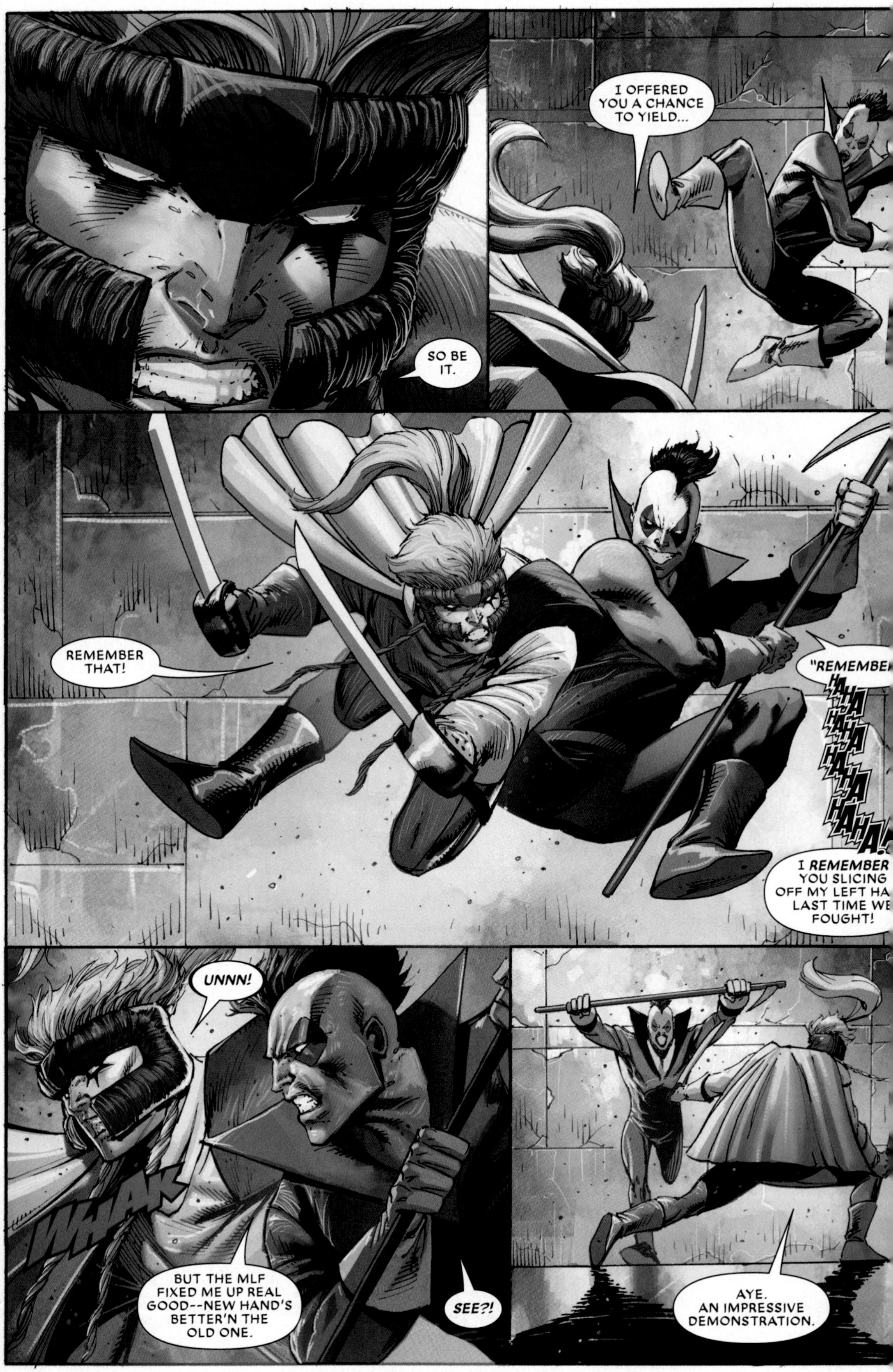
I OFFERED YOU A CHANCE TO YIELD...
SO BE IT.
REMEMBER THAT!
"REMEMBE
HAHAHAHAHAHAHAHA!
I REMEMBER YOU SLICING OFF MY LEFT HA LAST TIME WE FOUGHT!
UNNN!
WHAK
BUT THE MLF FIXED ME UP REAL GOOD--NEW HAND'S BETTER'N THE OLD ONE.
SEE?!
AYE. AN IMPRESSIVE DEMONSTRATION.

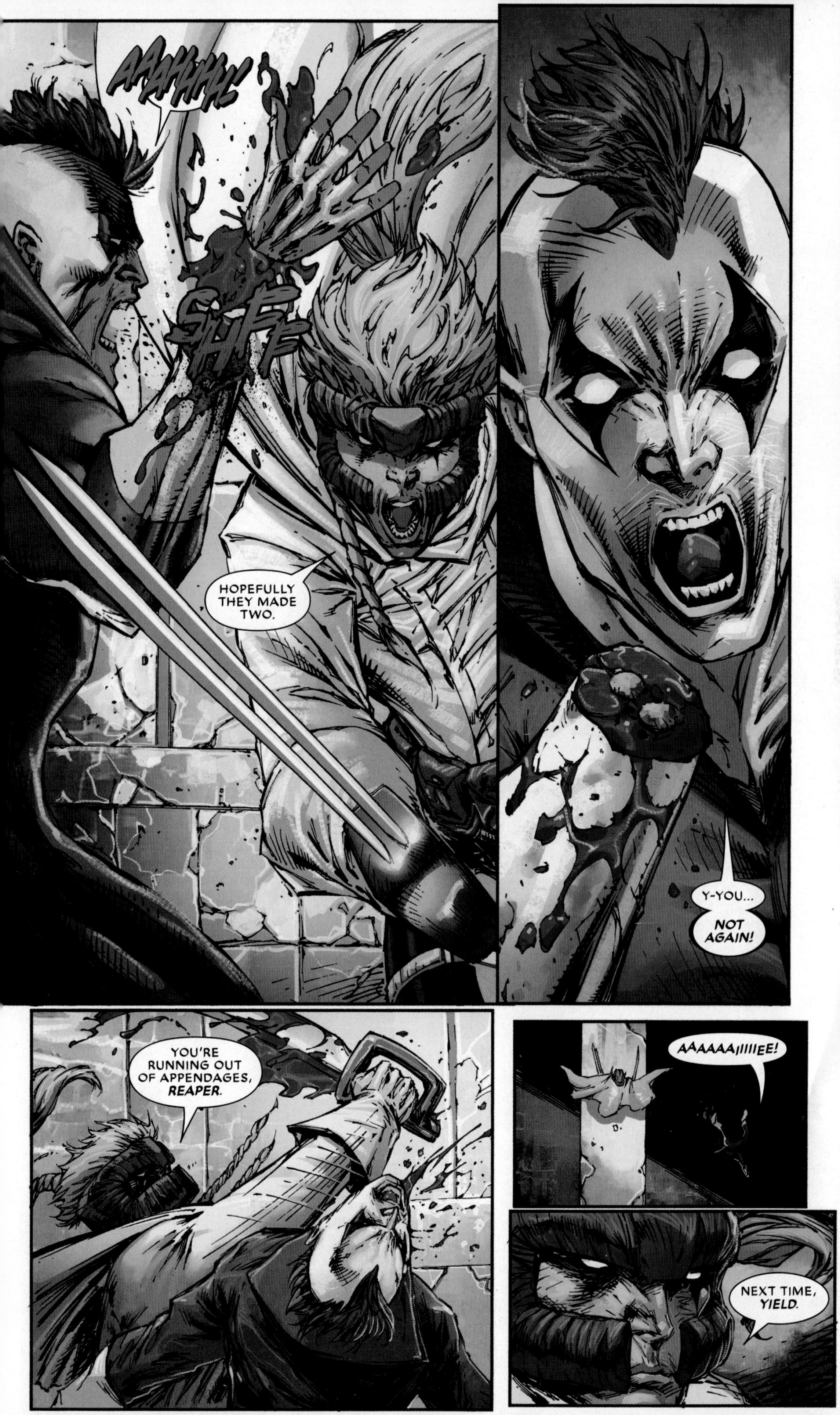
AAAHHHH!
SHF
HOPEFULLY THEY MADE TWO.
Y-YOU... NOT AGAIN!
YOU'RE RUNNING OUT OF APPENDAGES, REAPER.
AAAAAAIIIIIEE!
NEXT TIME, YIELD.

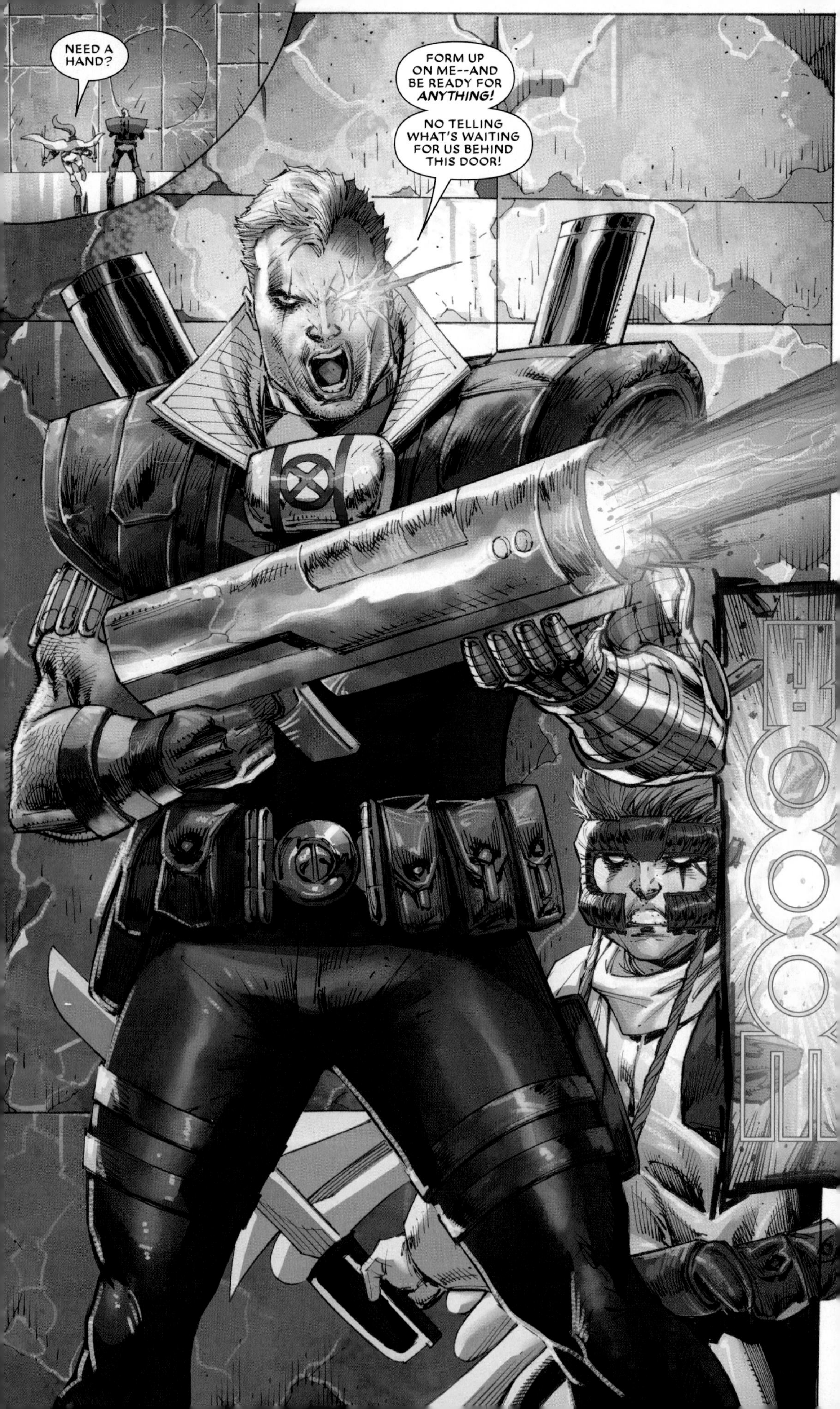
NEED A HAND?
FORM UP ON ME--AND BE READY FOR *ANYTHING!*
NO TELLING WHAT'S WAITING FOR US BEHIND THIS DOOR!

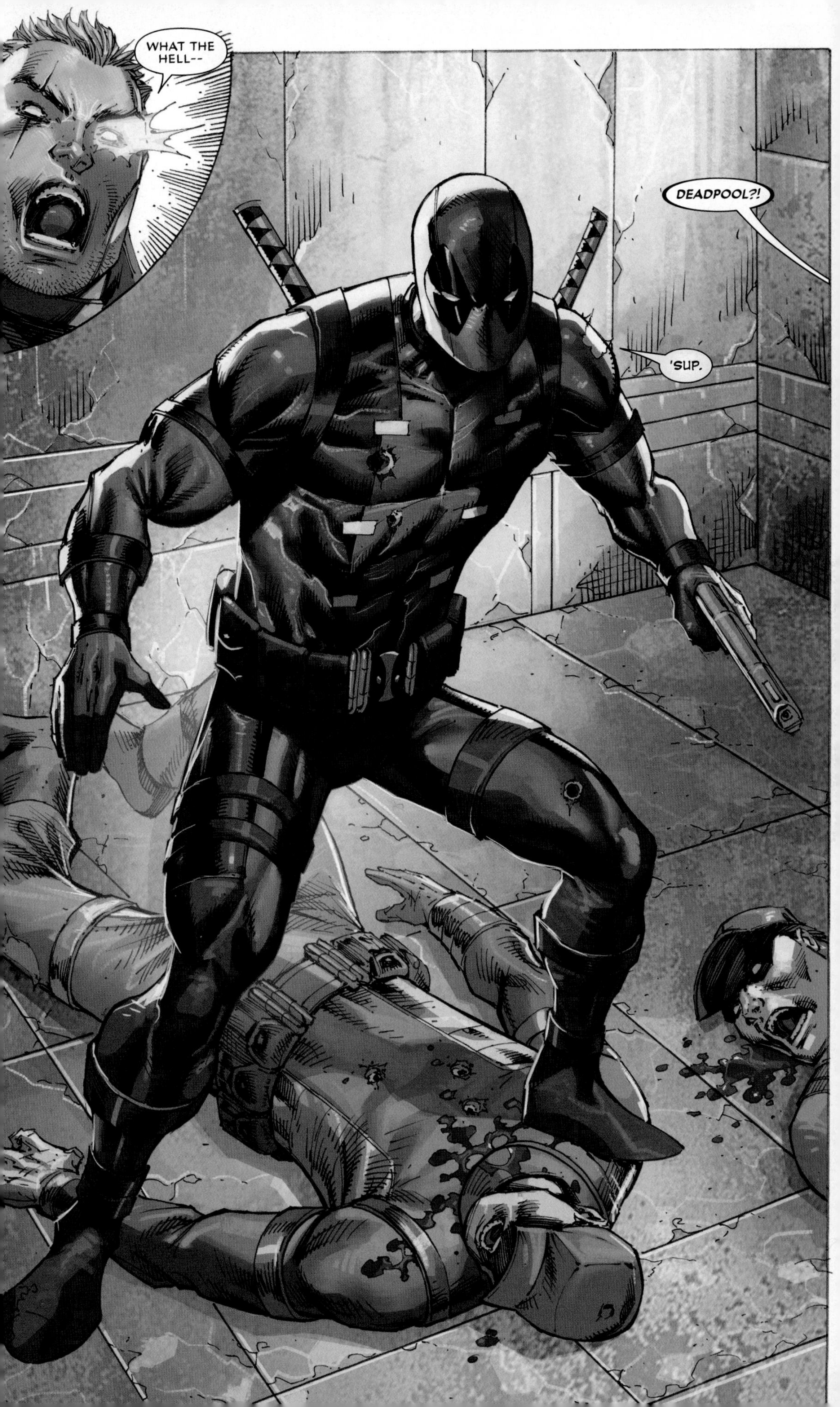
WHAT THE HELL--
DEADPOOL?!
'SUP.

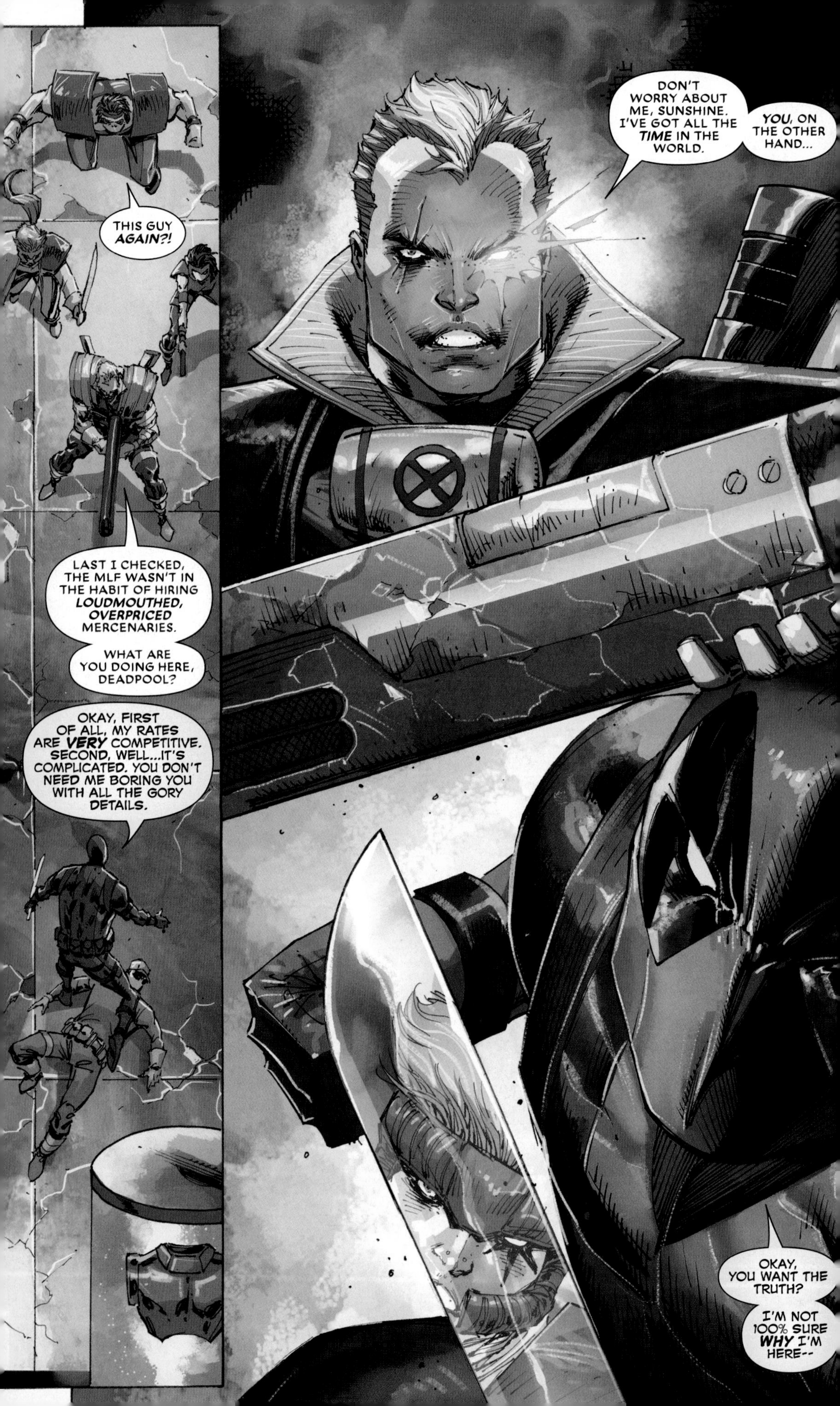
THIS GUY AGAIN?!
LAST I CHECKED, THE MLF WASN'T IN THE HABIT OF HIRING LOUDMOUTHED, OVERPRICED MERCENARIES.
WHAT ARE YOU DOING HERE, DEADPOOL?
OKAY, FIRST OF ALL, MY RATES ARE VERY COMPETITIVE. SECOND, WELL...IT'S COMPLICATED. YOU DON'T NEED ME BORING YOU WITH ALL THE GORY DETAILS.
DON'T WORRY ABOUT ME, SUNSHINE. I'VE GOT ALL THE TIME IN THE WORLD.
YOU, ON THE OTHER HAND...
OKAY, YOU WANT THE TRUTH?
I'M NOT 100% SURE WHY I'M HERE--

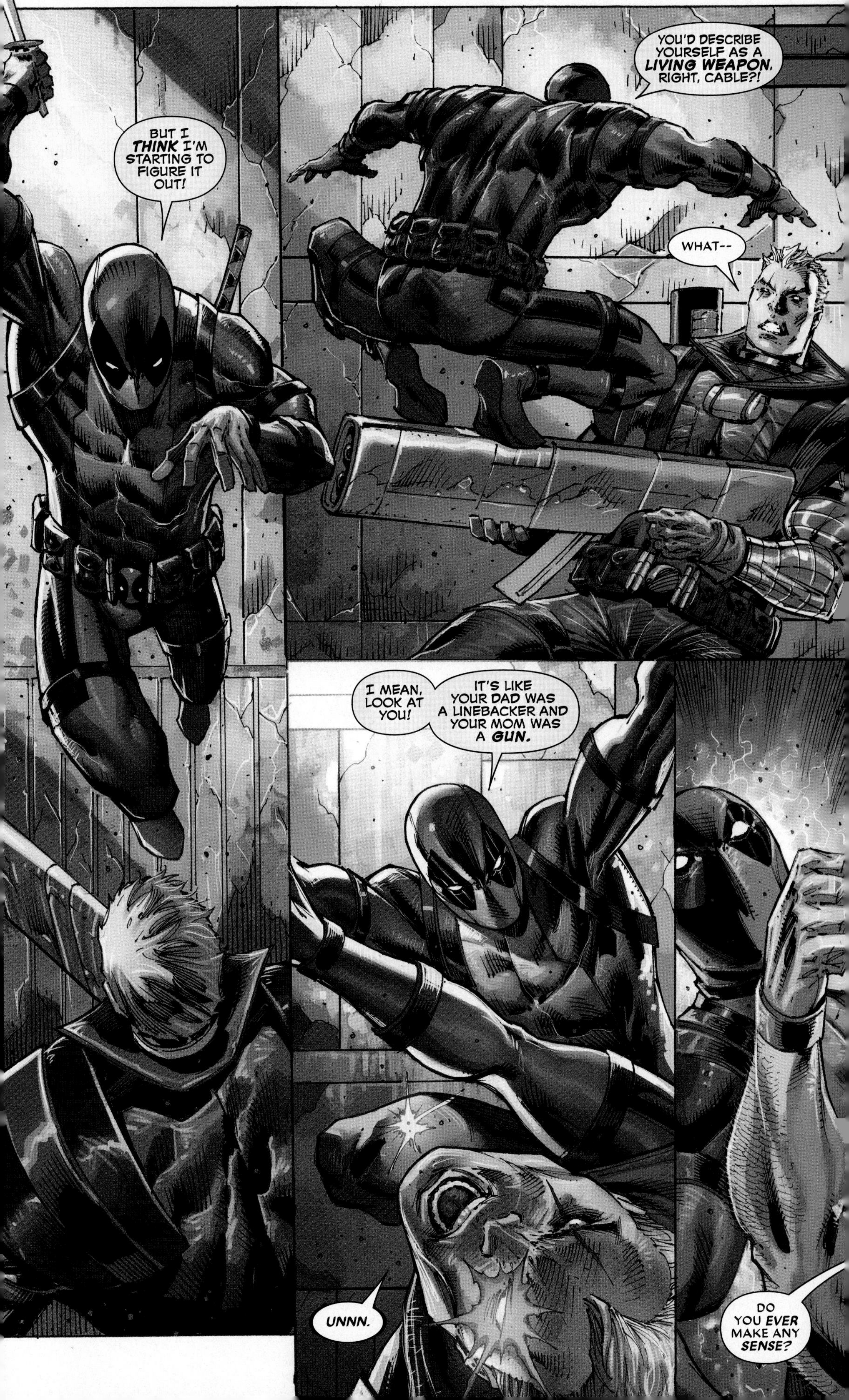
BUT I THINK I'M STARTING TO FIGURE IT OUT!
YOU'D DESCRIBE YOURSELF AS A LIVING WEAPON, RIGHT, CABLE?!
WHAT--
I MEAN, LOOK AT YOU!
IT'S LIKE YOUR DAD WAS A LINEBACKER AND YOUR MOM WAS A GUN.
UNNN.
DO YOU EVER MAKE ANY SENSE?

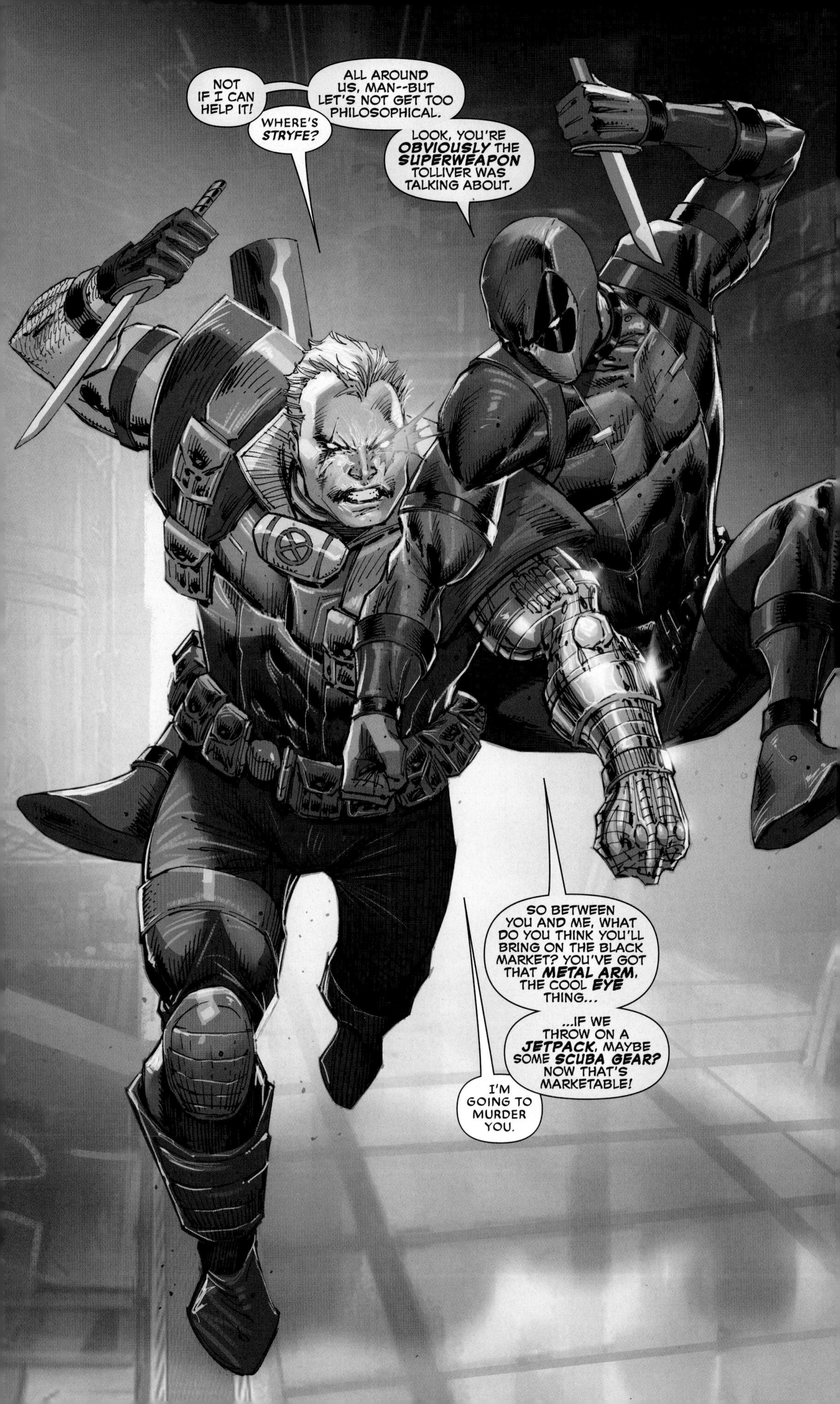

NOT IF I CAN HELP IT!
ALL AROUND US, MAN--BUT LET'S NOT GET TOO PHILOSOPHICAL.
WHERE'S STRYFE?
LOOK, YOU'RE OBVIOUSLY THE SUPERWEAPON TOLLIVER WAS TALKING ABOUT.
SO BETWEEN YOU AND ME, WHAT DO YOU THINK YOU'LL BRING ON THE BLACK MARKET? YOU'VE GOT THAT METAL ARM, THE COOL EYE THING...
...IF WE THROW ON A JETPACK, MAYBE SOME SCUBA GEAR? NOW THAT'S MARKETABLE!
I'M GOING TO MURDER YOU.

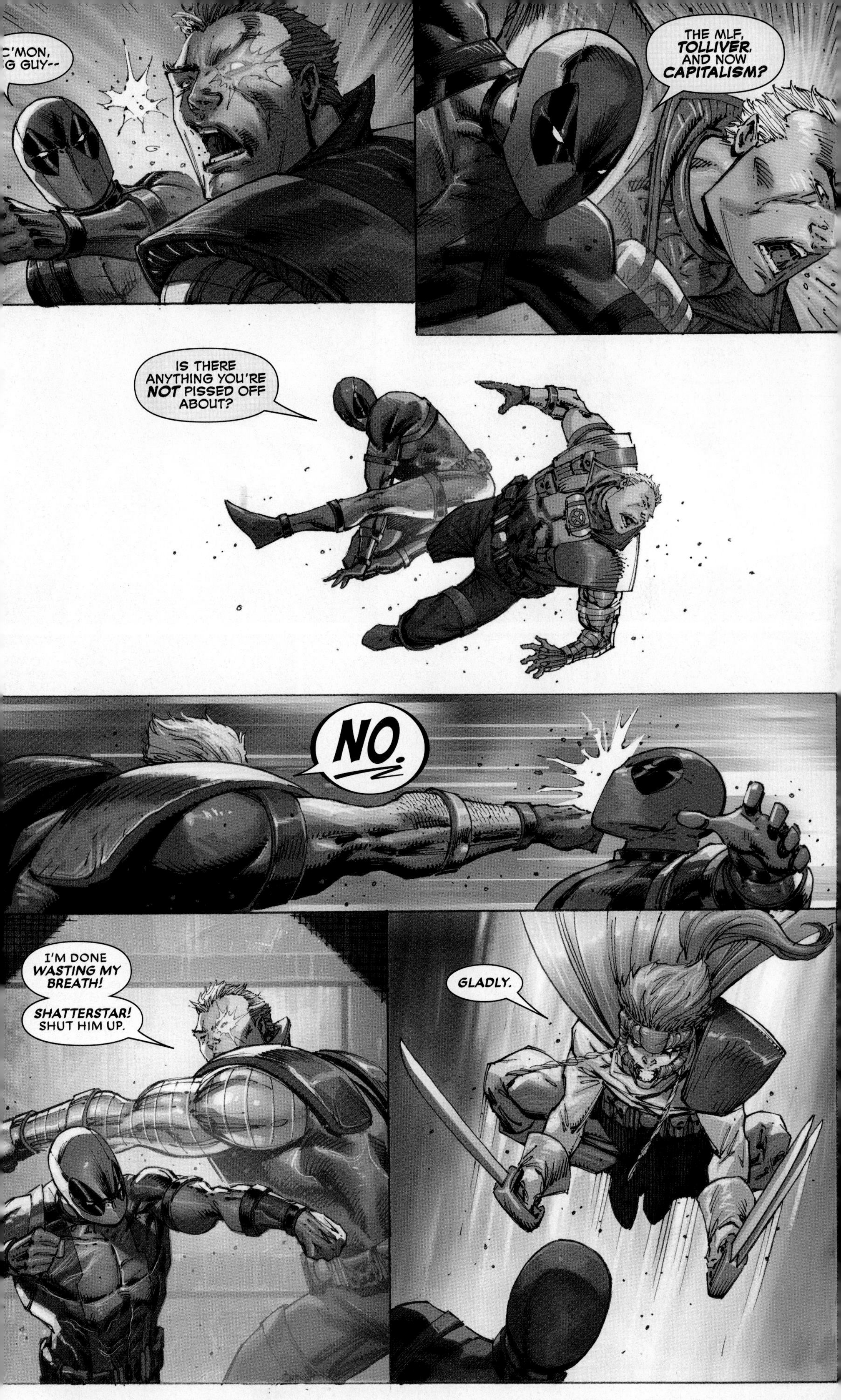
C'MON, G GUY--
THE MLF, TOLLIVER, AND NOW CAPITALISM?
IS THERE ANYTHING YOU'RE NOT PISSED OFF ABOUT?
NO.
I'M DONE WASTING MY BREATH!
SHATTERSTAR! SHUT HIM UP.
GLADLY.

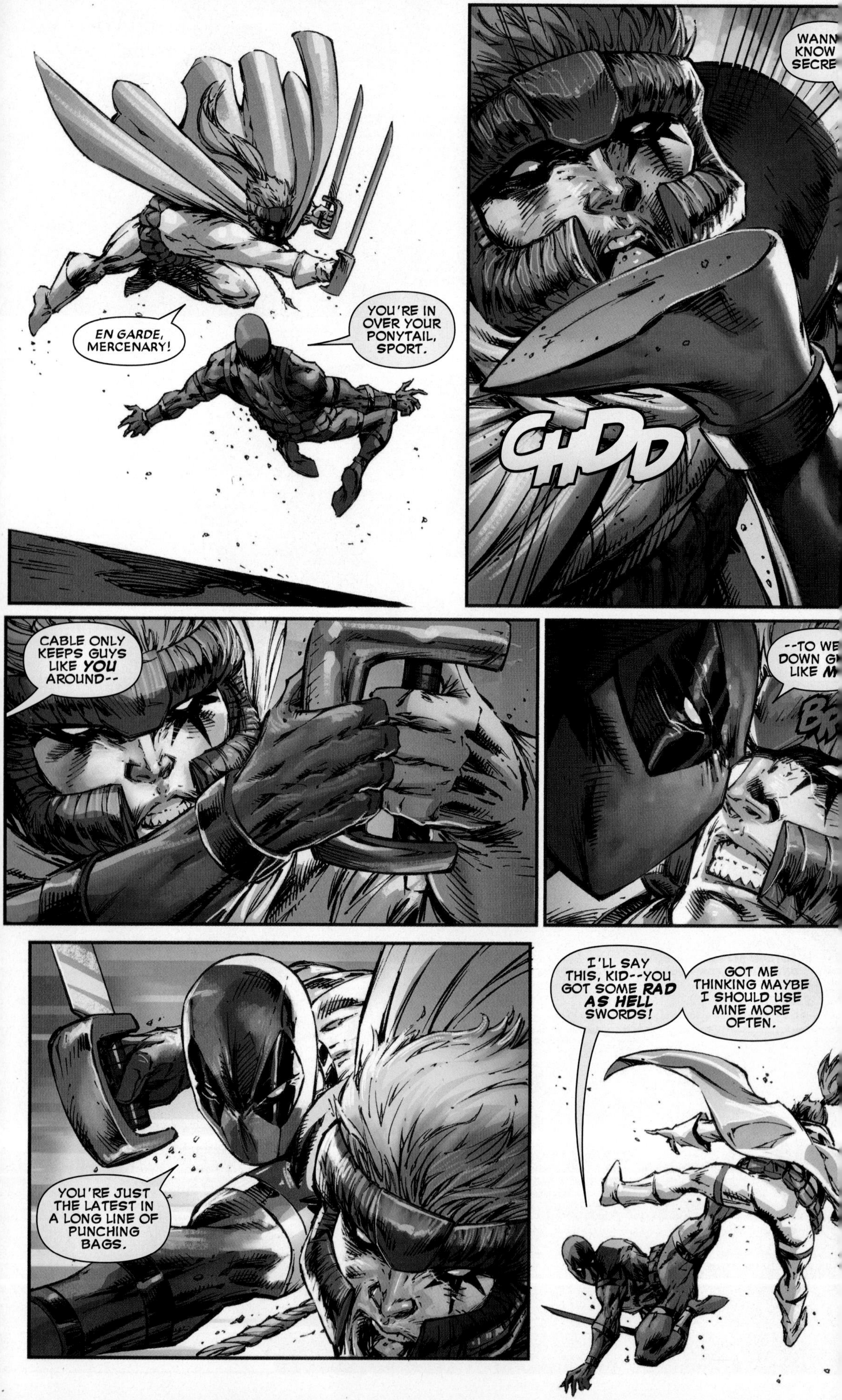
EN GARDE, MERCENARY!
YOU'RE IN OVER YOUR PONYTAIL, SPORT.
WANN KNOW SECRE
CHDD
CABLE ONLY KEEPS GUYS LIKE *YOU* AROUND--
--TO WE DOWN G LIKE
YOU'RE JUST THE LATEST IN A LONG LINE OF PUNCHING BAGS.
I'LL SAY THIS, KID--YOU GOT SOME ***RAD AS HELL*** SWORDS!
GOT ME THINKING MAYBE I SHOULD USE MINE MORE OFTEN.

I WON THOSE BLADES IN THE *HELL GAMES* OF MOJOWORLD!

UNHAND THEM--*NOW!*

HEY! LOOK WHAT YOU DID, JACKASS--

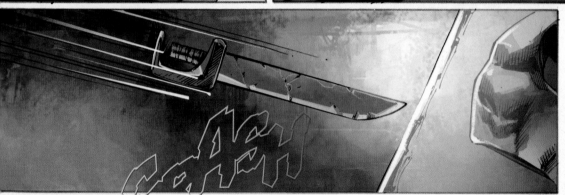

NOW THERE'S GONNA BE GLASS ALL OVER AND--

--IS THAT *APOCALYPSE'S* ARMOR?

OHHHHHHH.

WE'RE NOT DONE, MERCENARY! *SHATTERSTAR* DEMANDS--

GO TO SLEEP, KID. FIGHT'S OVER.

POP

YEP, THIS IS THE REAL DEAL. *DEFINITELY* WHAT TOLLIVER WAS AFTER.

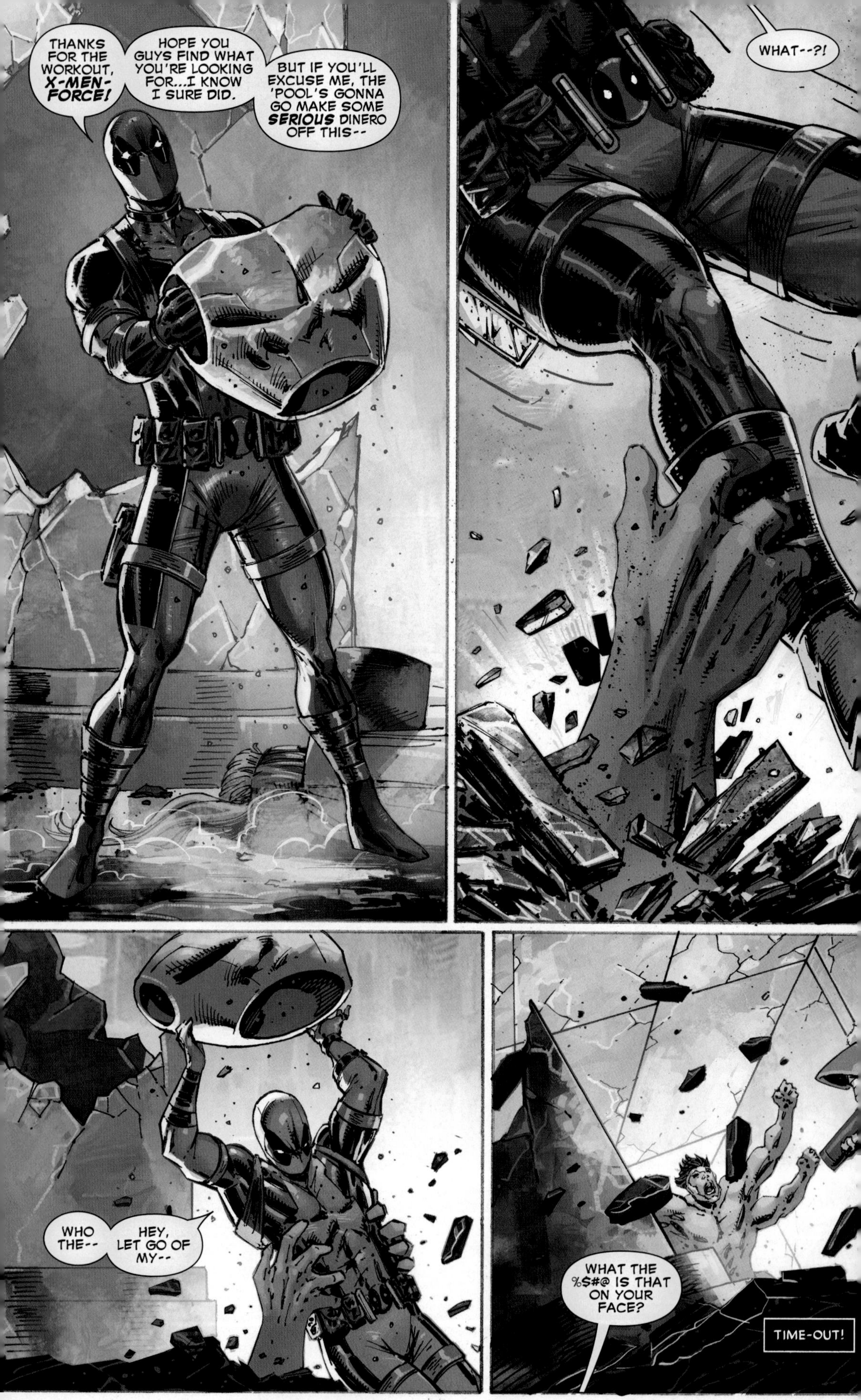
THANKS FOR THE WORKOUT, X-MEN-FORCE!
HOPE YOU GUYS FIND WHAT YOU'RE LOOKING FOR...I KNOW I SURE DID.
BUT IF YOU'LL EXCUSE ME, THE 'POOL'S GONNA GO MAKE SOME SERIOUS DINERO OFF THIS--
WHAT--?!
WHO THE--
HEY, LET GO OF MY--
WHAT THE %$#@ IS THAT ON YOUR FACE?
TIME-OUT!

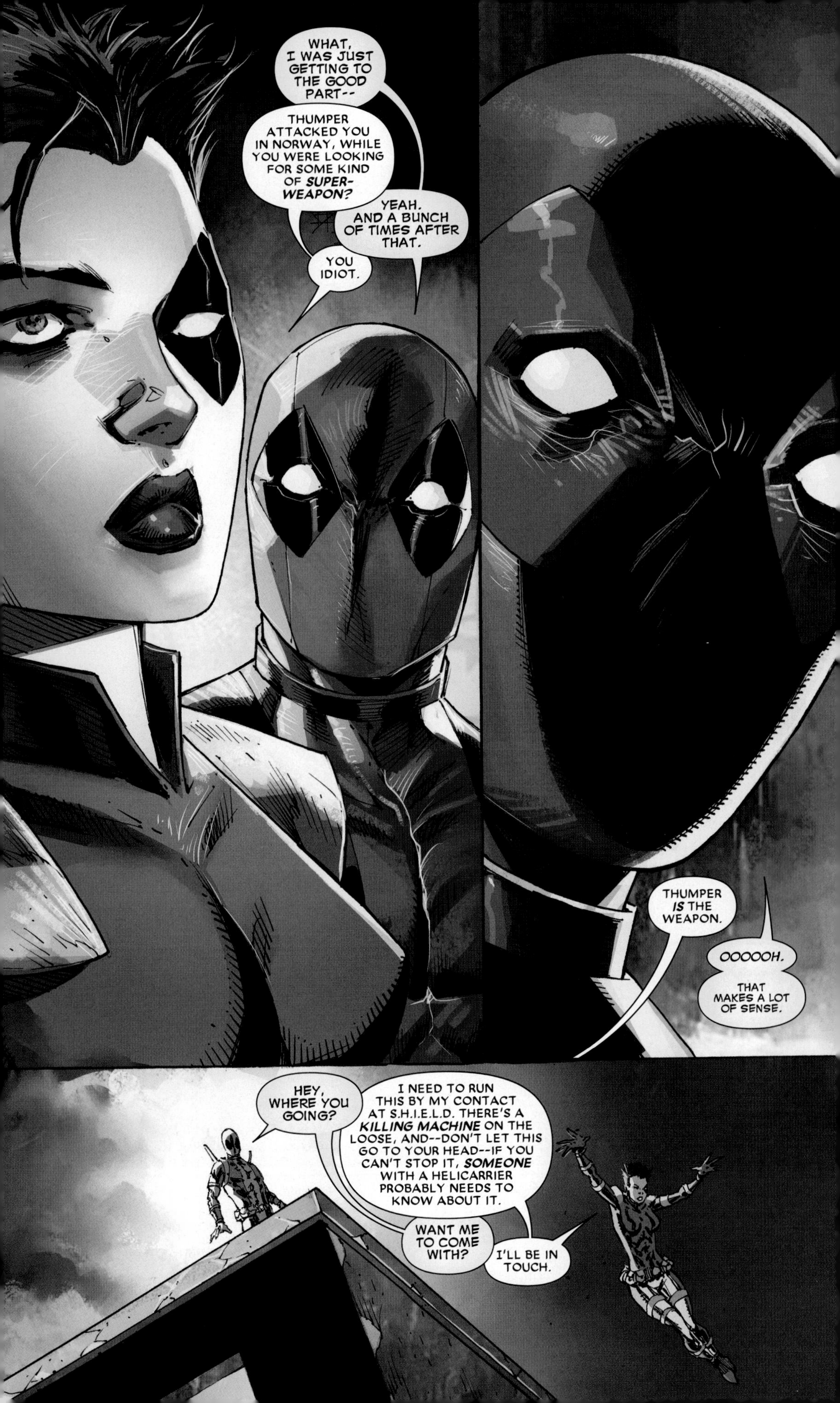
WHAT, I WAS JUST GETTING TO THE GOOD PART--
THUMPER ATTACKED YOU IN NORWAY, WHILE YOU WERE LOOKING FOR SOME KIND OF *SUPER-WEAPON?*
YEAH. AND A BUNCH OF TIMES AFTER THAT.
YOU IDIOT.
THUMPER *IS* THE WEAPON.
OOOOOH.
THAT MAKES A LOT OF SENSE.
HEY, WHERE YOU GOING?
I NEED TO RUN THIS BY MY CONTACT AT S.H.I.E.L.D. THERE'S A *KILLING MACHINE* ON THE LOOSE, AND--DON'T LET THIS GO TO YOUR HEAD--IF YOU CAN'T STOP IT, *SOMEONE* WITH A HELICARRIER PROBABLY NEEDS TO KNOW ABOUT IT.
WANT ME TO COME WITH?
I'LL BE IN TOUCH.

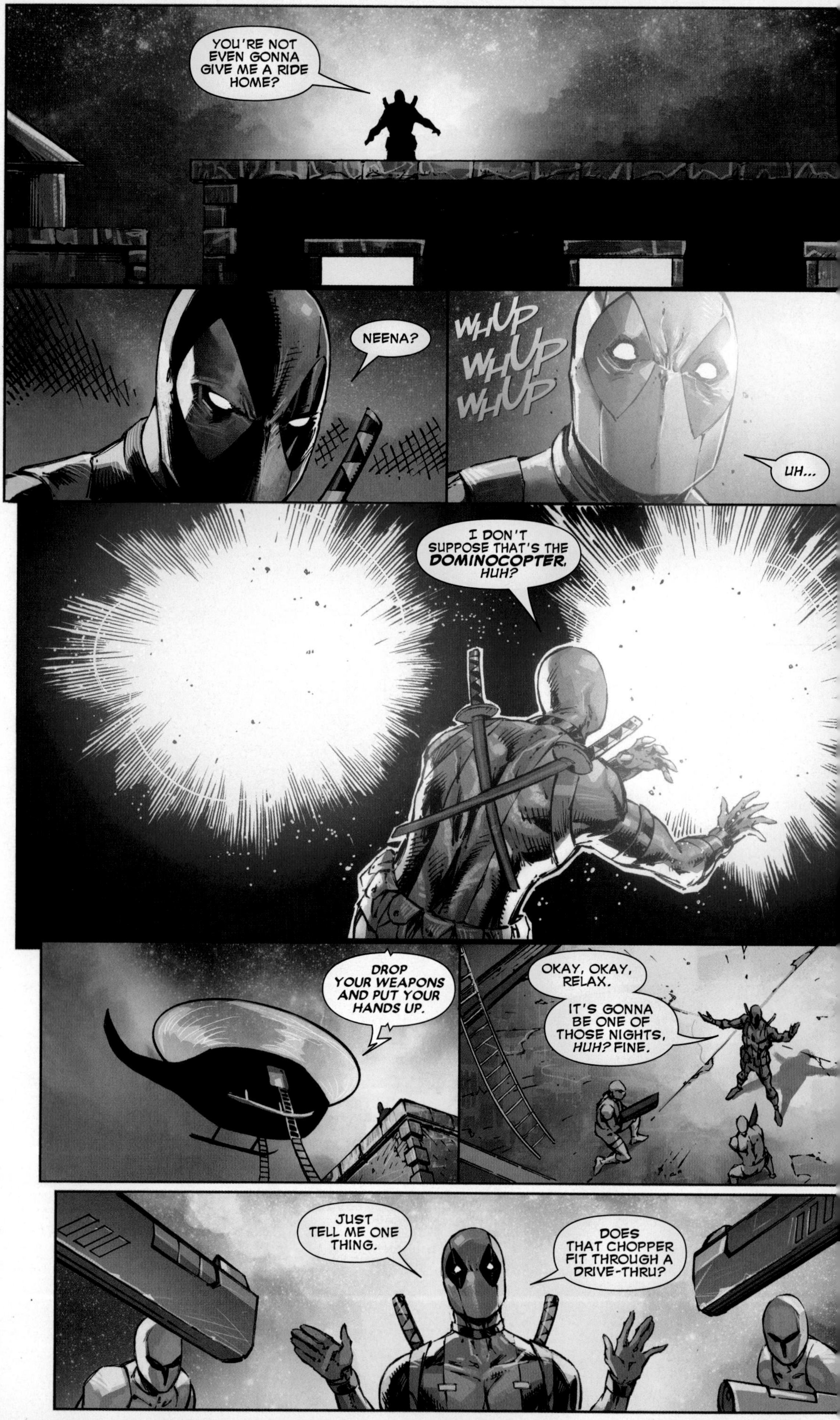

YOU'RE NOT EVEN GONNA GIVE ME A RIDE HOME?
NEENA?
WHUP WHUP WHUP
UH...
I DON'T SUPPOSE THAT'S THE DOMINOCOPTER, HUH?
DROP YOUR WEAPONS AND PUT YOUR HANDS UP.
OKAY, OKAY, RELAX.
IT'S GONNA BE ONE OF THOSE NIGHTS, HUH? FINE.
JUST TELL ME ONE THING.
DOES THAT CHOPPER FIT THROUGH A DRIVE-THRU?

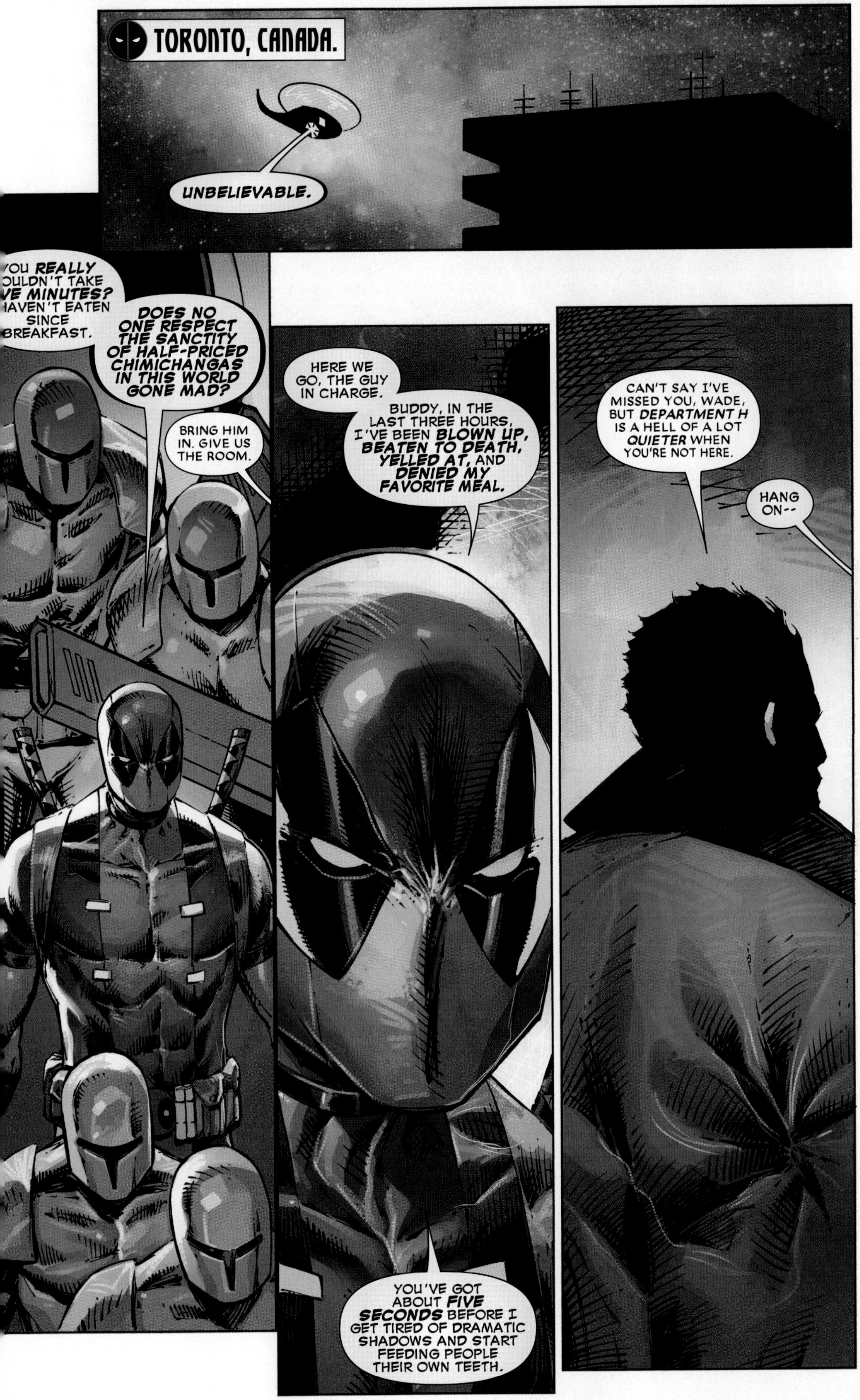
TORONTO, CANADA.
UNBELIEVABLE.
YOU REALLY OULDN'T TAKE VE MINUTES? HAVEN'T EATEN SINCE BREAKFAST.
DOES NO ONE RESPECT THE SANCTITY OF HALF-PRICED CHIMICHANGAS IN THIS WORLD GONE MAD?
BRING HIM IN. GIVE US THE ROOM.
HERE WE GO, THE GUY IN CHARGE.
BUDDY, IN THE LAST THREE HOURS, I'VE BEEN BLOWN UP, BEATEN TO DEATH, YELLED AT, AND DENIED MY FAVORITE MEAL.
YOU'VE GOT ABOUT FIVE SECONDS BEFORE I GET TIRED OF DRAMATIC SHADOWS AND START FEEDING PEOPLE THEIR OWN TEETH.
CAN'T SAY I'VE MISSED YOU, WADE, BUT DEPARTMENT H IS A HELL OF A LOT QUIETER WHEN YOU'RE NOT HERE.
HANG ON--

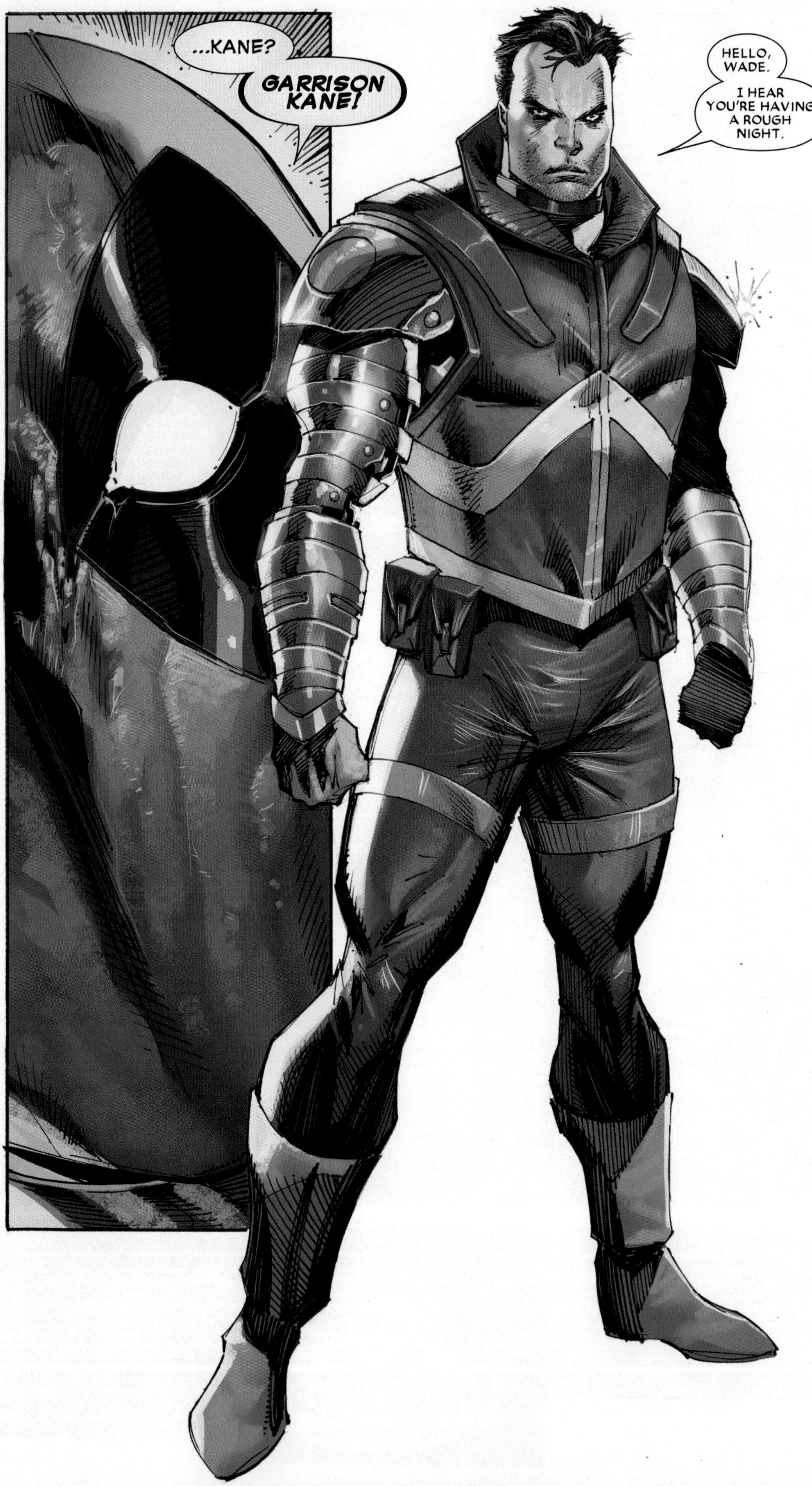

...KANE?
GARRISON KANE!
HELLO, WADE.
I HEAR YOU'RE HAVING A ROUGH NIGHT.

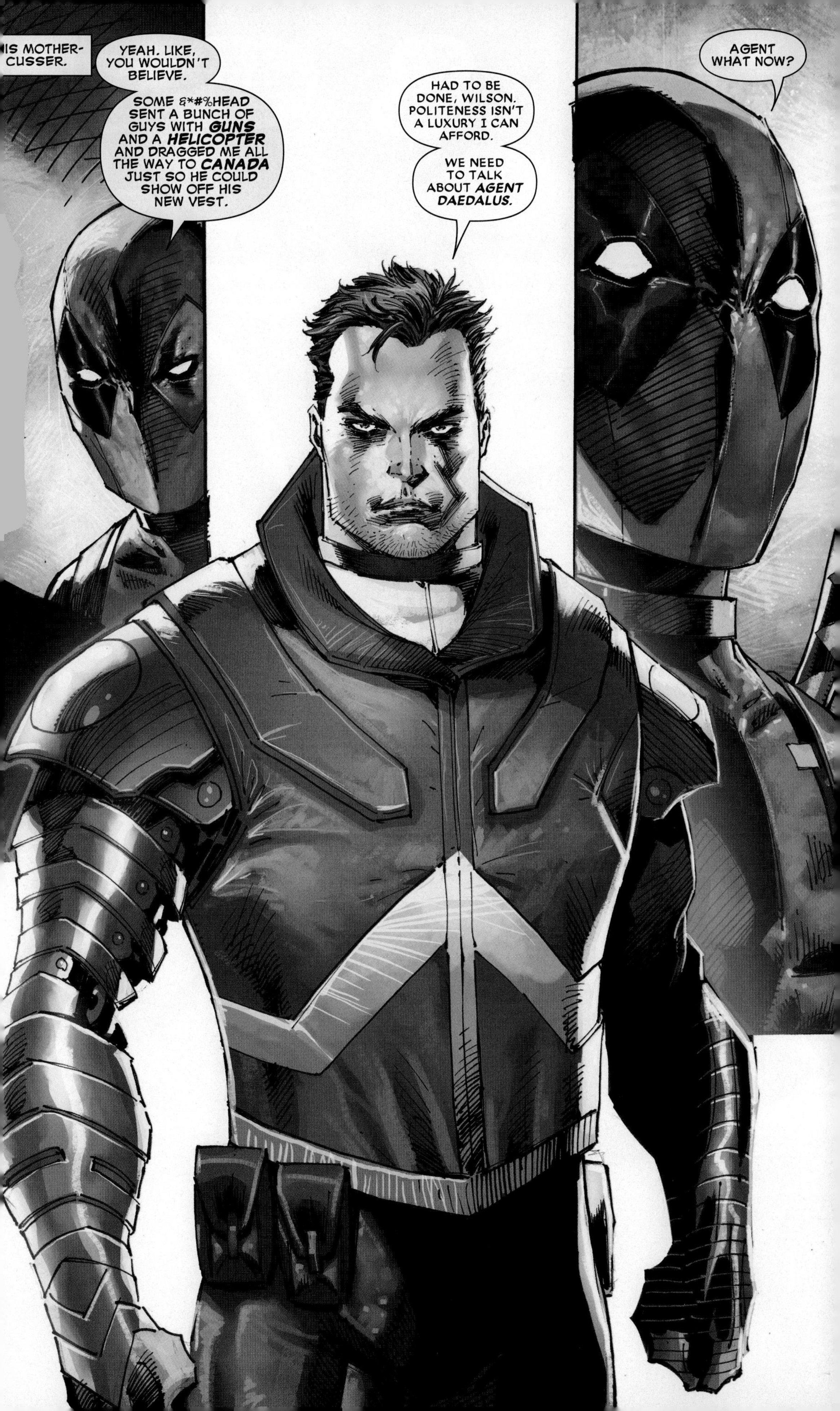
IS MOTHER-
CUSSER.
YEAH. LIKE, YOU WOULDN'T BELIEVE.
SOME &*#%HEAD SENT A BUNCH OF GUYS WITH GUNS AND A HELICOPTER AND DRAGGED ME ALL THE WAY TO CANADA JUST SO HE COULD SHOW OFF HIS NEW VEST.
HAD TO BE DONE, WILSON. POLITENESS ISN'T A LUXURY I CAN AFFORD.
WE NEED TO TALK ABOUT AGENT DAEDALUS.
AGENT WHAT NOW?

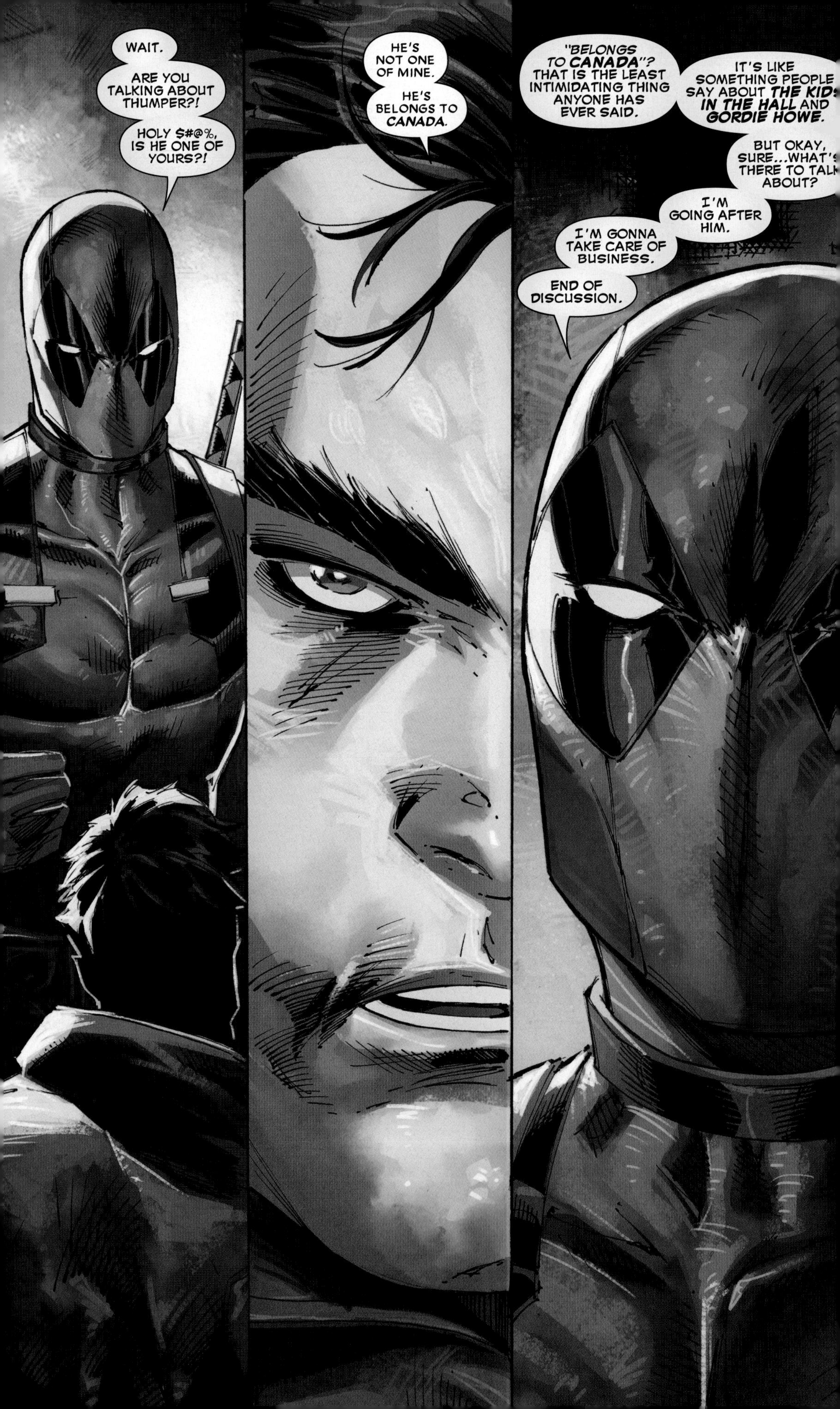
WAIT.
ARE YOU TALKING ABOUT THUMPER?!
HOLY $#@%, IS HE ONE OF YOURS?!
HE'S NOT ONE OF MINE.
HE'S BELONGS TO CANADA.
"BELONGS TO CANADA"? THAT IS THE LEAST INTIMIDATING THING ANYONE HAS EVER SAID.
IT'S LIKE SOMETHING PEOPLE SAY ABOUT THE KIDS IN THE HALL AND GORDIE HOWE.
BUT OKAY, SURE...WHAT'S THERE TO TALK ABOUT?
I'M GOING AFTER HIM.
I'M GONNA TAKE CARE OF BUSINESS.
END OF DISCUSSION.

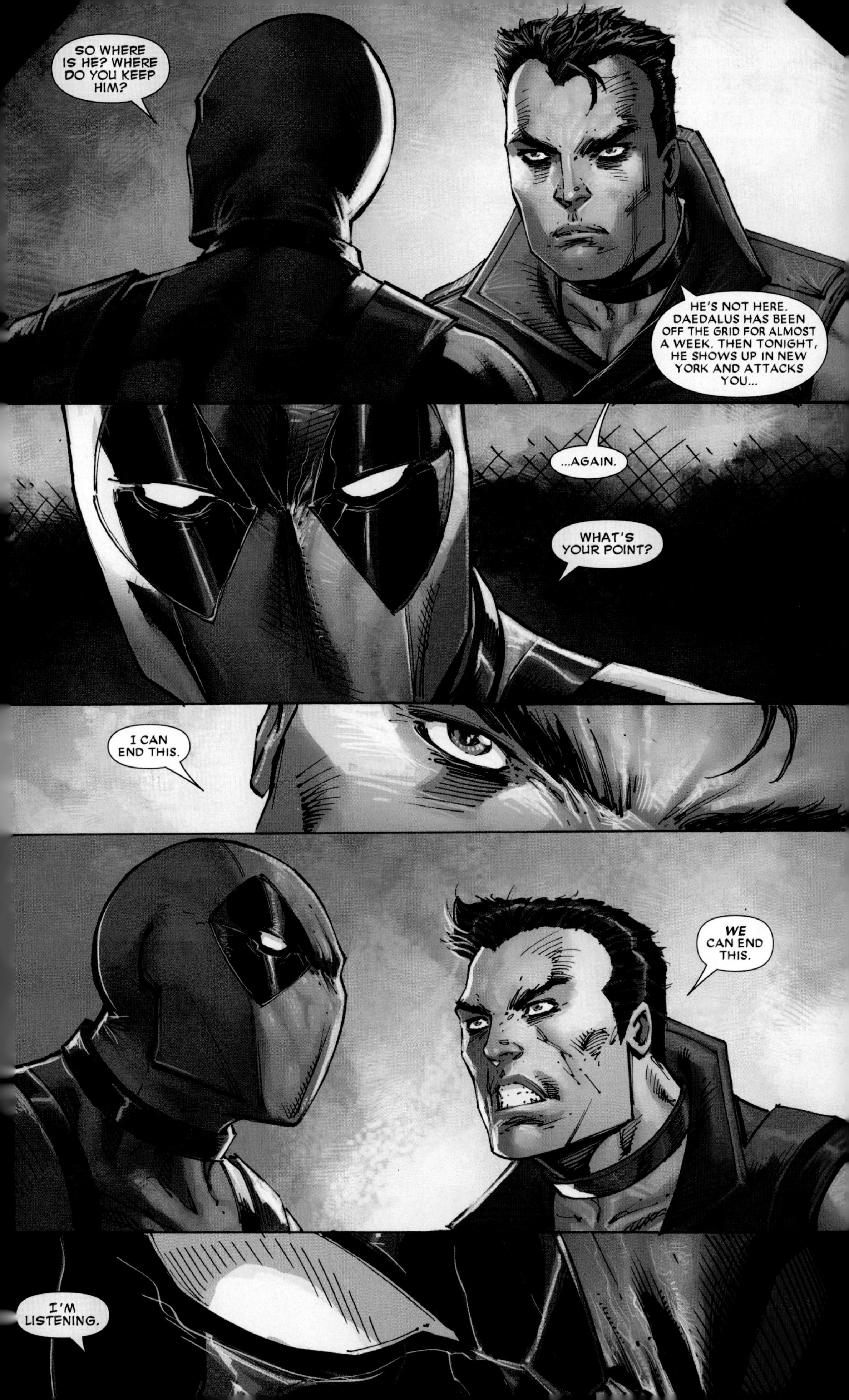
SO WHERE IS HE? WHERE DO YOU KEEP HIM?
HE'S NOT HERE. DAEDALUS HAS BEEN OFF THE GRID FOR ALMOST A WEEK. THEN TONIGHT, HE SHOWS UP IN NEW YORK AND ATTACKS YOU...
...AGAIN.
WHAT'S YOUR POINT?
I CAN END THIS.
WE CAN END THIS.
I'M LISTENING.

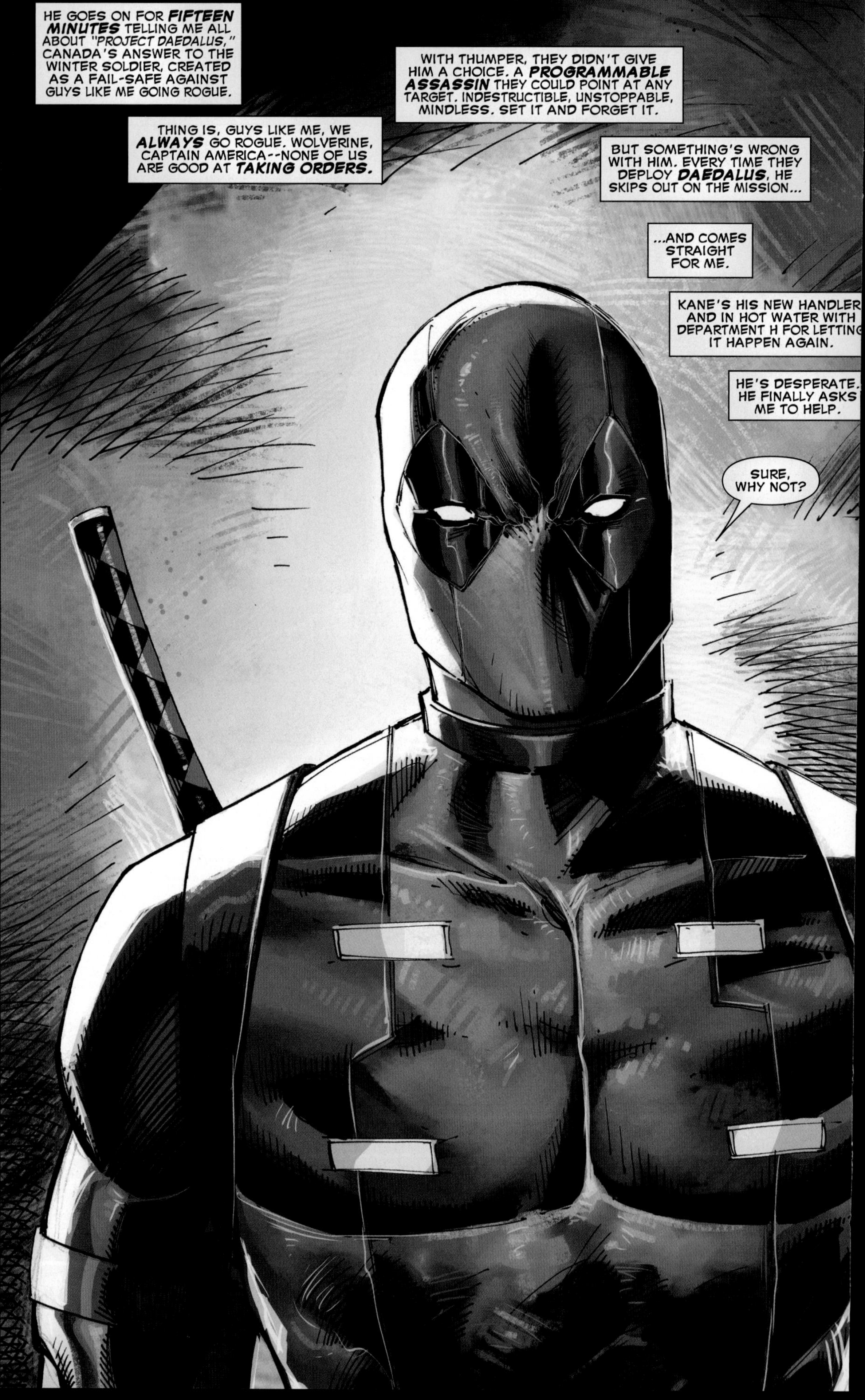
HE GOES ON FOR FIFTEEN MINUTES TELLING ME ALL ABOUT "PROJECT DAEDALUS," CANADA'S ANSWER TO THE WINTER SOLDIER, CREATED AS A FAIL-SAFE AGAINST GUYS LIKE ME GOING ROGUE.
THING IS, GUYS LIKE ME, WE ALWAYS GO ROGUE. WOLVERINE, CAPTAIN AMERICA--NONE OF US ARE GOOD AT TAKING ORDERS.
WITH THUMPER, THEY DIDN'T GIVE HIM A CHOICE. A PROGRAMMABLE ASSASSIN THEY COULD POINT AT ANY TARGET. INDESTRUCTIBLE, UNSTOPPABLE, MINDLESS. SET IT AND FORGET IT.
BUT SOMETHING'S WRONG WITH HIM. EVERY TIME THEY DEPLOY DAEDALUS, HE SKIPS OUT ON THE MISSION...
...AND COMES STRAIGHT FOR ME.
KANE'S HIS NEW HANDLER AND IN HOT WATER WITH DEPARTMENT H FOR LETTING IT HAPPEN AGAIN.
HE'S DESPERATE. HE FINALLY ASKS ME TO HELP.
SURE, WHY NOT?

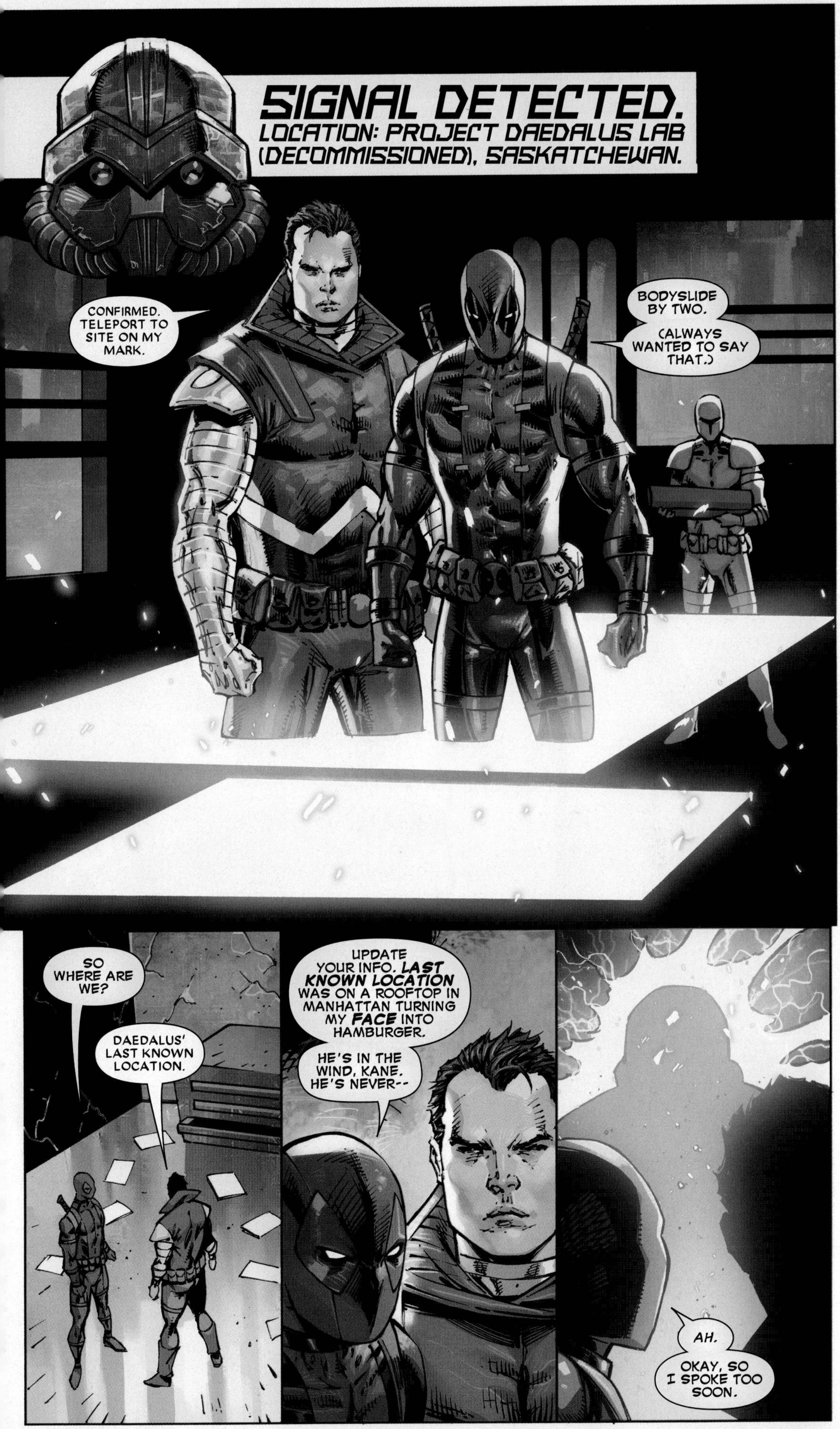
SIGNAL DETECTED.
LOCATION: PROJECT DAEDALUS LAB (DECOMMISSIONED), SASKATCHEWAN.
CONFIRMED. TELEPORT TO SITE ON MY MARK.
BODYSLIDE BY TWO.
(ALWAYS WANTED TO SAY THAT.)
SO WHERE ARE WE?
DAEDALUS' LAST KNOWN LOCATION.
UPDATE YOUR INFO. LAST KNOWN LOCATION WAS ON A ROOFTOP IN MANHATTAN TURNING MY FACE INTO HAMBURGER.
HE'S IN THE WIND, KANE. HE'S NEVER--
AH.
OKAY, SO I SPOKE TOO SOON.

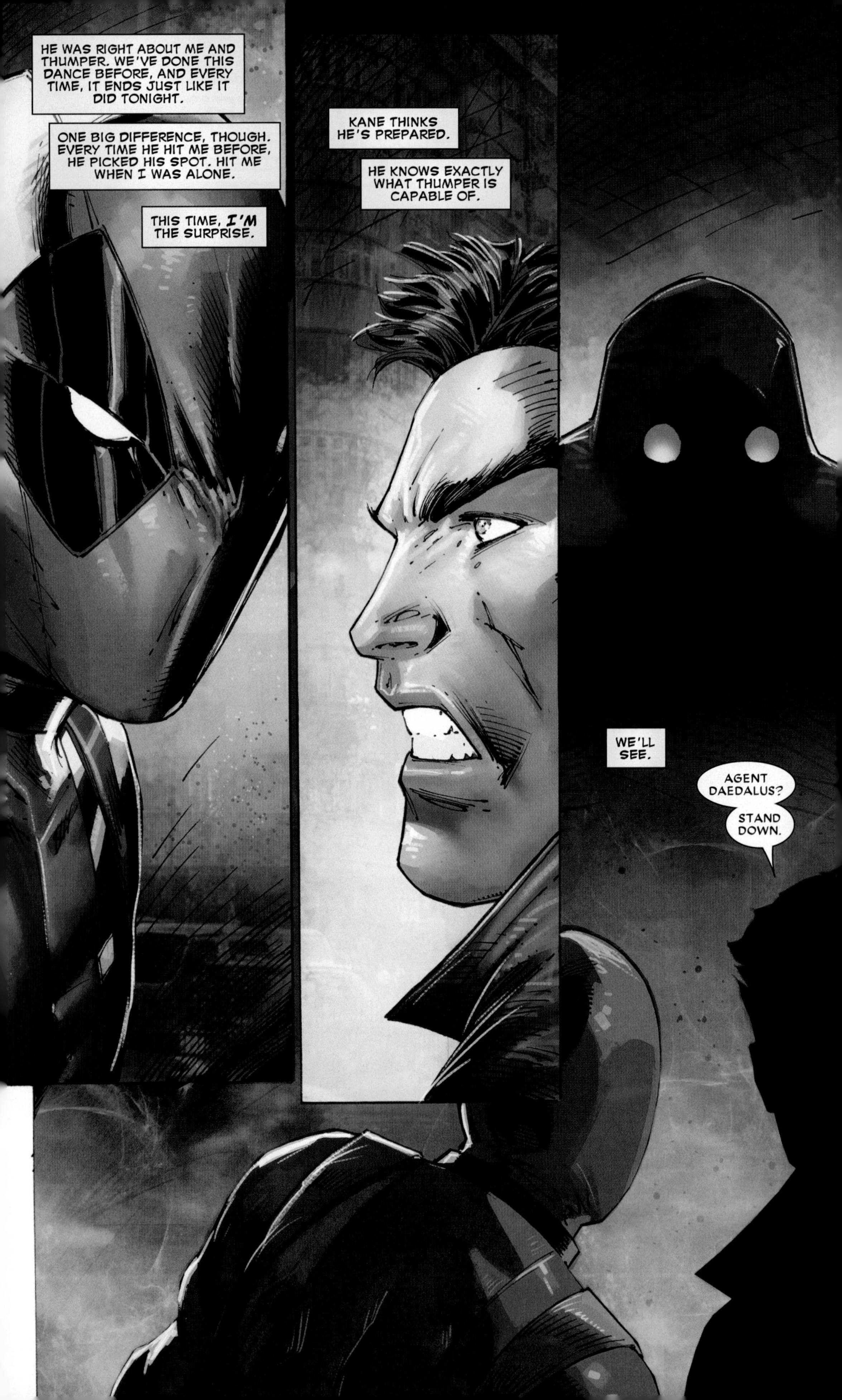
HE WAS RIGHT ABOUT ME AND THUMPER. WE'VE DONE THIS DANCE BEFORE, AND EVERY TIME, IT ENDS JUST LIKE IT DID TONIGHT.
ONE BIG DIFFERENCE, THOUGH. EVERY TIME HE HIT ME BEFORE, HE PICKED HIS SPOT. HIT ME WHEN I WAS ALONE.
THIS TIME, *I'M* THE SURPRISE.
KANE THINKS HE'S PREPARED.
HE KNOWS EXACTLY WHAT THUMPER IS CAPABLE OF.
WE'LL SEE.
AGENT DAEDALUS?
STAND DOWN.

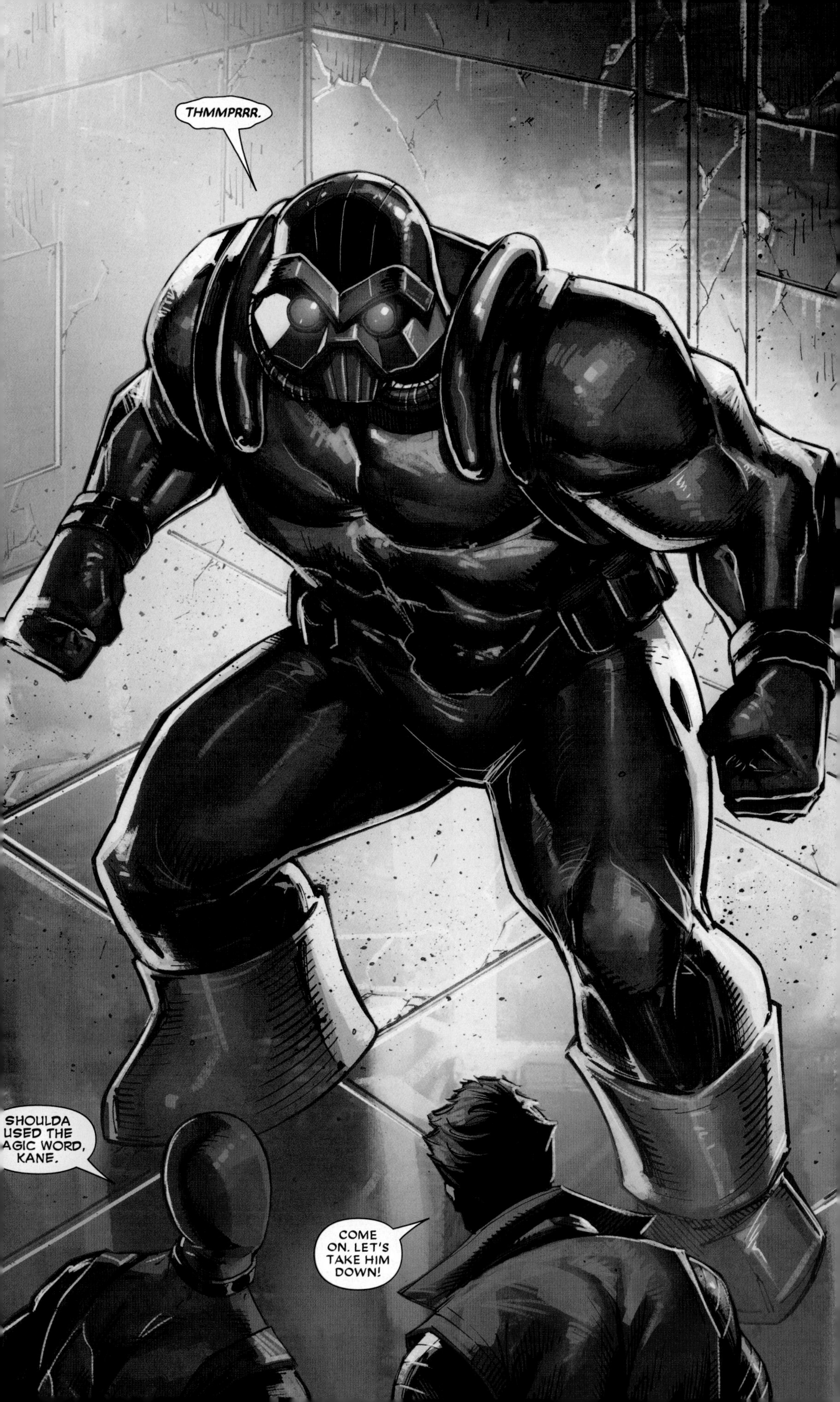
THMMPRRR.
SHOULDA USED THE AGIC WORD, KANE.
COME ON. LET'S TAKE HIM DOWN!

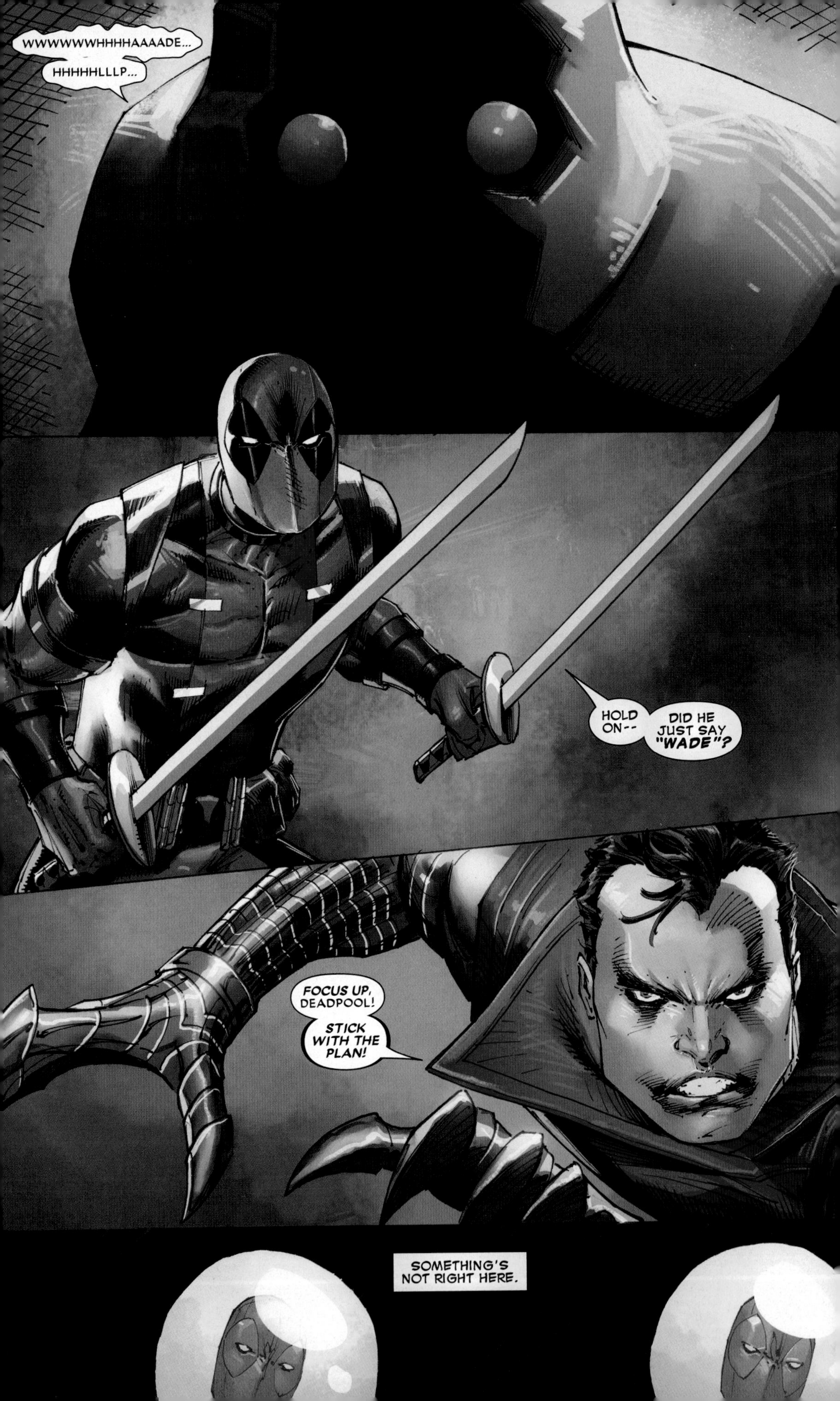

WWWWWWWHHHHAAAADE...
HHHHHLLLP...
HOLD ON--
DID HE JUST SAY "WADE"?
FOCUS UP, DEADPOOL!
STICK WITH THE PLAN!
SOMETHING'S NOT RIGHT HERE.

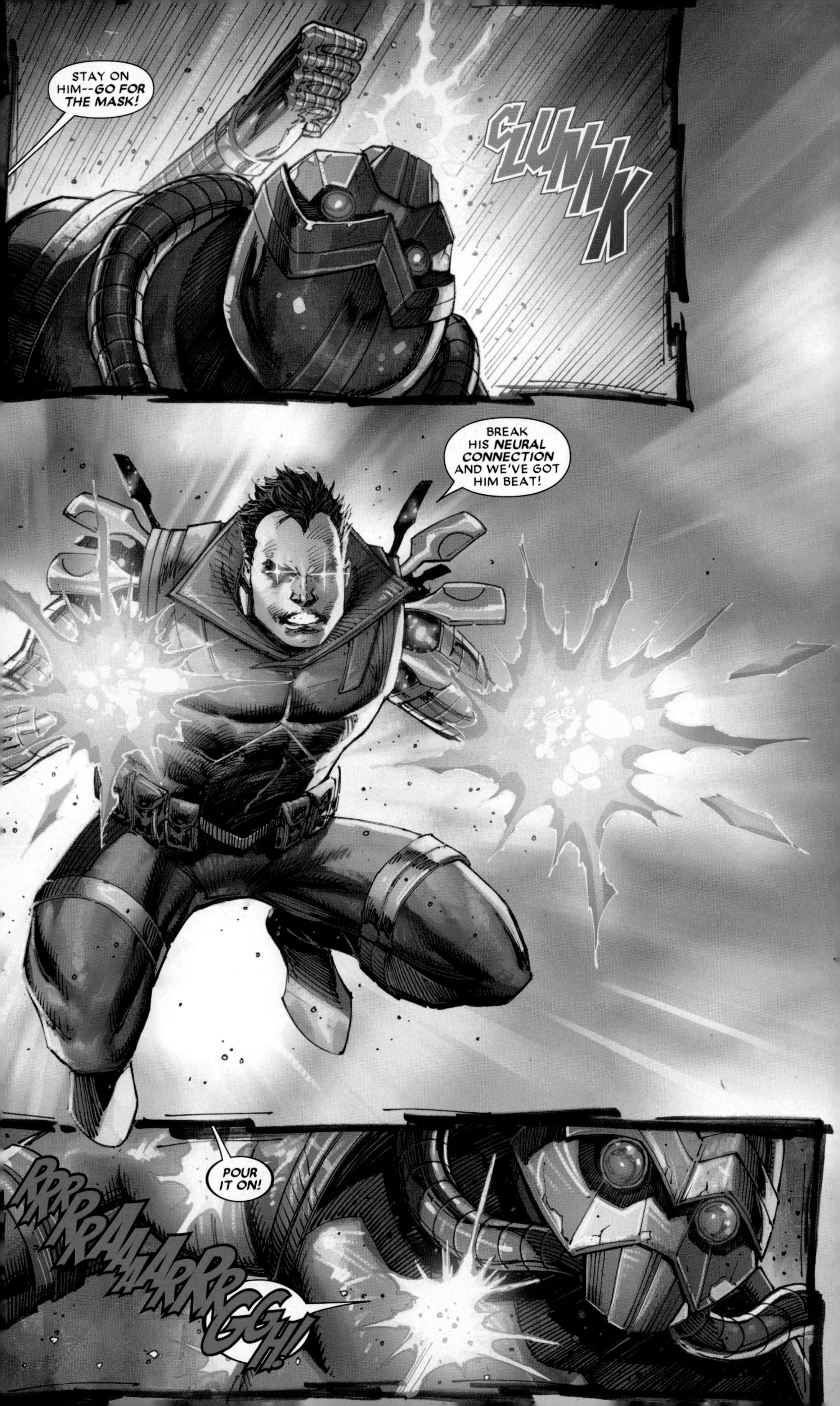
STAY ON HIM--GO FOR THE MASK!
CLUNNK
BREAK HIS NEURAL CONNECTION AND WE'VE GOT HIM BEAT!
POUR IT ON!
RRRRRAAAARRRGGH!

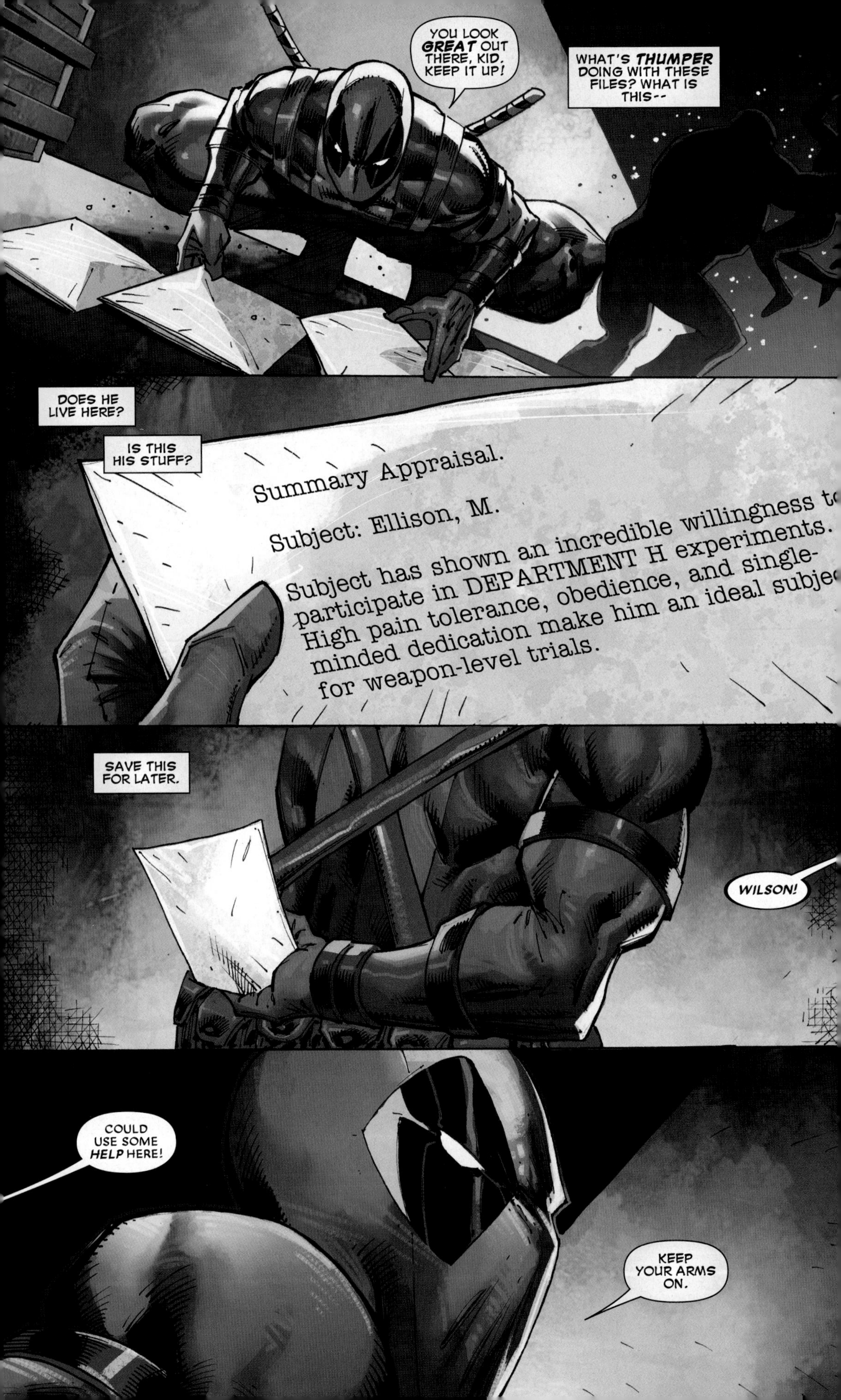

YOU LOOK GREAT OUT THERE, KID. KEEP IT UP!
WHAT'S THUMPER DOING WITH THESE FILES? WHAT IS THIS--
DOES HE LIVE HERE?
IS THIS HIS STUFF?
Summary Appraisal.
Subject: Ellison, M.
Subject has shown an incredible willingness to participate in DEPARTMENT H experiments. High pain tolerance, obedience, and single-minded dedication make him an ideal subject for weapon-level trials.
SAVE THIS FOR LATER.
WILSON!
COULD USE SOME HELP HERE!
KEEP YOUR ARMS ON.

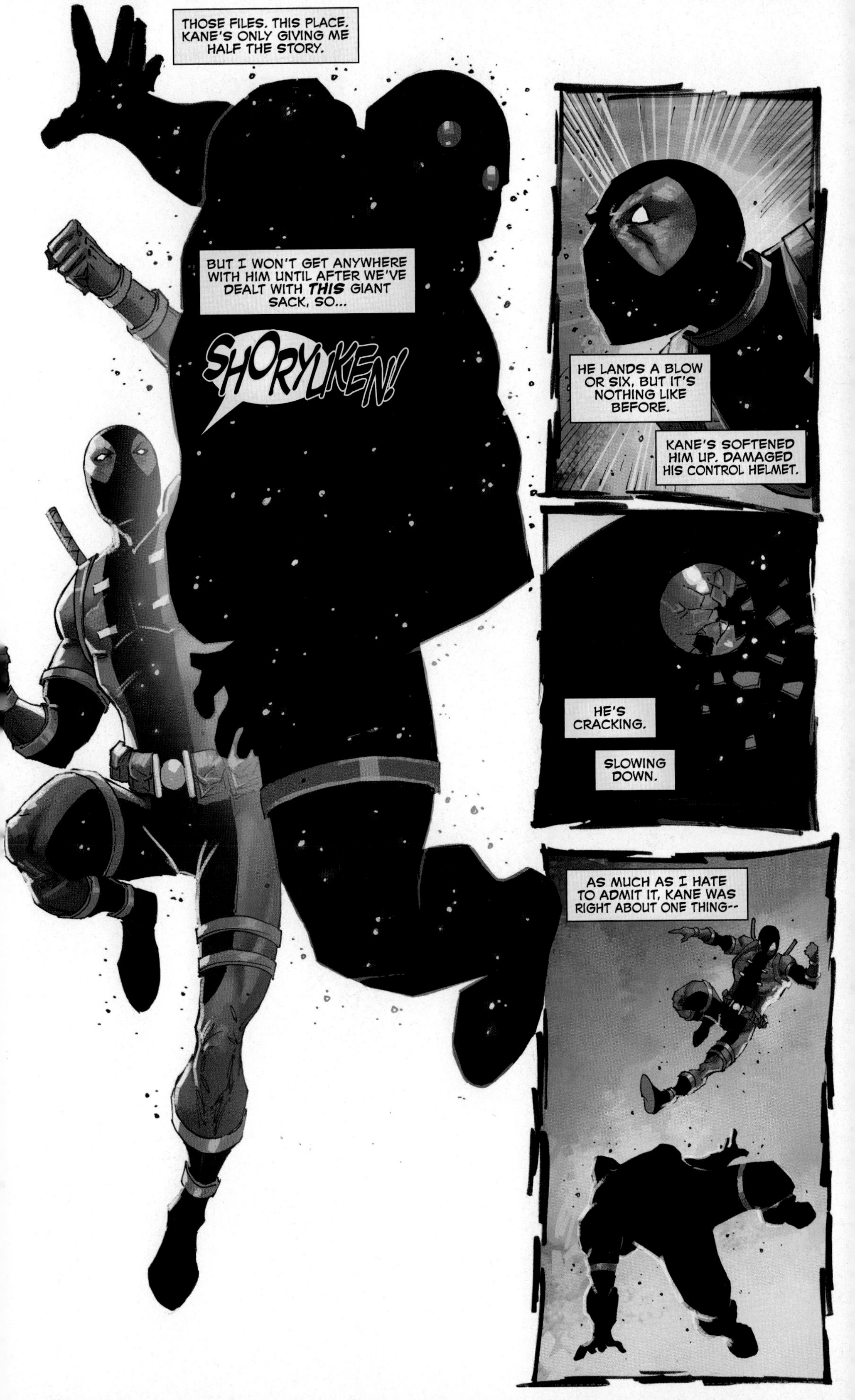
THOSE FILES. THIS PLACE. KANE'S ONLY GIVING ME HALF THE STORY.
BUT I WON'T GET ANYWHERE WITH HIM UNTIL AFTER WE'VE DEALT WITH THIS GIANT SACK, SO...
SHORYUKEN!!
HE LANDS A BLOW OR SIX, BUT IT'S NOTHING LIKE BEFORE.
KANE'S SOFTENED HIM UP. DAMAGED HIS CONTROL HELMET.
HE'S CRACKING.
SLOWING DOWN.
AS MUCH AS I HATE TO ADMIT IT, KANE WAS RIGHT ABOUT ONE THING--

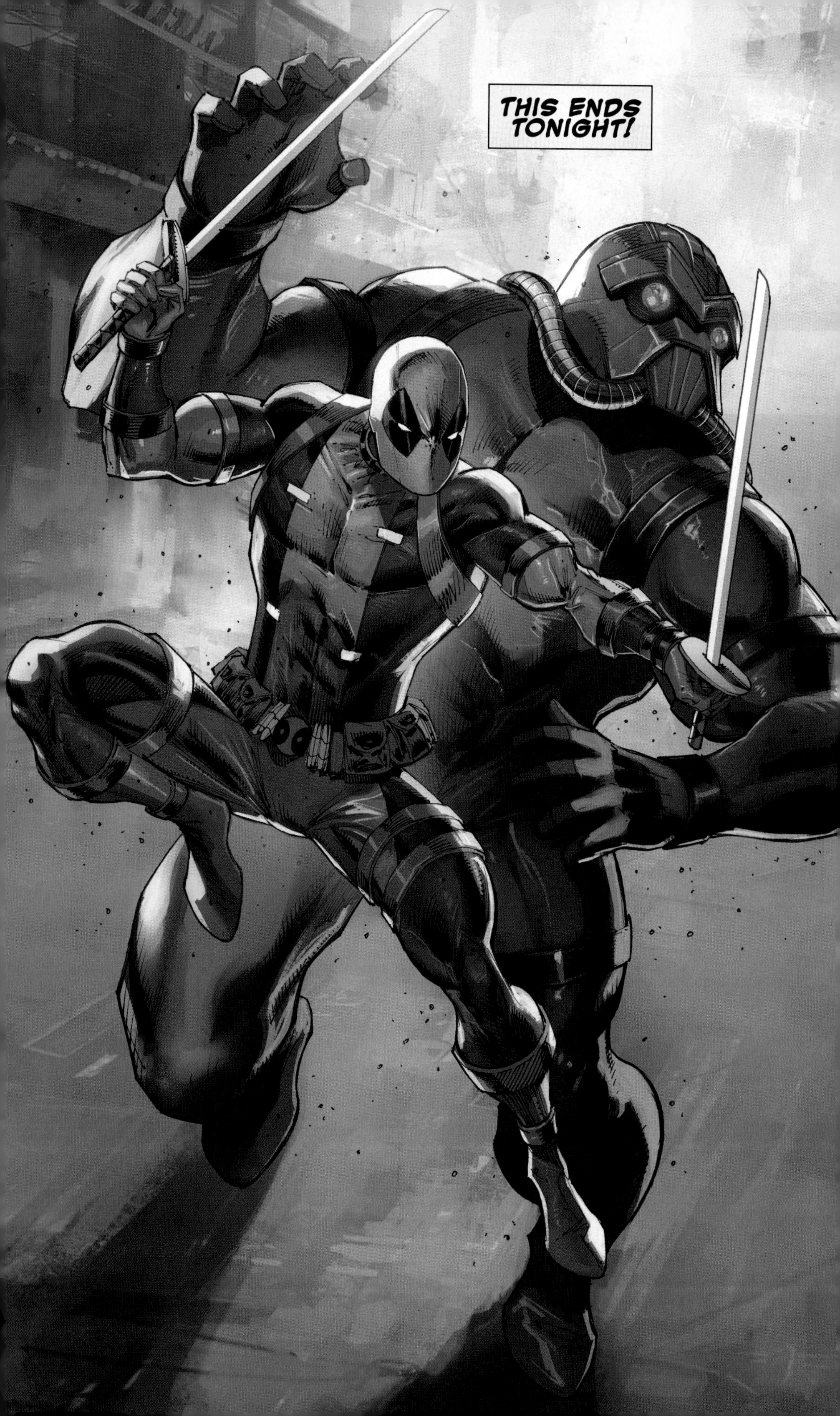
THIS ENDS TONIGHT!

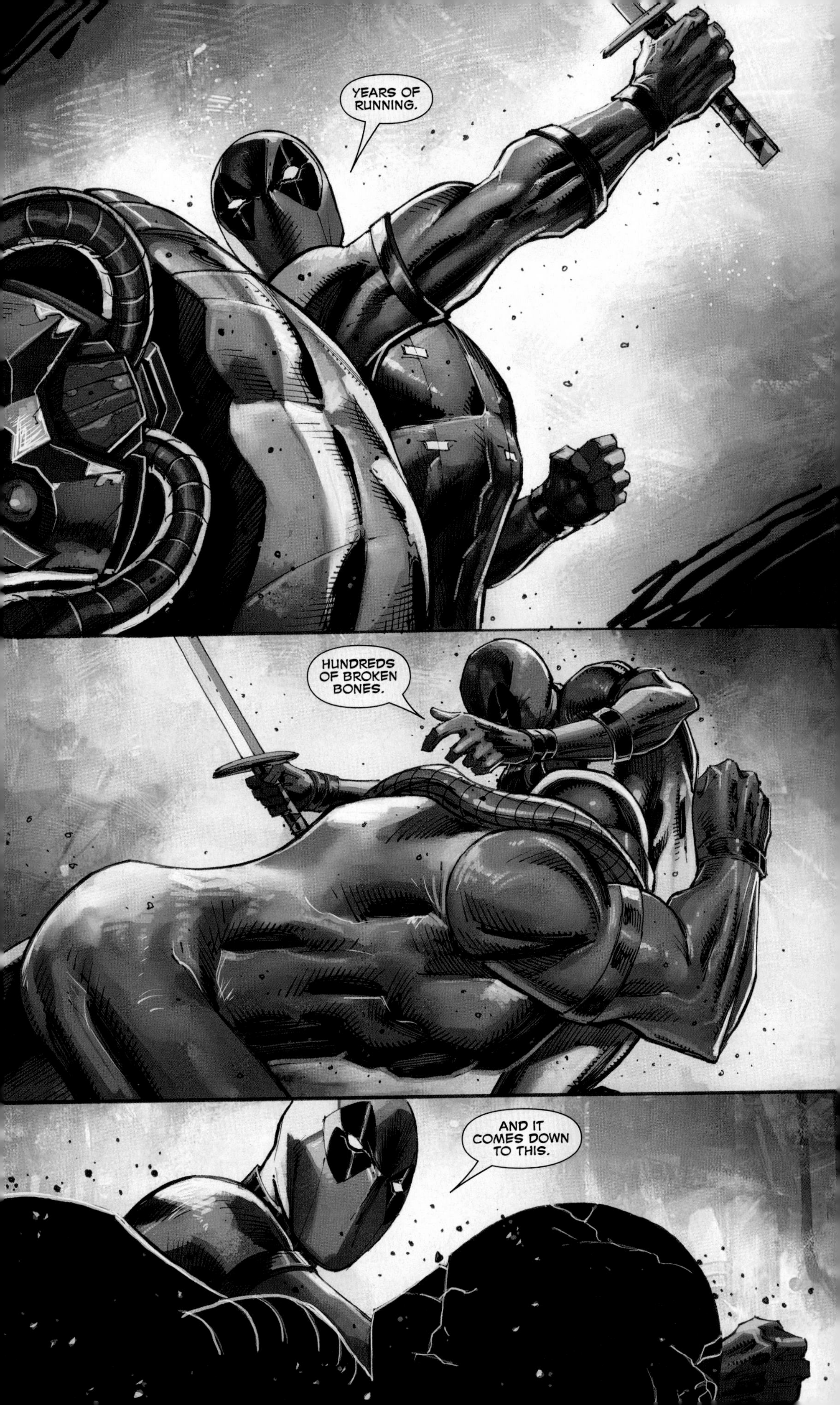
YEARS OF RUNNING.
HUNDREDS OF BROKEN BONES.
AND IT COMES DOWN TO THIS.

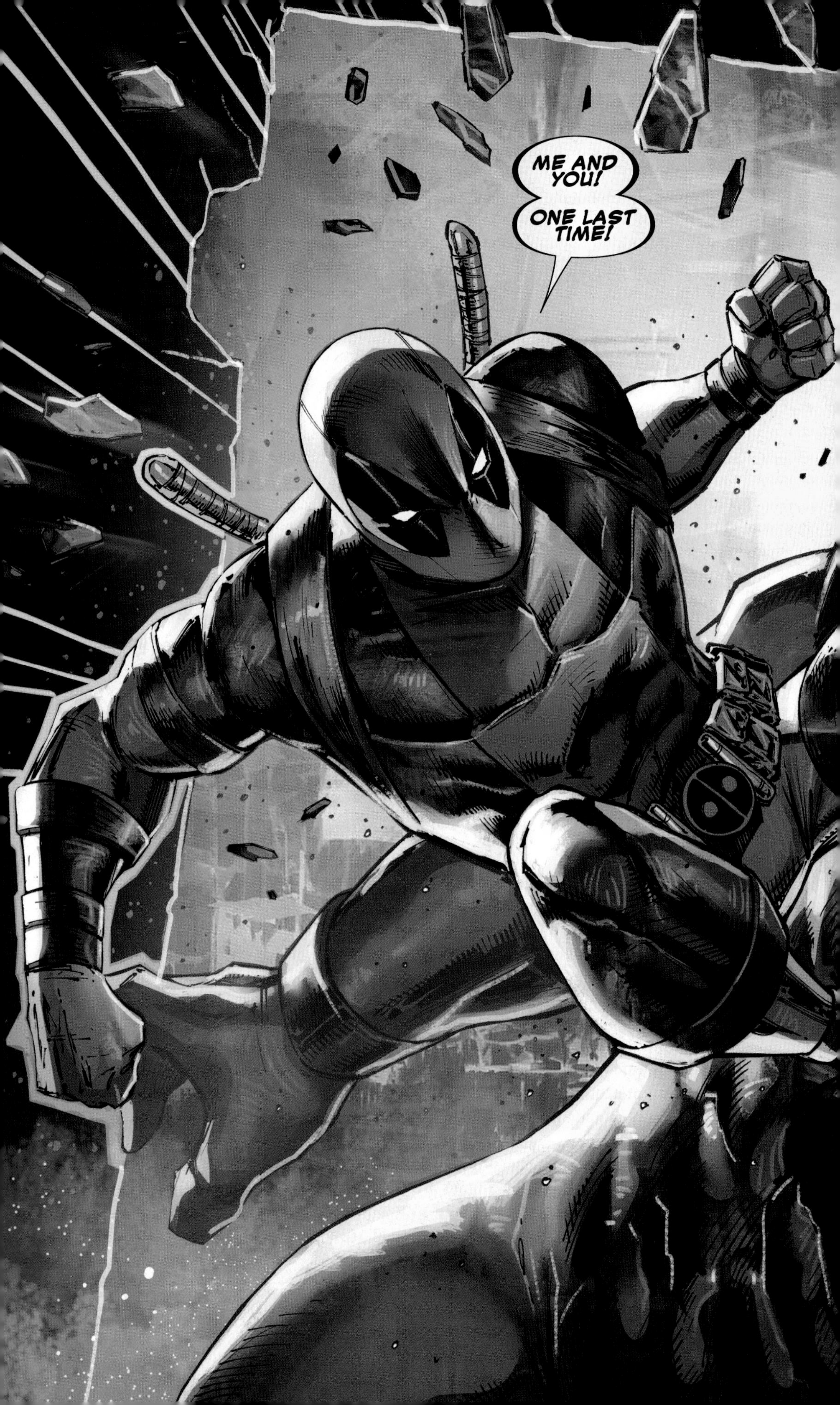
ME AND YOU!
ONE LAST TIME!

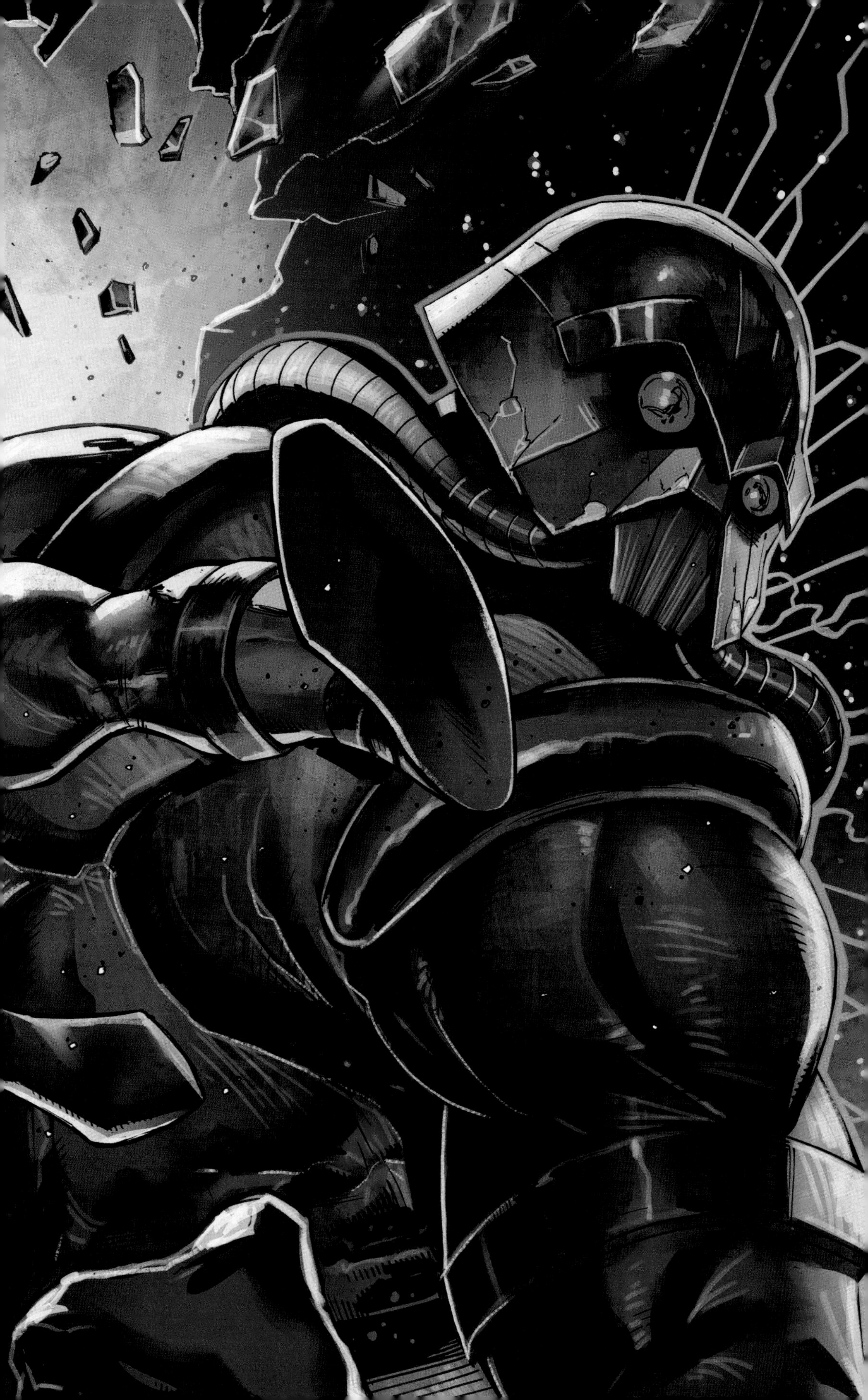

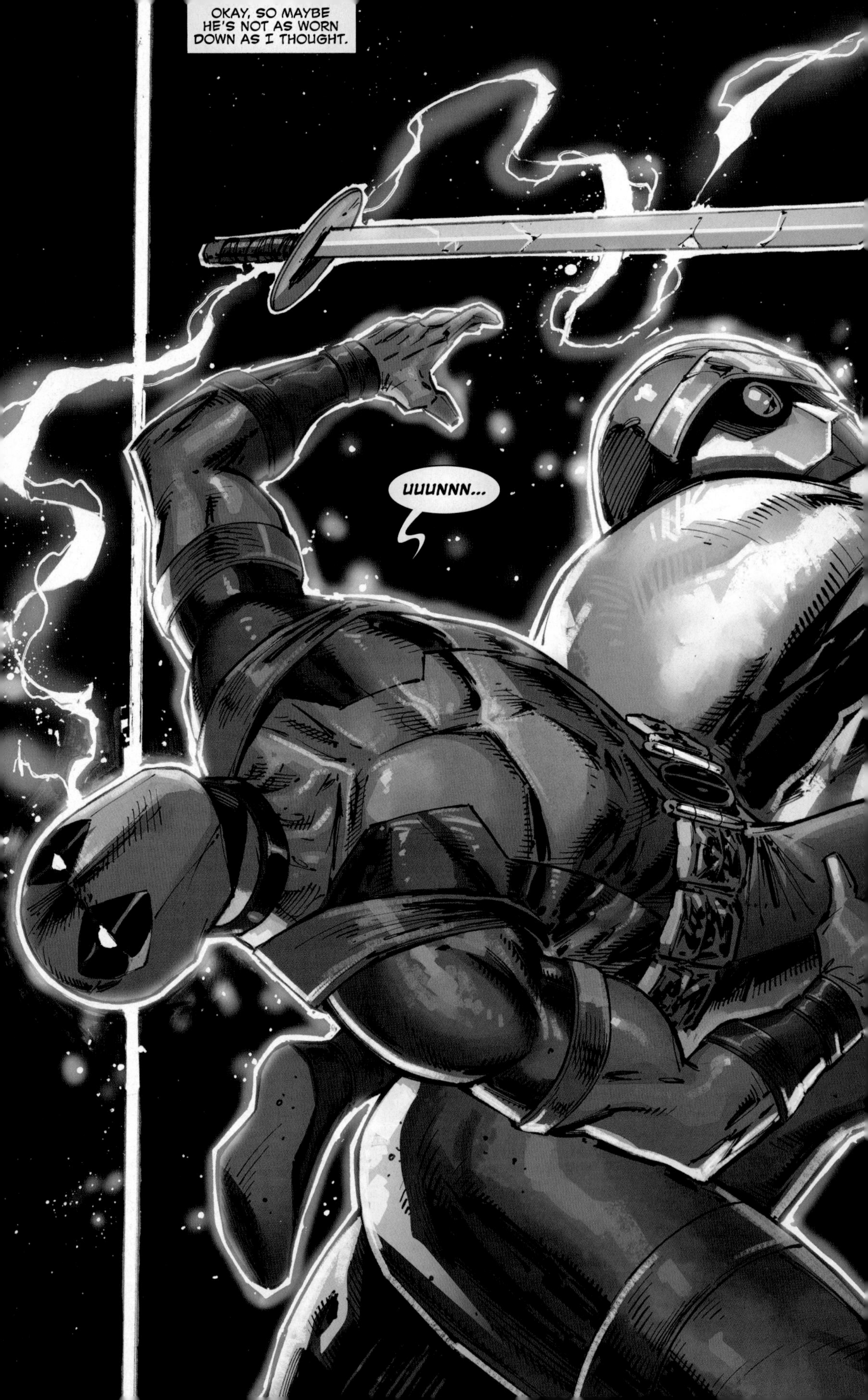
OKAY, SO MAYBE HE'S NOT AS WORN DOWN AS I THOUGHT.
UUUNNN...

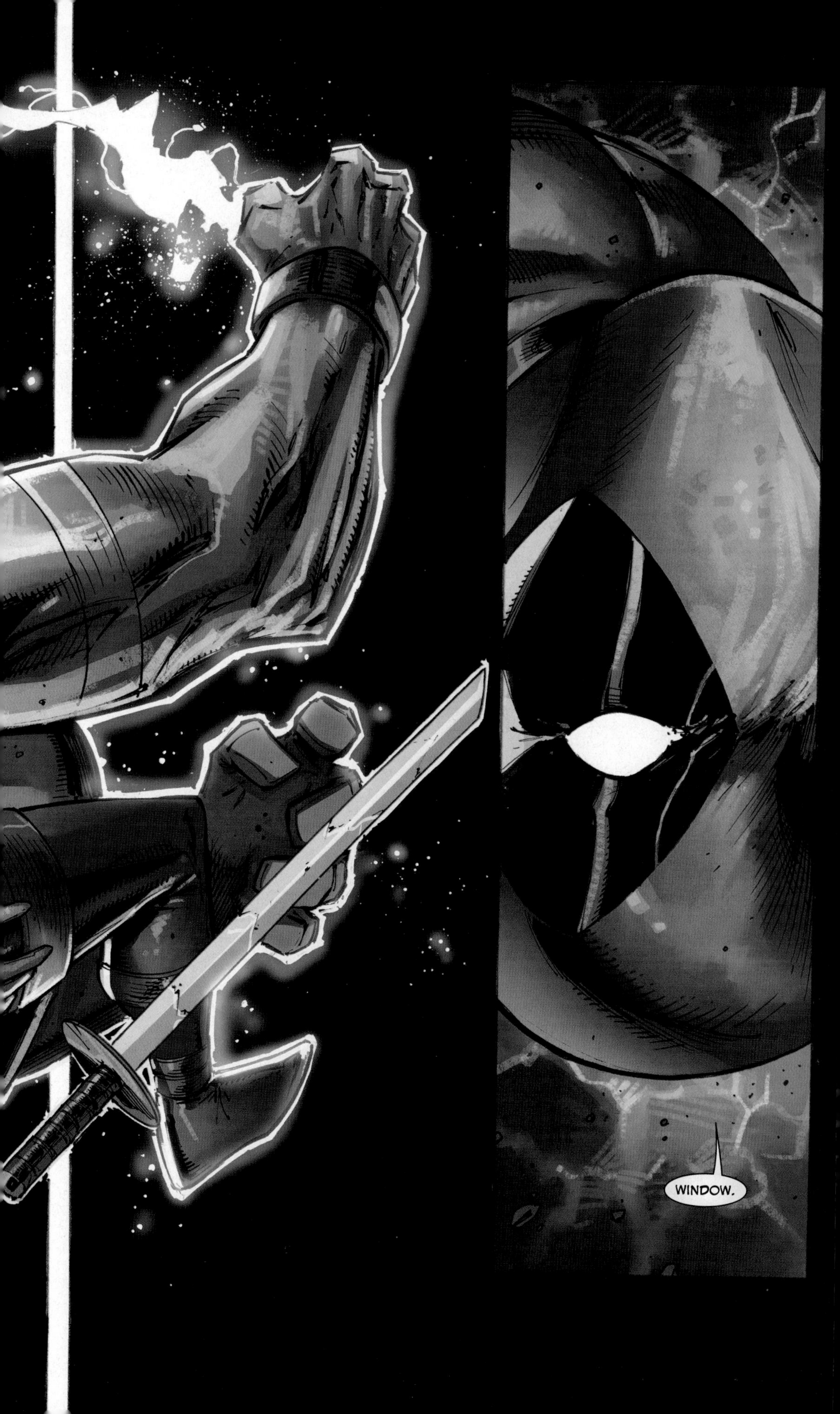
WINDOW.

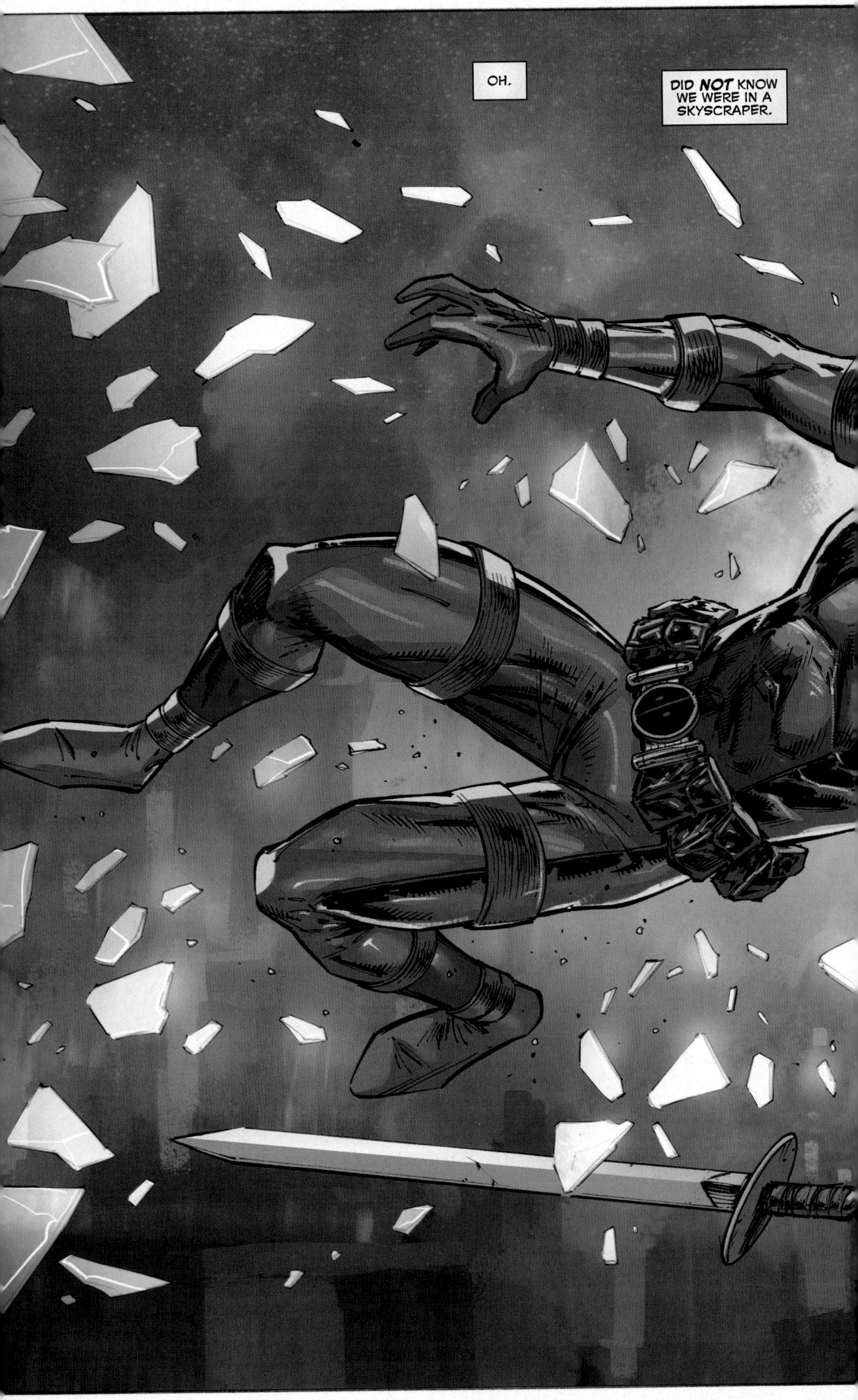
OH.
DID NOT KNOW WE WERE IN A SKYSCRAPER.

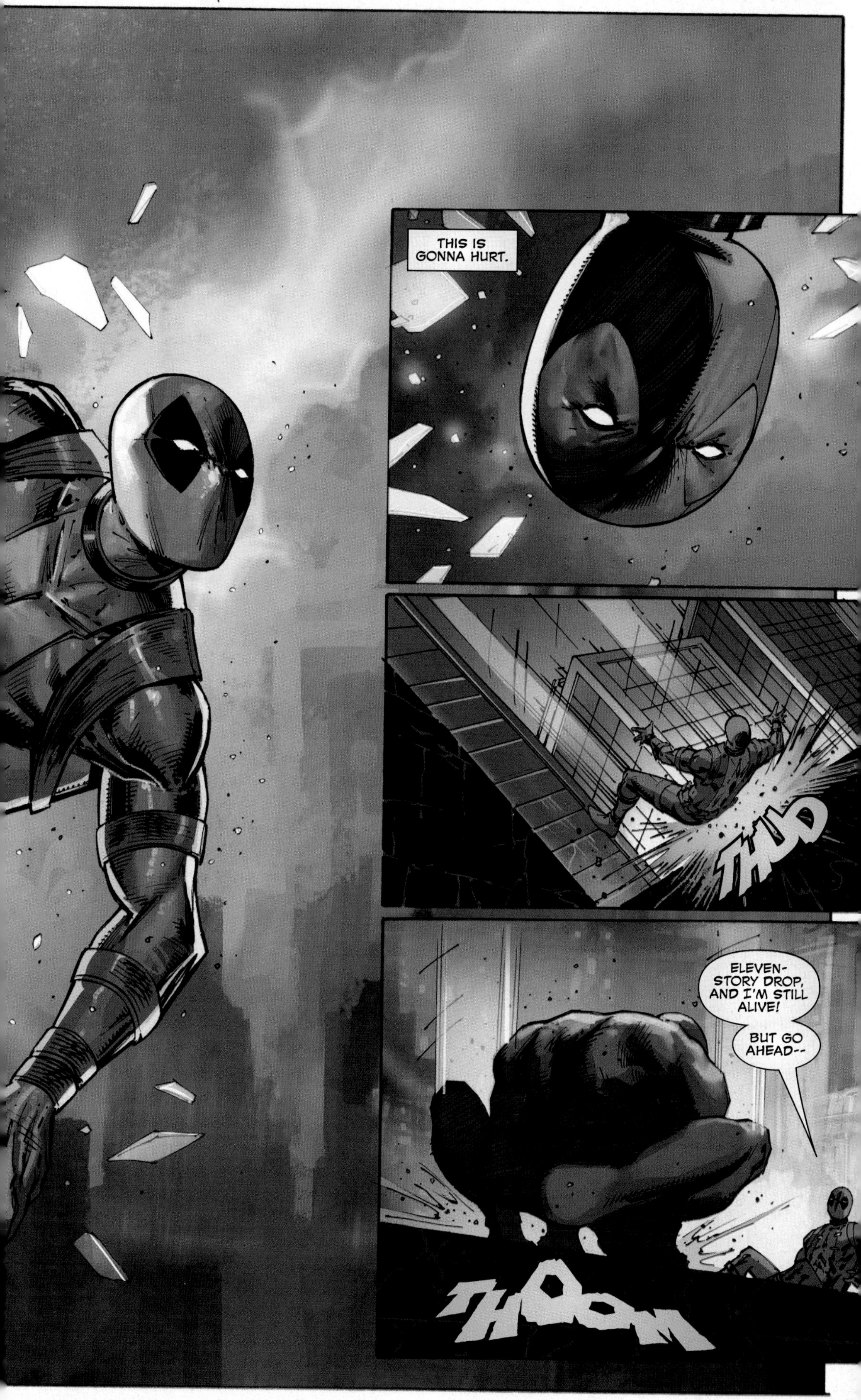
THIS IS GONNA HURT.
THUD
ELEVEN-STORY DROP, AND I'M STILL ALIVE!
BUT GO AHEAD--
THOOM

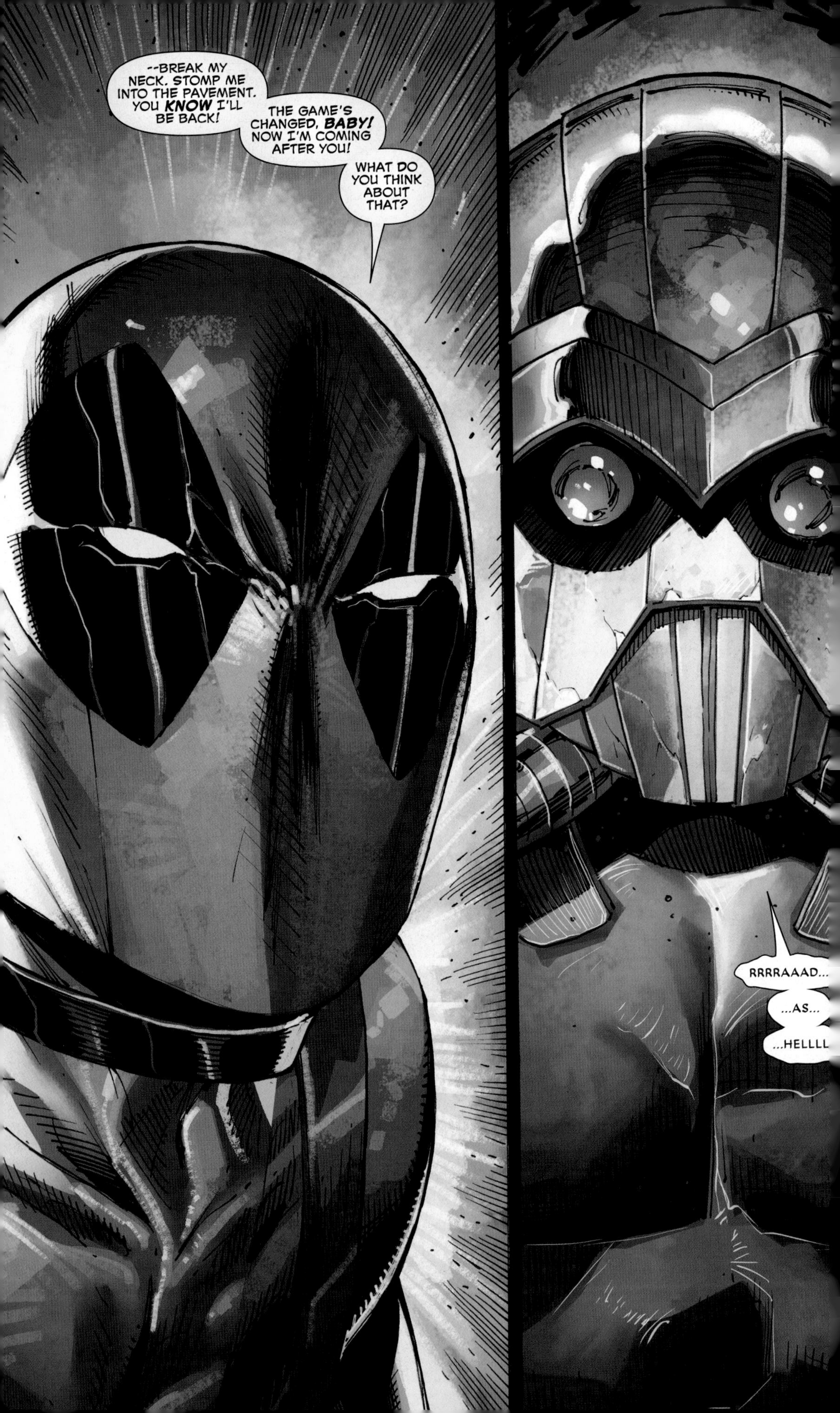
--BREAK MY NECK. STOMP ME INTO THE PAVEMENT. YOU **KNOW** I'LL BE BACK!
THE GAME'S CHANGED, **BABY!** NOW I'M COMING AFTER YOU!
WHAT DO YOU THINK ABOUT THAT?
RRRRAAAD...
...AS...
...HELLLL

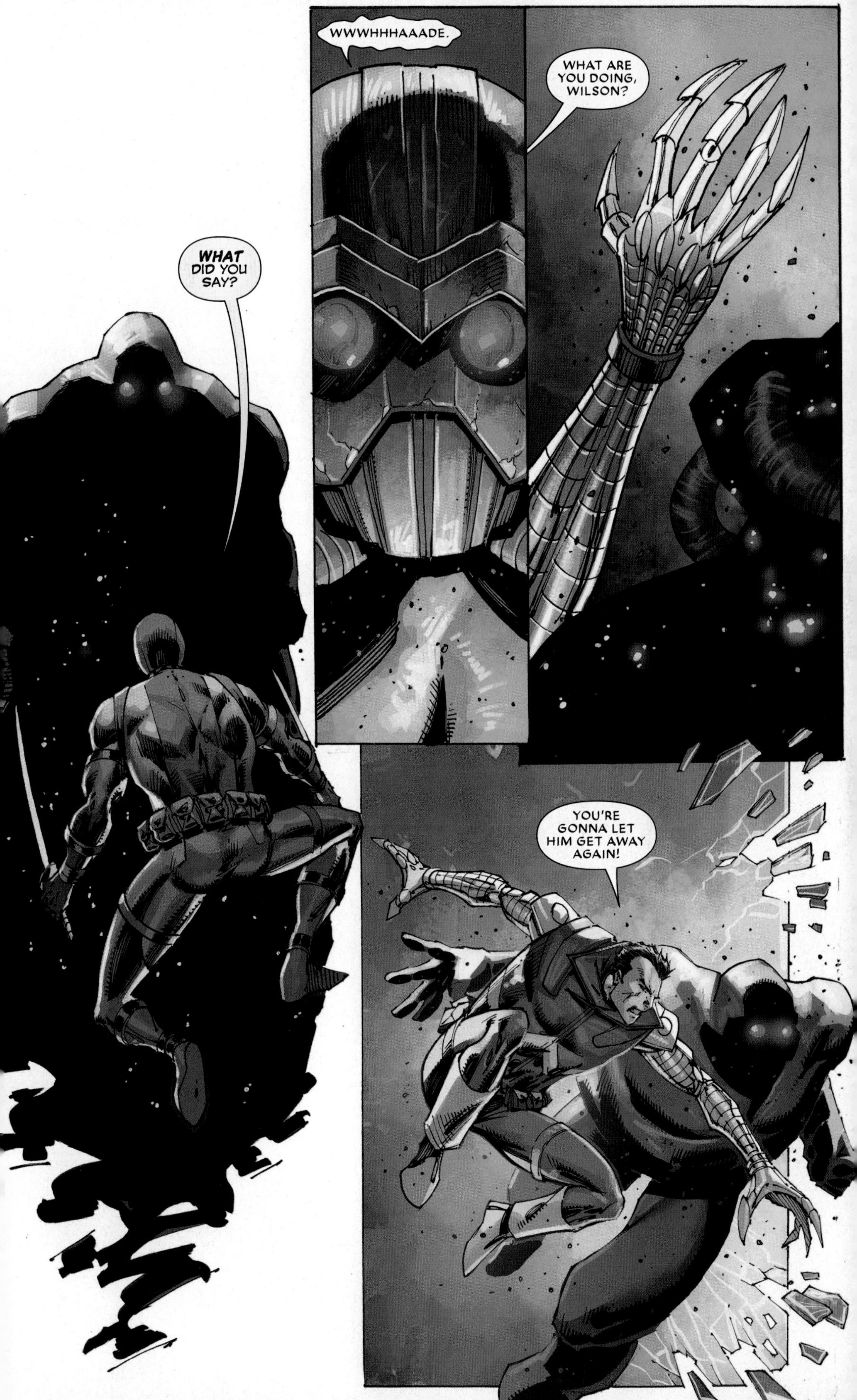
WHAT DID YOU SAY?
WWWHHHAAADE.
WHAT ARE YOU DOING, WILSON?
YOU'RE GONNA LET HIM GET AWAY AGAIN!

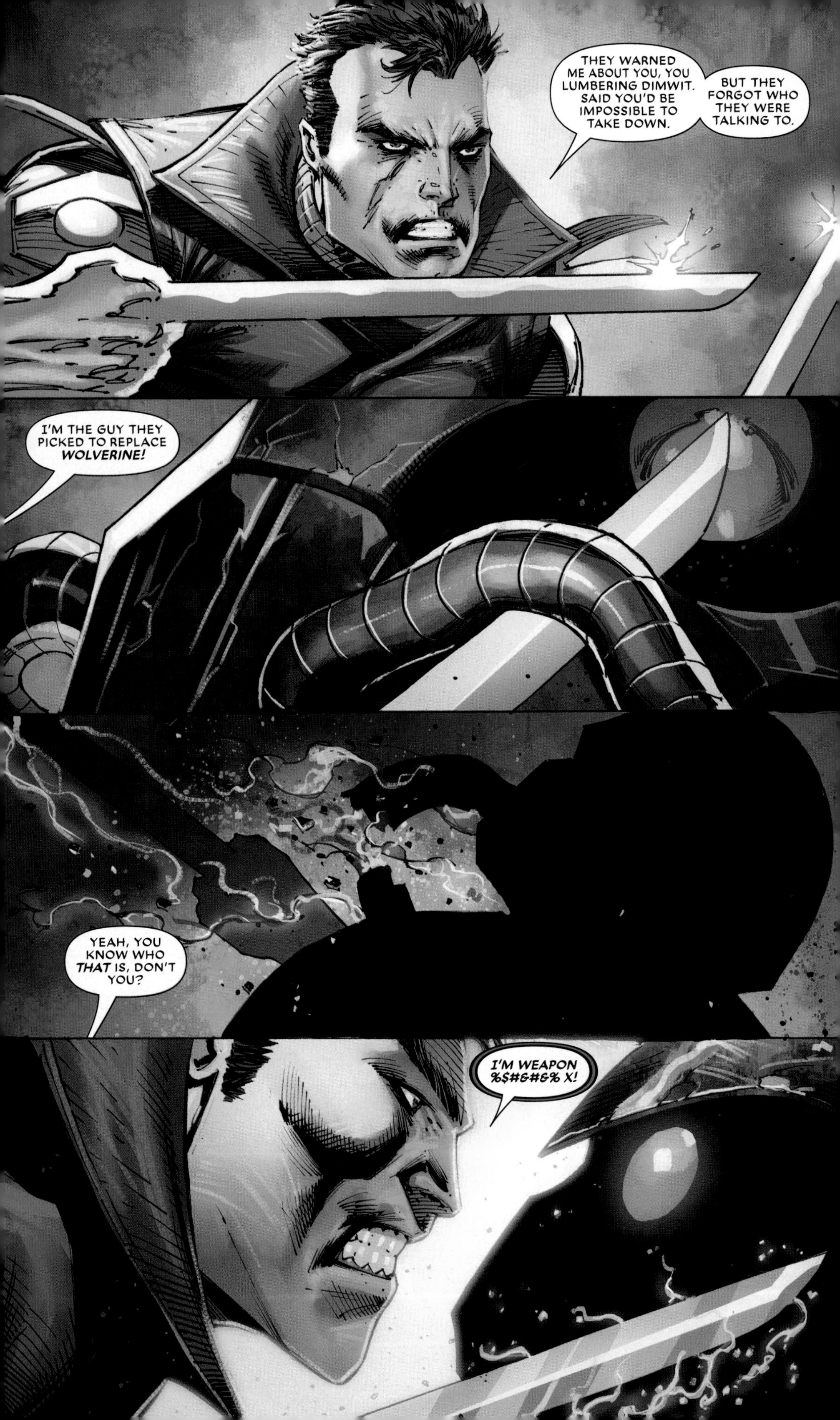
THEY WARNED ME ABOUT YOU, YOU LUMBERING DIMWIT. SAID YOU'D BE IMPOSSIBLE TO TAKE DOWN.
BUT THEY FORGOT WHO THEY WERE TALKING TO.
I'M THE GUY THEY PICKED TO REPLACE *WOLVERINE!*
YEAH, YOU KNOW WHO *THAT* IS, DON'T YOU?
I'M WEAPON %$#&#&% X!

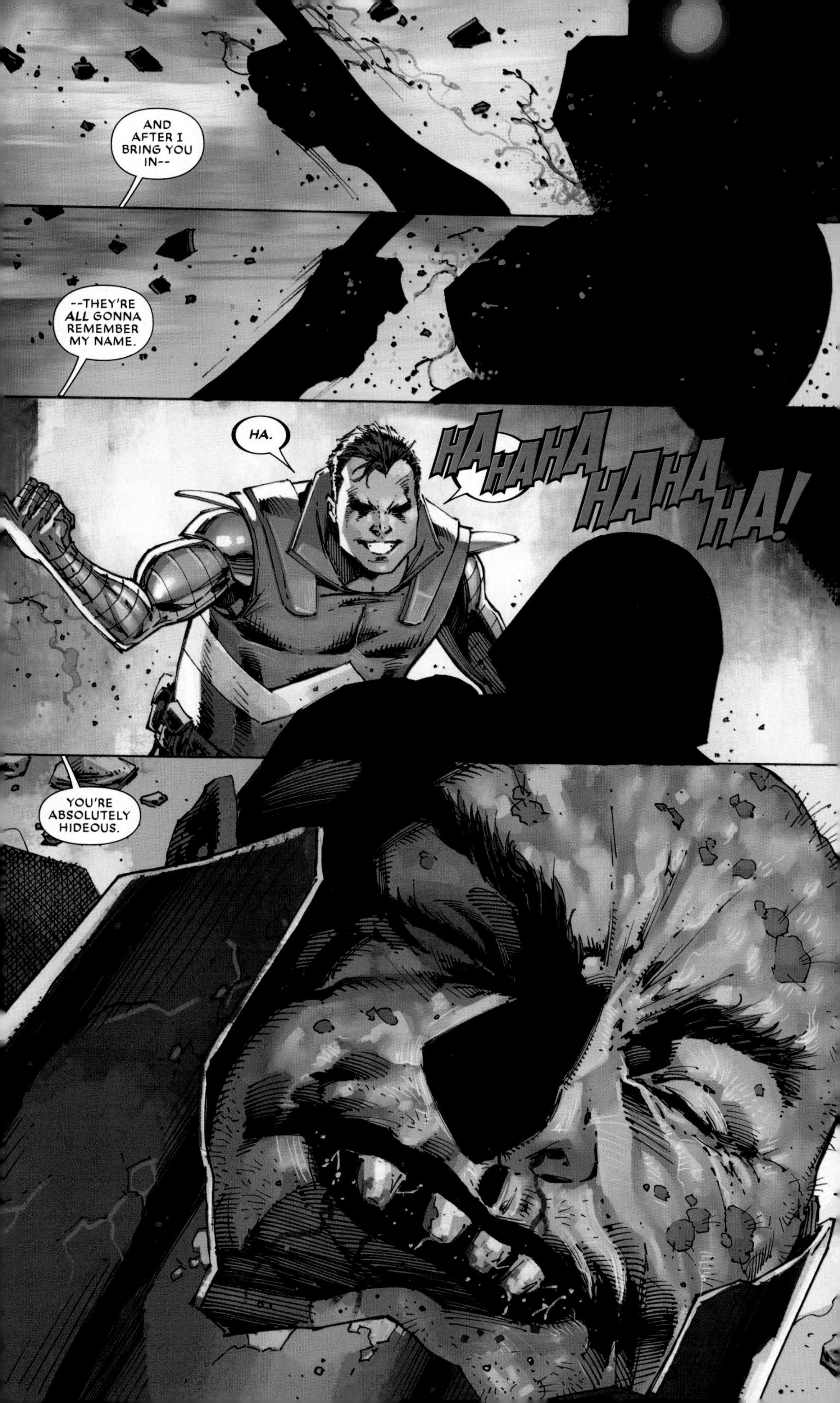
AND AFTER I BRING YOU IN--
--THEY'RE ALL GONNA REMEMBER MY NAME.
HA.
HAHAHAHAHAHAHA!
YOU'RE ABSOLUTELY HIDEOUS.

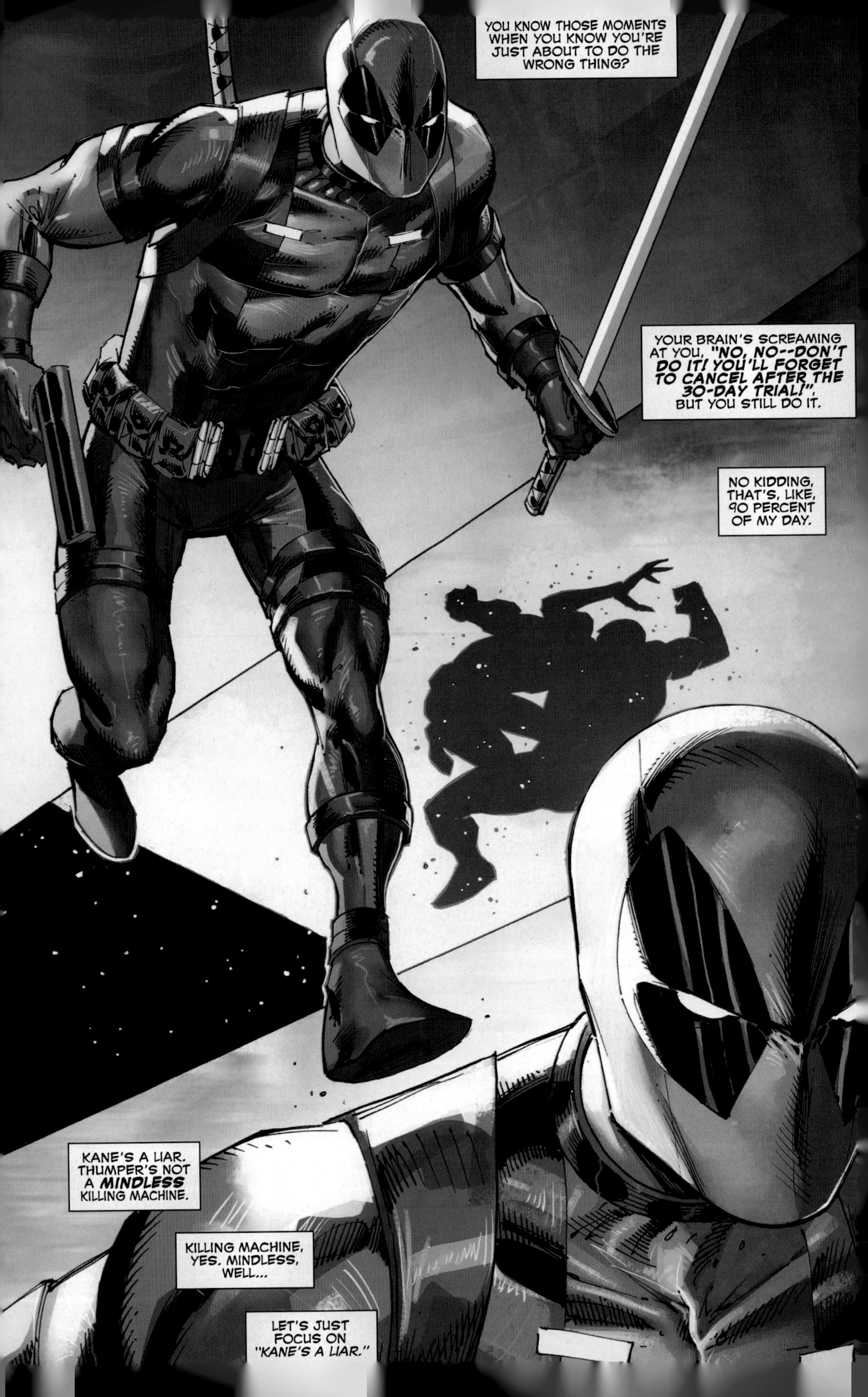

YOU KNOW THOSE MOMENTS WHEN YOU KNOW YOU'RE JUST ABOUT TO DO THE WRONG THING?
YOUR BRAIN'S SCREAMING AT YOU, "NO, NO--DON'T DO IT! YOU'LL FORGET TO CANCEL AFTER THE 30-DAY TRIAL!", BUT YOU STILL DO IT.
NO KIDDING, THAT'S, LIKE, 90 PERCENT OF MY DAY.
KANE'S A LIAR. THUMPER'S NOT A MINDLESS KILLING MACHINE.
KILLING MACHINE, YES. MINDLESS, WELL...
LET'S JUST FOCUS ON "KANE'S A LIAR."

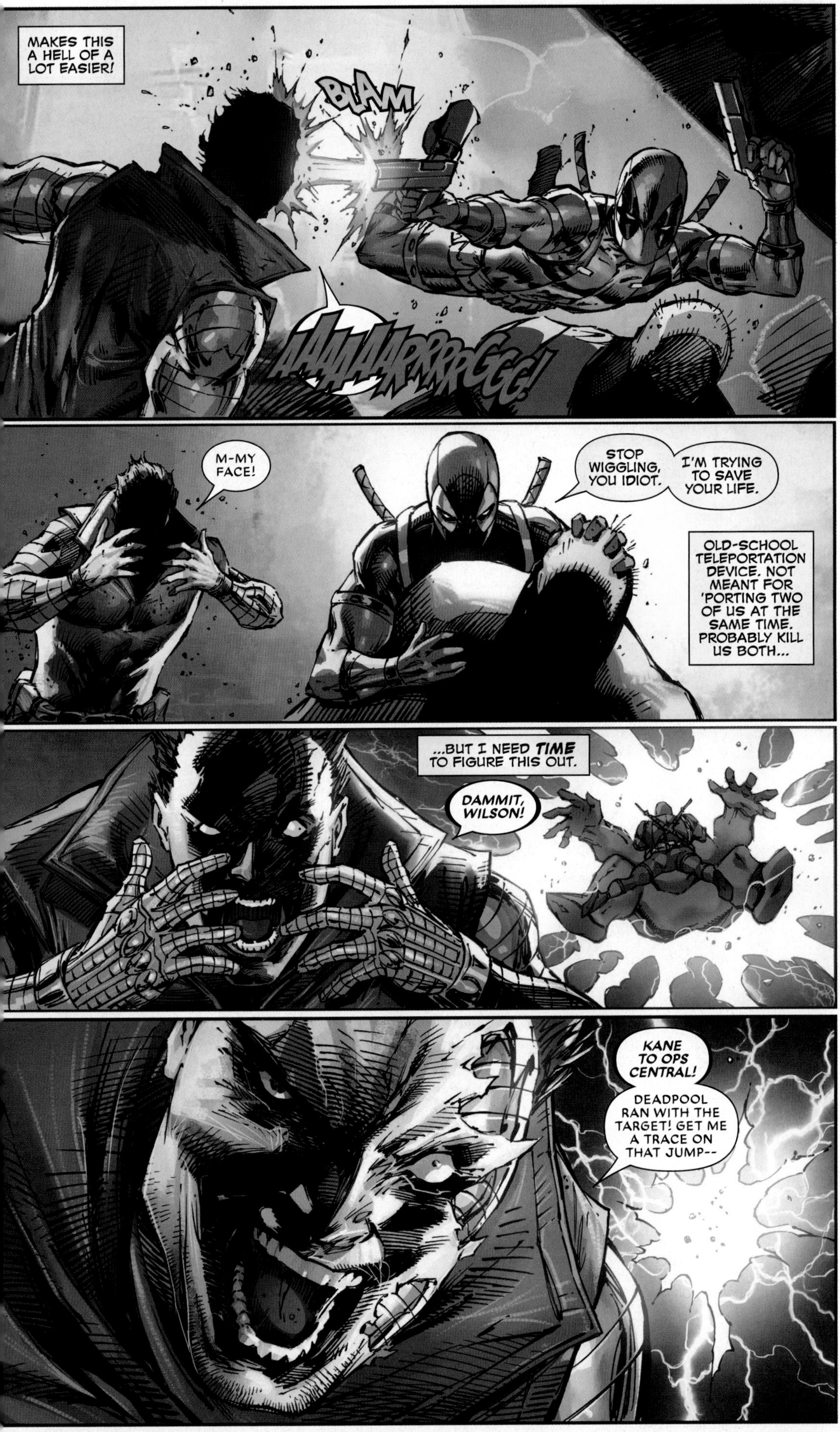
MAKES THIS A HELL OF A LOT EASIER!
BLAM
AAAAAARRRRGGG!
M-MY FACE!
STOP WIGGLING, YOU IDIOT.
I'M TRYING TO SAVE YOUR LIFE.
OLD-SCHOOL TELEPORTATION DEVICE. NOT MEANT FOR 'PORTING TWO OF US AT THE SAME TIME. PROBABLY KILL US BOTH...
...BUT I NEED *TIME* TO FIGURE THIS OUT.
DAMMIT, WILSON!
KANE TO OPS CENTRAL!
DEADPOOL RAN WITH THE TARGET! GET ME A TRACE ON THAT JUMP--

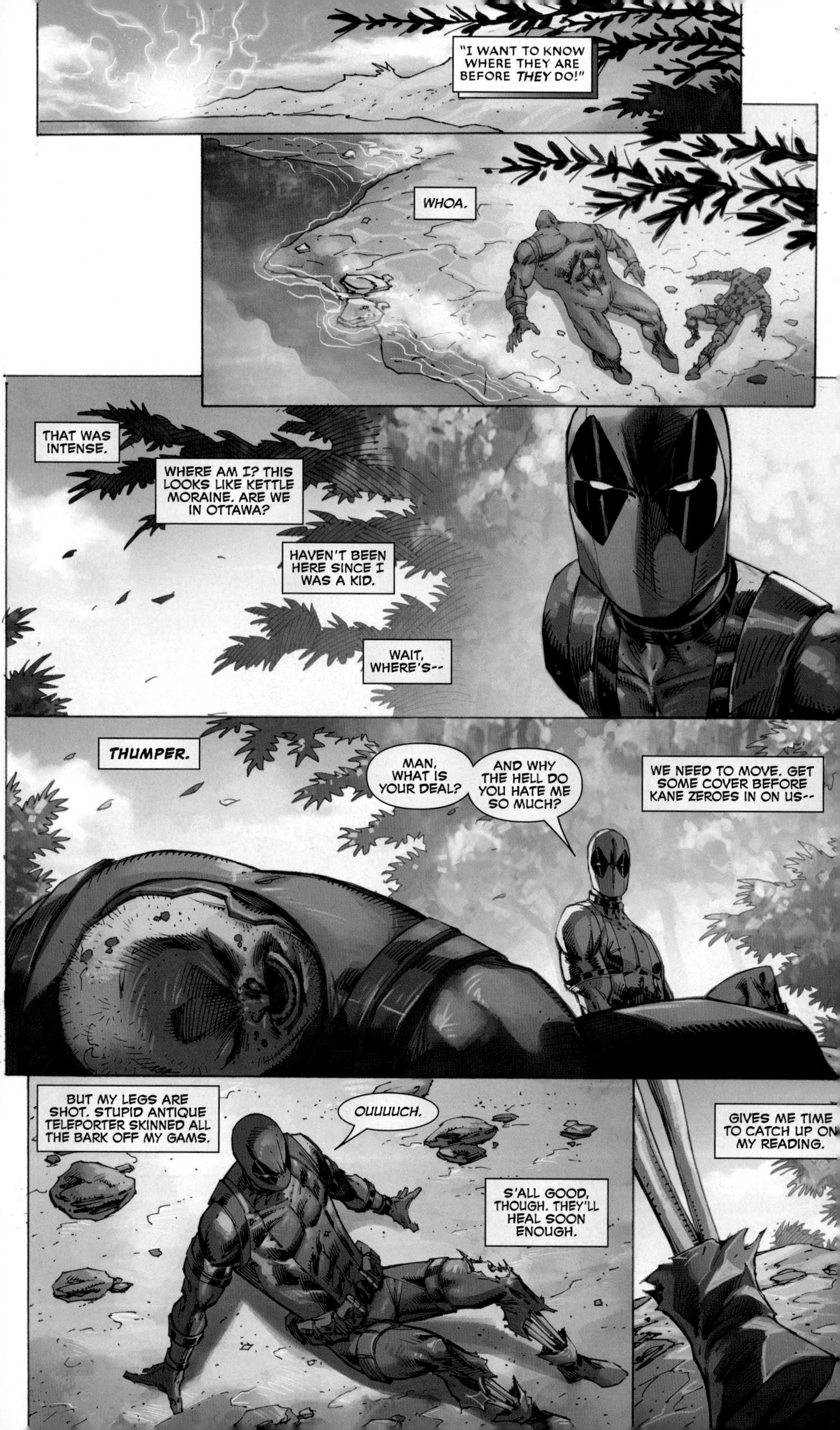
"I WANT TO KNOW WHERE THEY ARE BEFORE THEY DO!"
WHOA.
THAT WAS INTENSE.
WHERE AM I? THIS LOOKS LIKE KETTLE MORAINE. ARE WE IN OTTAWA?
HAVEN'T BEEN HERE SINCE I WAS A KID.
WAIT, WHERE'S--
THUMPER.
MAN, WHAT IS YOUR DEAL?
AND WHY THE HELL DO YOU HATE ME SO MUCH?
WE NEED TO MOVE. GET SOME COVER BEFORE KANE ZEROES IN ON US--
BUT MY LEGS ARE SHOT. STUPID ANTIQUE TELEPORTER SKINNED ALL THE BARK OFF MY GAMS.
OUUUUCH.
S'ALL GOOD, THOUGH. THEY'LL HEAL SOON ENOUGH.
GIVES ME TIME TO CATCH UP ON MY READING.

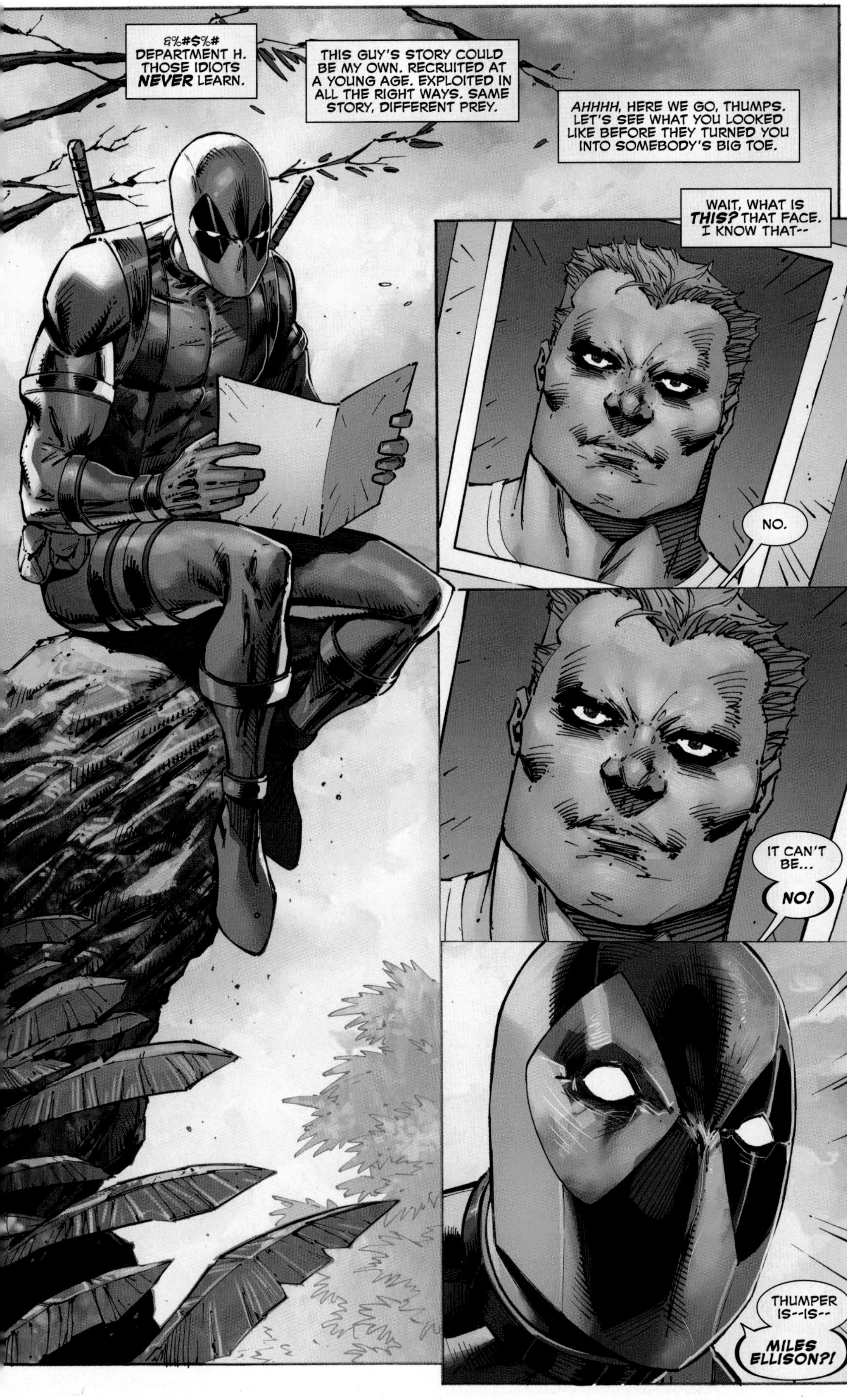
&%#$%# DEPARTMENT H. THOSE IDIOTS NEVER LEARN.
THIS GUY'S STORY COULD BE MY OWN. RECRUITED AT A YOUNG AGE. EXPLOITED IN ALL THE RIGHT WAYS. SAME STORY, DIFFERENT PREY.
AHHHH, HERE WE GO, THUMPS. LET'S SEE WHAT YOU LOOKED LIKE BEFORE THEY TURNED YOU INTO SOMEBODY'S BIG TOE.
WAIT, WHAT IS THIS? THAT FACE. I KNOW THAT--
NO.
IT CAN'T BE...
NO!
THUMPER IS--IS--
MILES ELLISON?!

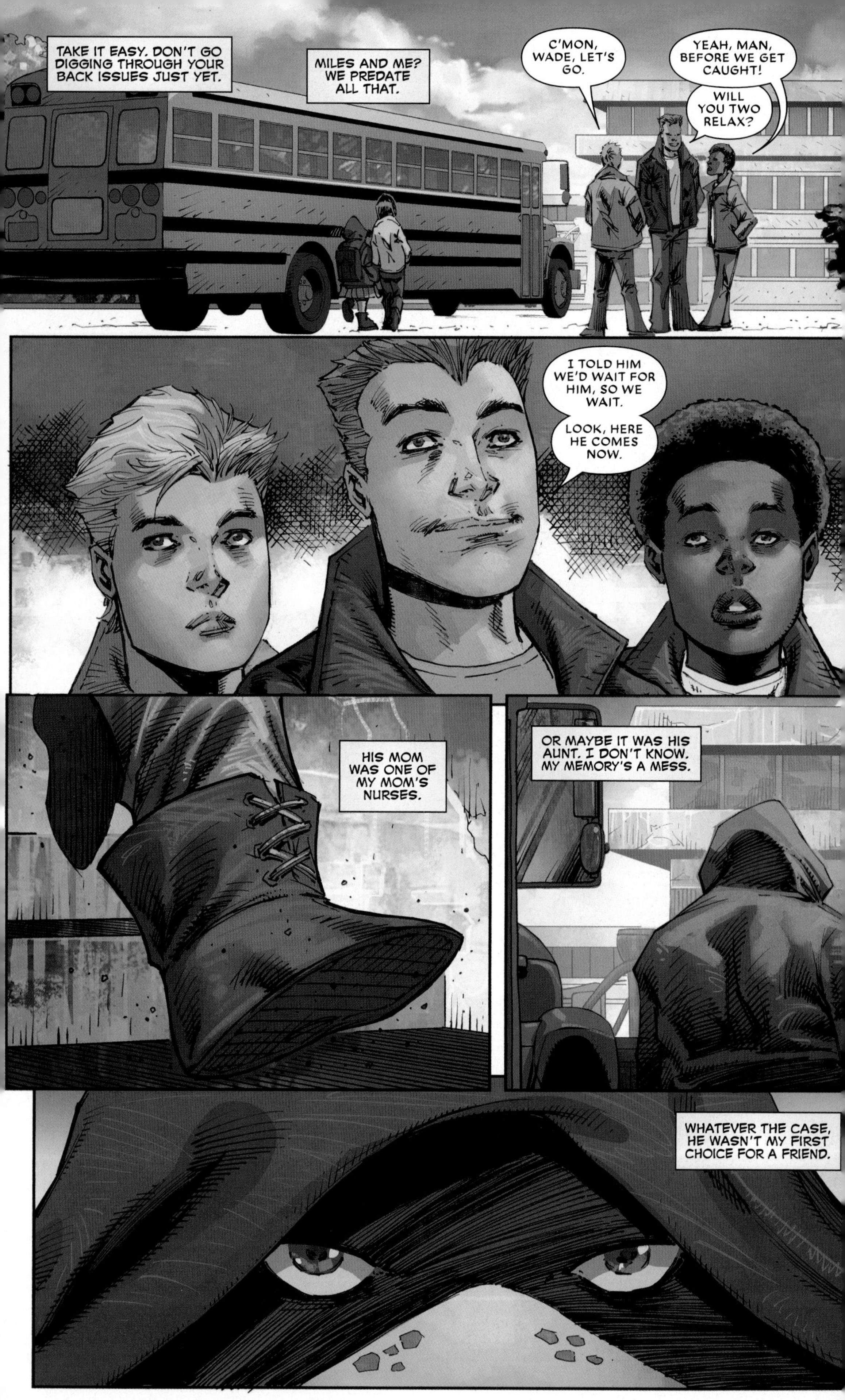

TAKE IT EASY. DON'T GO DIGGING THROUGH YOUR BACK ISSUES JUST YET.
MILES AND ME? WE PREDATE ALL THAT.
C'MON, WADE, LET'S GO.
YEAH, MAN, BEFORE WE GET CAUGHT!
WILL YOU TWO RELAX?
I TOLD HIM WE'D WAIT FOR HIM, SO WE WAIT.
LOOK, HERE HE COMES NOW.
HIS MOM WAS ONE OF MY MOM'S NURSES.
OR MAYBE IT WAS HIS AUNT. I DON'T KNOW. MY MEMORY'S A MESS.
WHATEVER THE CASE, HE WASN'T MY FIRST CHOICE FOR A FRIEND.

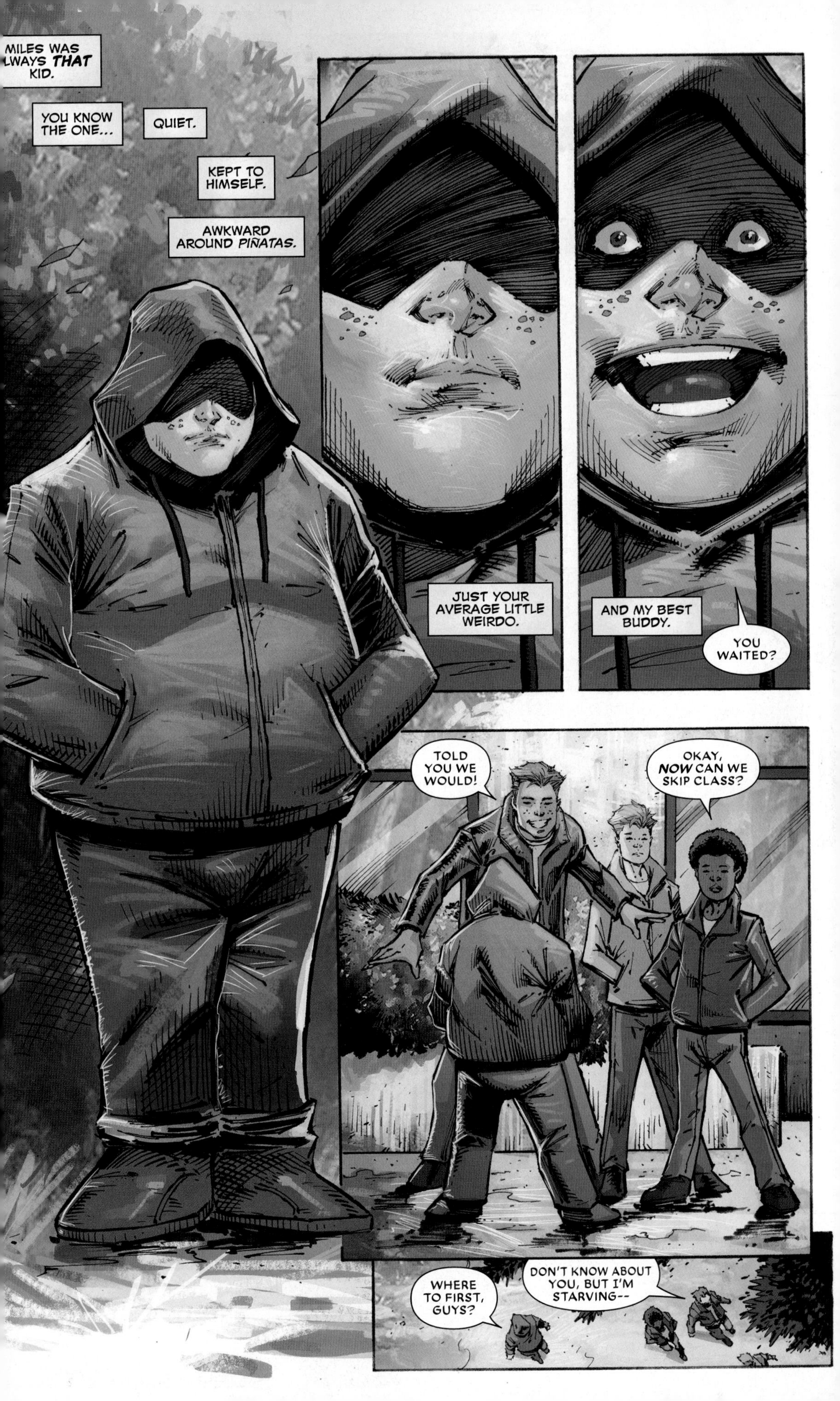
MILES WAS
LWAYS *THAT*
KID.
YOU KNOW THE ONE...
QUIET.
KEPT TO HIMSELF.
AWKWARD AROUND *PIÑATAS*.
JUST YOUR AVERAGE LITTLE WEIRDO.
AND MY BEST BUDDY.
YOU WAITED?
TOLD YOU WE WOULD!
OKAY, *NOW* CAN WE SKIP CLASS?
WHERE TO FIRST, GUYS?
DON'T KNOW ABOUT YOU, BUT I'M STARVING--

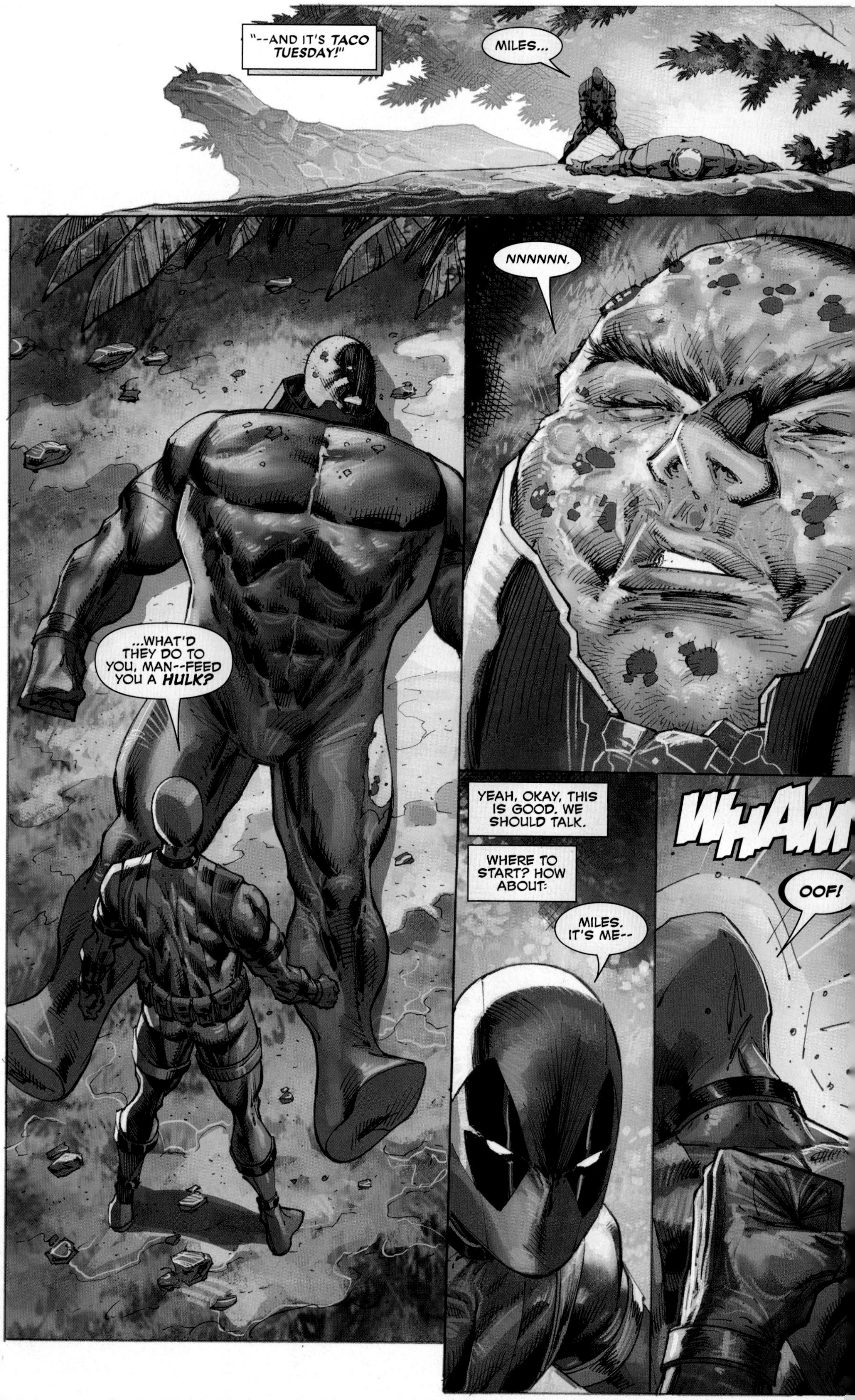
"--AND IT'S TACO TUESDAY!"
MILES...
...WHAT'D THEY DO TO YOU, MAN--FEED YOU A HULK?
NNNNNN.
YEAH, OKAY, THIS IS GOOD. WE SHOULD TALK.
WHERE TO START? HOW ABOUT:
MILES. IT'S ME--
WHAM
OOF!

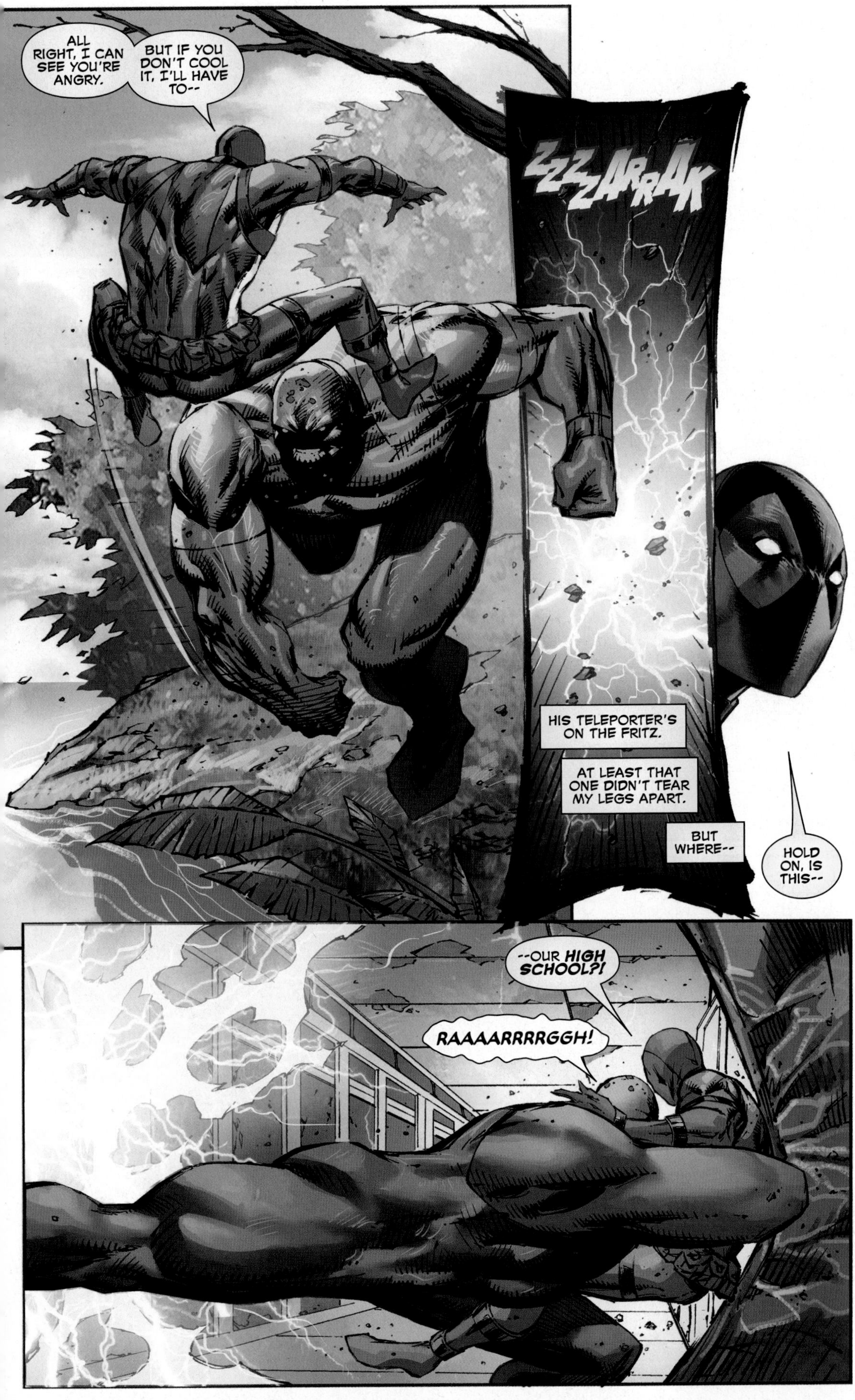

ALL RIGHT, I CAN SEE YOU'RE ANGRY.
BUT IF YOU DON'T COOL IT, I'LL HAVE TO--
ZZZZARRAK
HIS TELEPORTER'S ON THE FRITZ.
AT LEAST THAT ONE DIDN'T TEAR MY LEGS APART.
BUT WHERE--
HOLD ON, IS THIS--
--OUR HIGH SCHOOL?!
RAAAARRRRGGH!

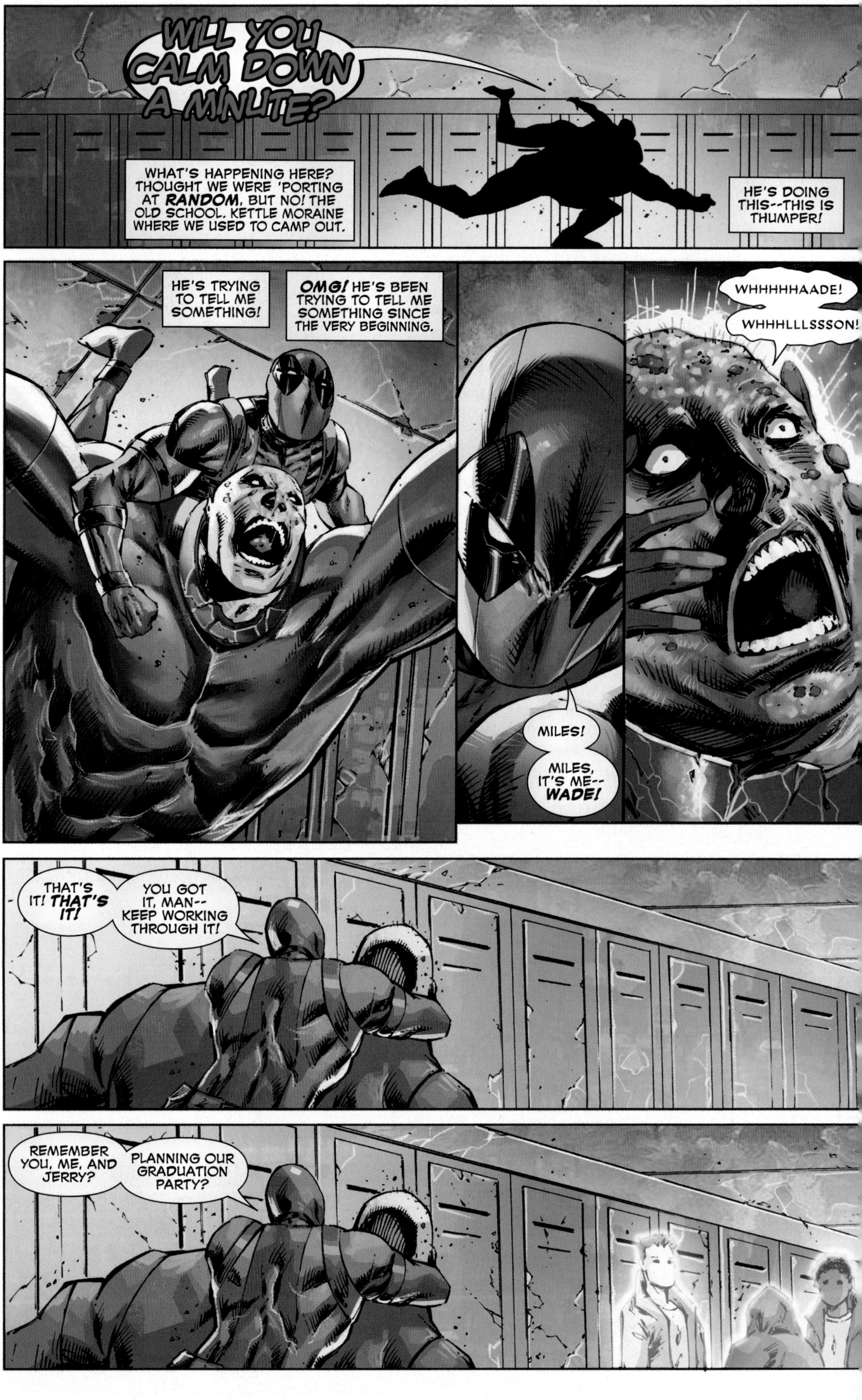
WILL YOU CALM DOWN A MINUTE?
WHAT'S HAPPENING HERE? THOUGHT WE WERE 'PORTING AT RANDOM, BUT NO! THE OLD SCHOOL. KETTLE MORAINE WHERE WE USED TO CAMP OUT.
HE'S DOING THIS--THIS IS THUMPER!
HE'S TRYING TO TELL ME SOMETHING!
OMG! HE'S BEEN TRYING TO TELL ME SOMETHING SINCE THE VERY BEGINNING.
WHHHHHAADE!
WHHHLLLSSSON!
MILES!
MILES, IT'S ME-- WADE!
THAT'S IT! THAT'S IT!
YOU GOT IT, MAN-- KEEP WORKING THROUGH IT!
REMEMBER YOU, ME, AND JERRY?
PLANNING OUR GRADUATION PARTY?

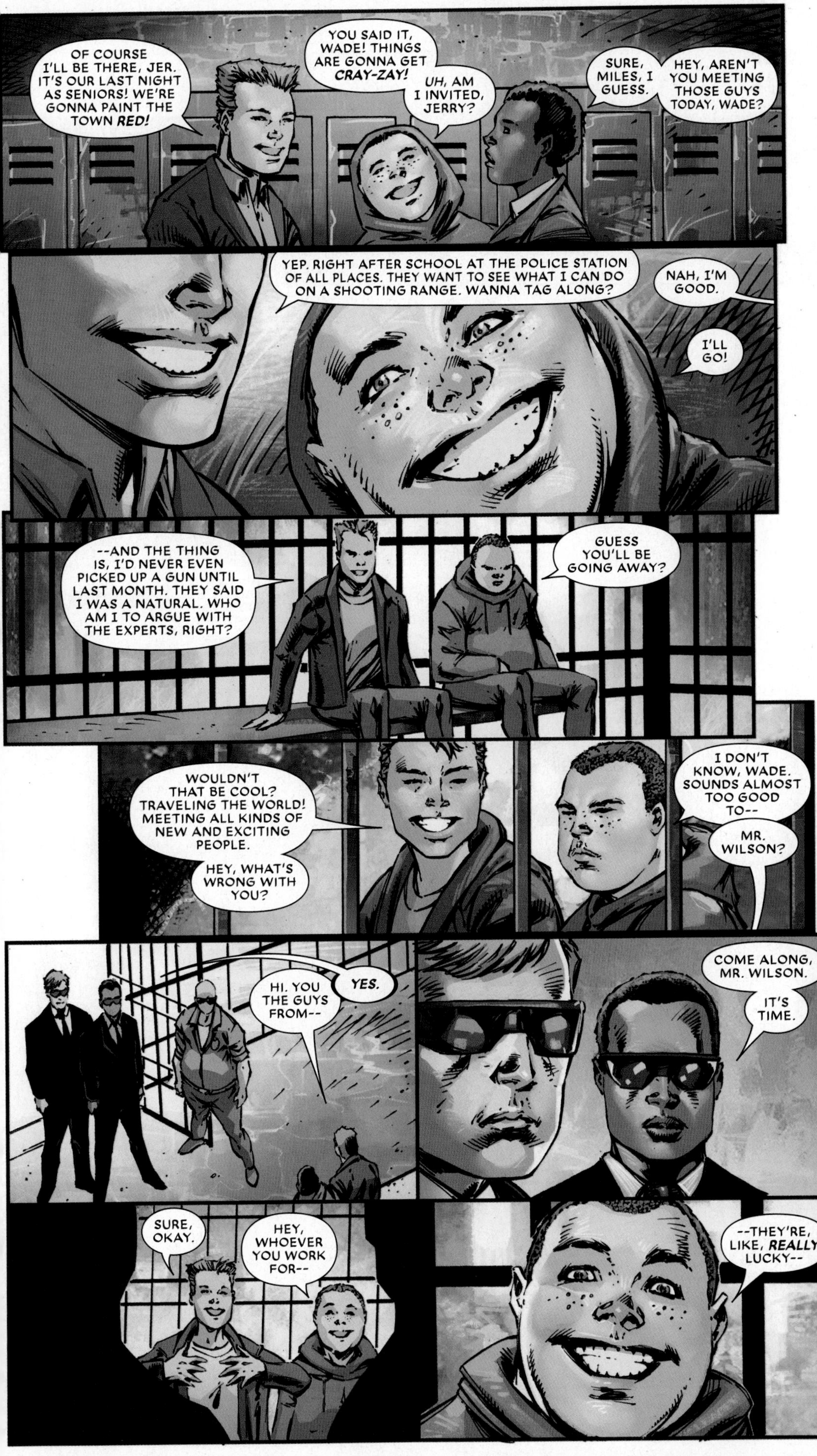
OF COURSE I'LL BE THERE, JER. IT'S OUR LAST NIGHT AS SENIORS! WE'RE GONNA PAINT THE TOWN RED!
YOU SAID IT, WADE! THINGS ARE GONNA GET CRAY-ZAY!
UH, AM I INVITED, JERRY?
SURE, MILES, I GUESS.
HEY, AREN'T YOU MEETING THOSE GUYS TODAY, WADE?
YEP. RIGHT AFTER SCHOOL AT THE POLICE STATION OF ALL PLACES. THEY WANT TO SEE WHAT I CAN DO ON A SHOOTING RANGE. WANNA TAG ALONG?
NAH, I'M GOOD.
I'LL GO!
--AND THE THING IS, I'D NEVER EVEN PICKED UP A GUN UNTIL LAST MONTH. THEY SAID I WAS A NATURAL. WHO AM I TO ARGUE WITH THE EXPERTS, RIGHT?
GUESS YOU'LL BE GOING AWAY?
WOULDN'T THAT BE COOL? TRAVELING THE WORLD! MEETING ALL KINDS OF NEW AND EXCITING PEOPLE.
HEY, WHAT'S WRONG WITH YOU?
I DON'T KNOW, WADE. SOUNDS ALMOST TOO GOOD TO--
MR. WILSON?
HI. YOU THE GUYS FROM--
YES.
COME ALONG, MR. WILSON.
IT'S TIME.
SURE, OKAY.
HEY, WHOEVER YOU WORK FOR--
--THEY'RE, LIKE, REALLY LUCKY--

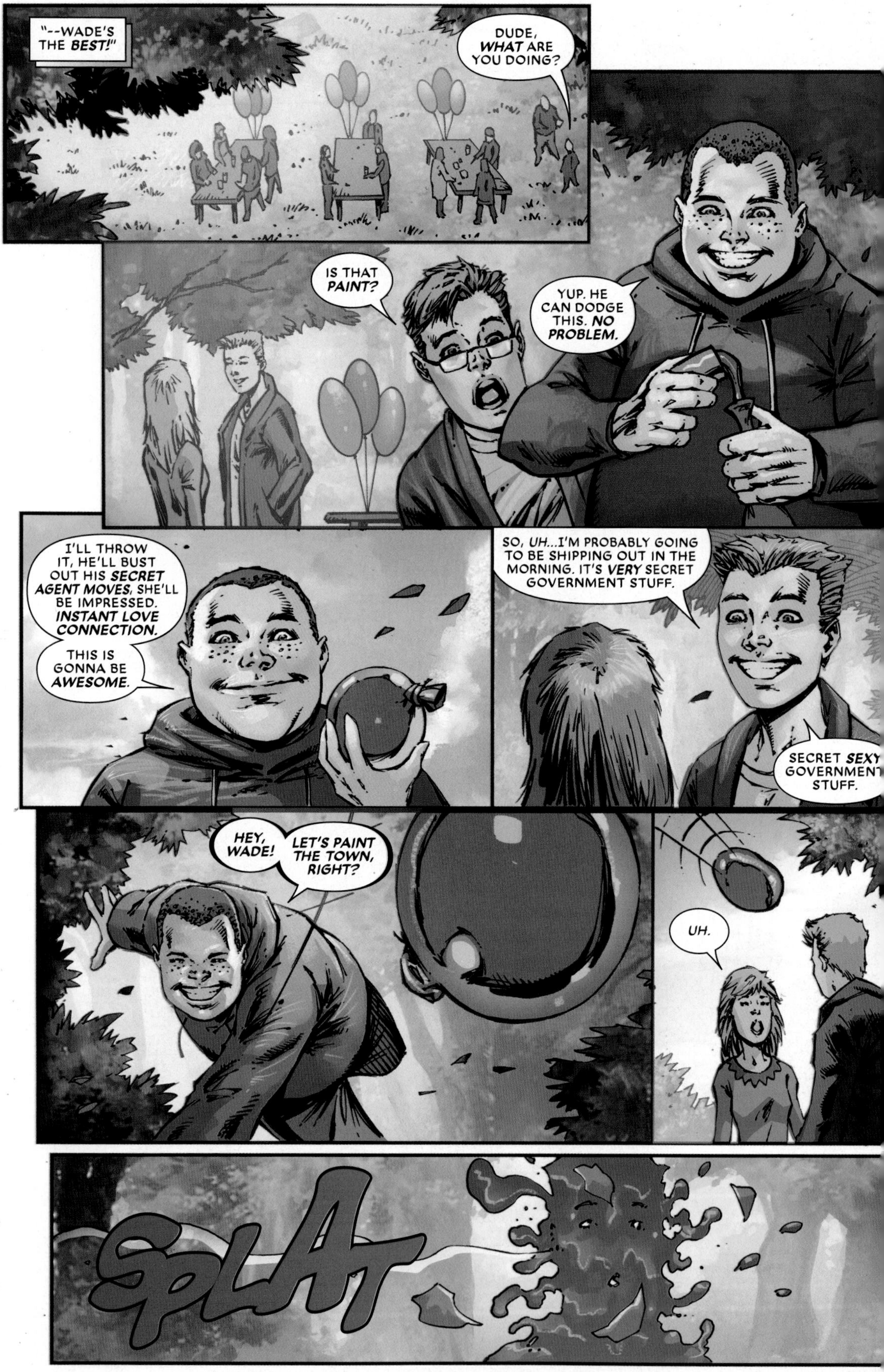
"--WADE'S THE BEST!"
DUDE, WHAT ARE YOU DOING?
IS THAT PAINT?
YUP. HE CAN DODGE THIS. NO PROBLEM.
I'LL THROW IT, HE'LL BUST OUT HIS SECRET AGENT MOVES, SHE'LL BE IMPRESSED. INSTANT LOVE CONNECTION.
THIS IS GONNA BE AWESOME.
SO, UH...I'M PROBABLY GOING TO BE SHIPPING OUT IN THE MORNING. IT'S VERY SECRET GOVERNMENT STUFF.
SECRET SEXY GOVERNMENT STUFF.
HEY, WADE!
LET'S PAINT THE TOWN, RIGHT?
UH.
SPLAT

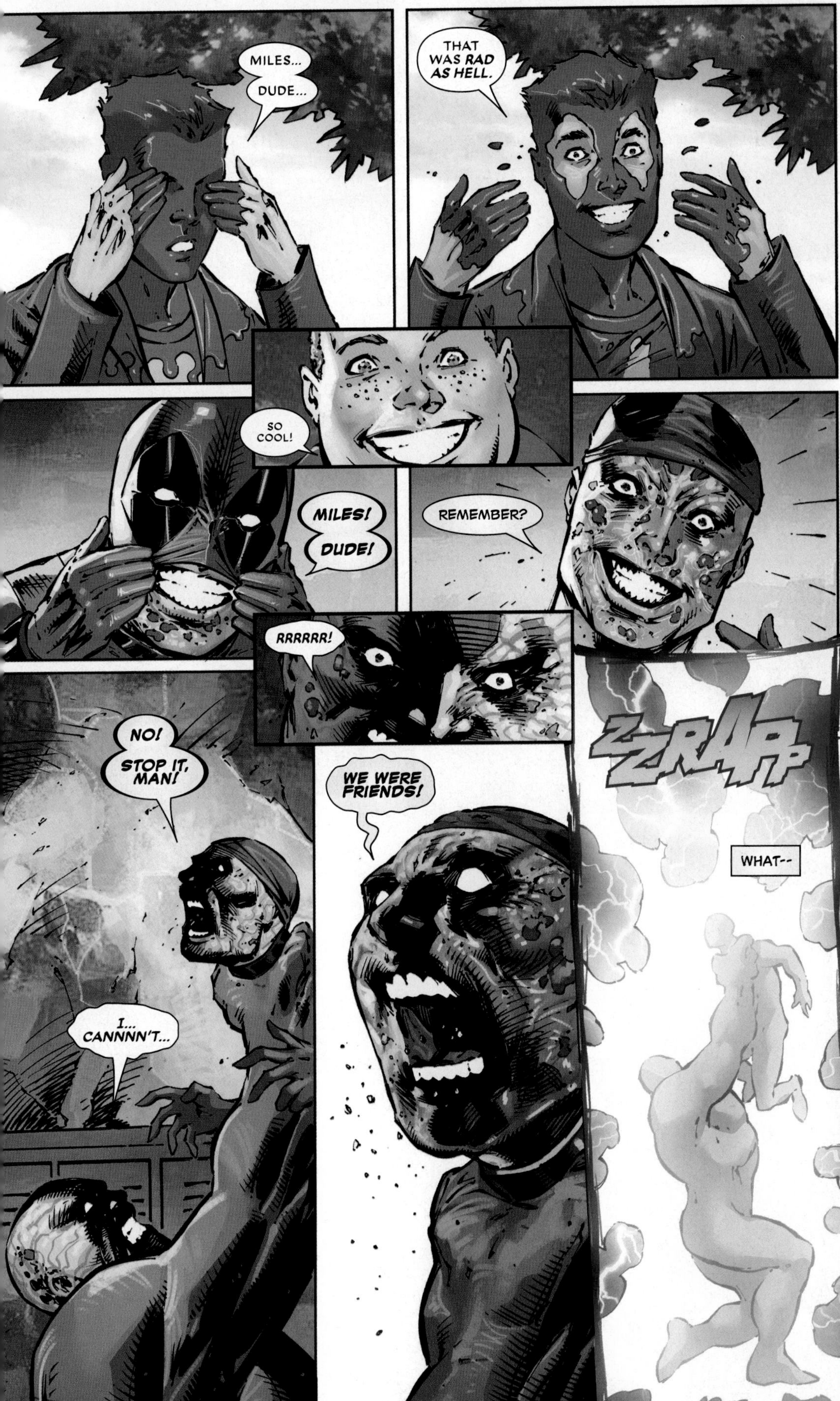
MILES...
DUDE...
THAT WAS RAD AS HELL.
SO COOL!
MILES! DUDE!
REMEMBER?
RRRRRR!
NO! STOP IT, MAN!
I... CANNNN'T...
WE WERE FRIENDS!
ZZRAPP
WHAT--

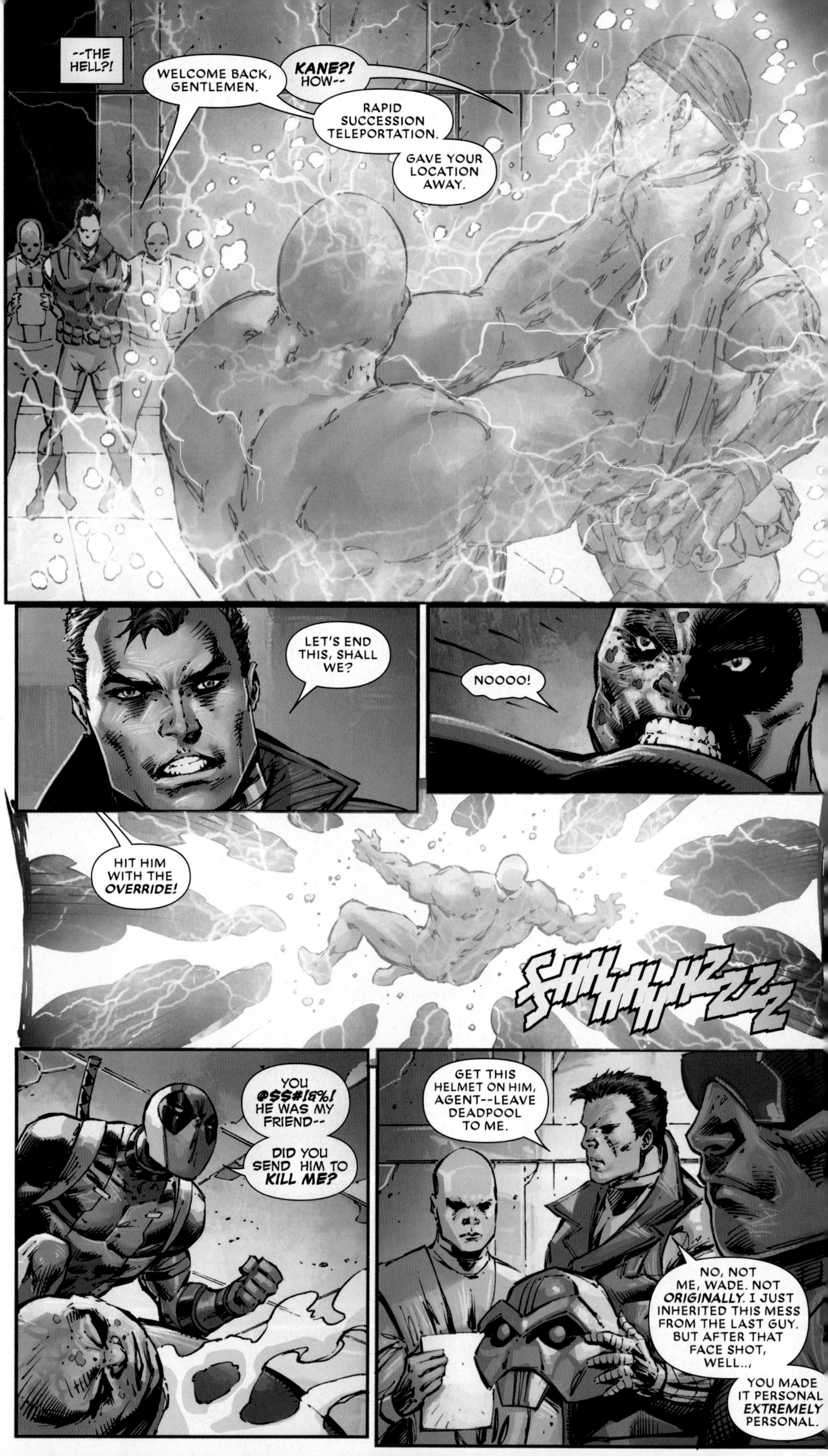
--THE HELL?!
WELCOME BACK, GENTLEMEN.
KANE?! HOW--
RAPID SUCCESSION TELEPORTATION.
GAVE YOUR LOCATION AWAY.
LET'S END THIS, SHALL WE?
NOOOO!
HIT HIM WITH THE OVERRIDE!
SHHHHHHZZZZ
YOU @$$#!&%! HE WAS MY FRIEND--
DID YOU SEND HIM TO KILL ME?
GET THIS HELMET ON HIM, AGENT--LEAVE DEADPOOL TO ME.
NO, NOT ME, WADE. NOT ORIGINALLY. I JUST INHERITED THIS MESS FROM THE LAST GUY. BUT AFTER THAT FACE SHOT, WELL..,
YOU MADE IT PERSONAL EXTREMELY PERSONAL.

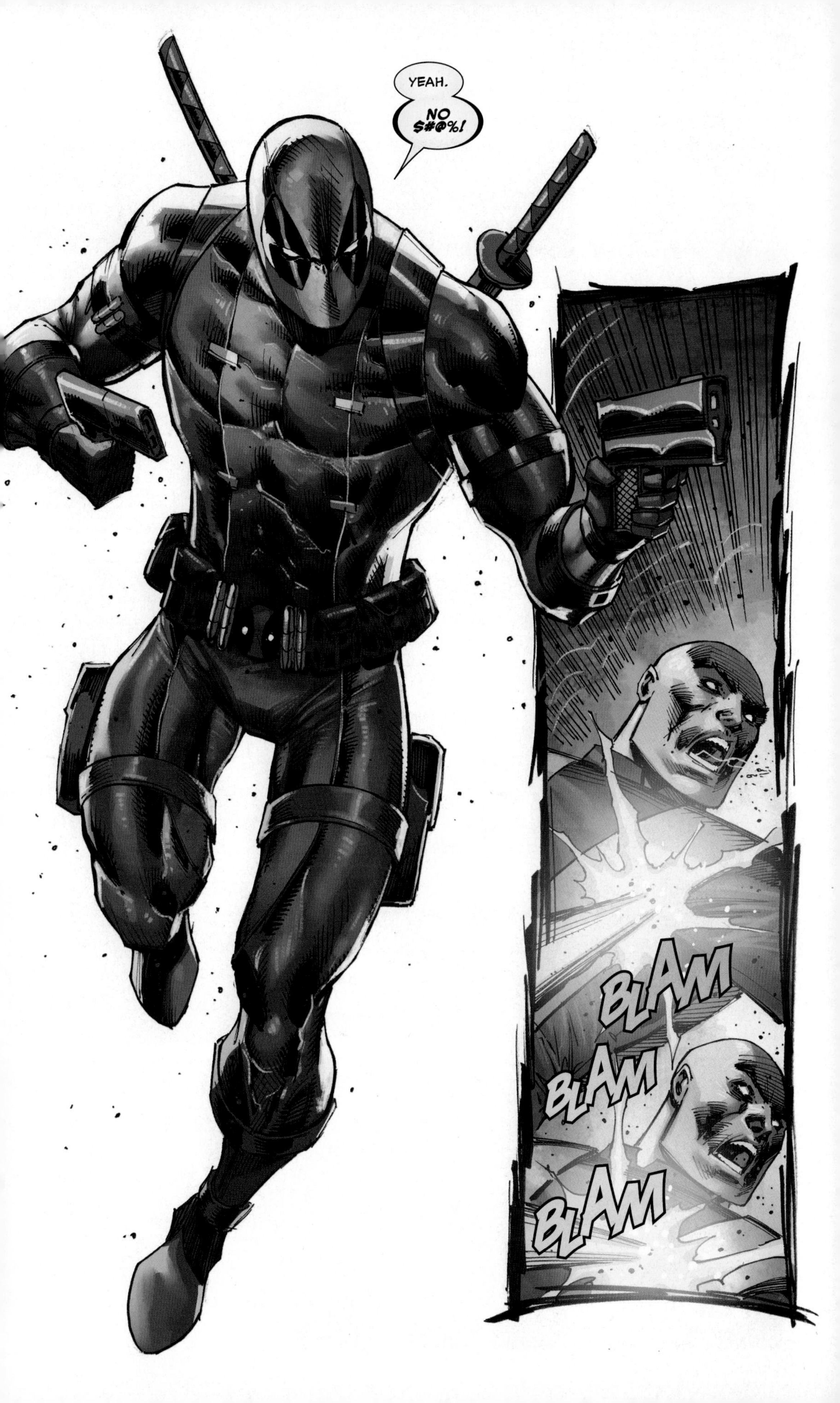
YEAH.
NO $#@%!
BLAM
BLAM
BLAM

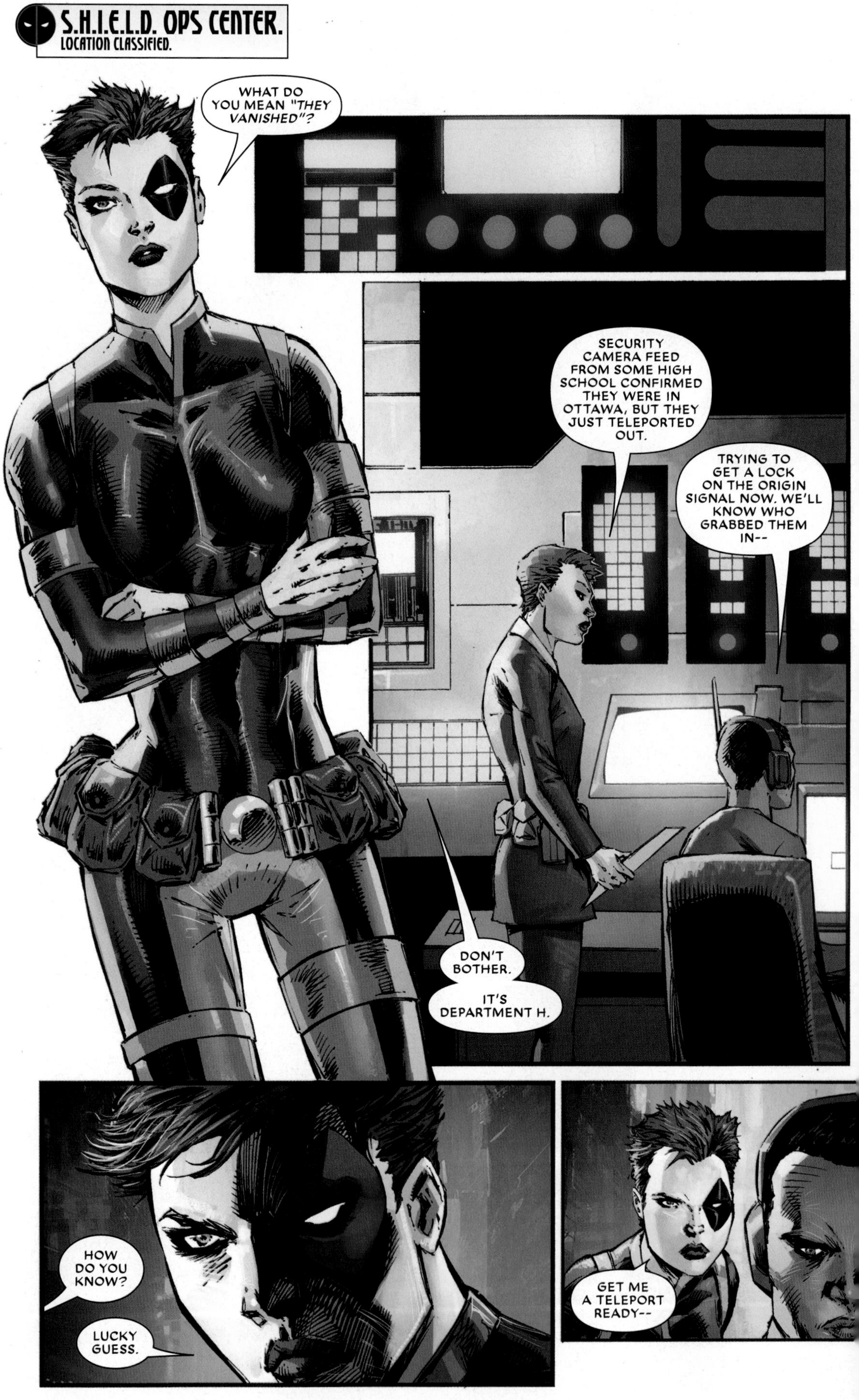
S.H.I.E.L.D. OPS CENTER.
LOCATION CLASSIFIED.
WHAT DO YOU MEAN "THEY VANISHED"?
SECURITY CAMERA FEED FROM SOME HIGH SCHOOL CONFIRMED THEY WERE IN OTTAWA, BUT THEY JUST TELEPORTED OUT.
TRYING TO GET A LOCK ON THE ORIGIN SIGNAL NOW. WE'LL KNOW WHO GRABBED THEM IN--
DON'T BOTHER.
IT'S DEPARTMENT H.
HOW DO YOU KNOW?
LUCKY GUESS.
GET ME A TELEPORT READY--

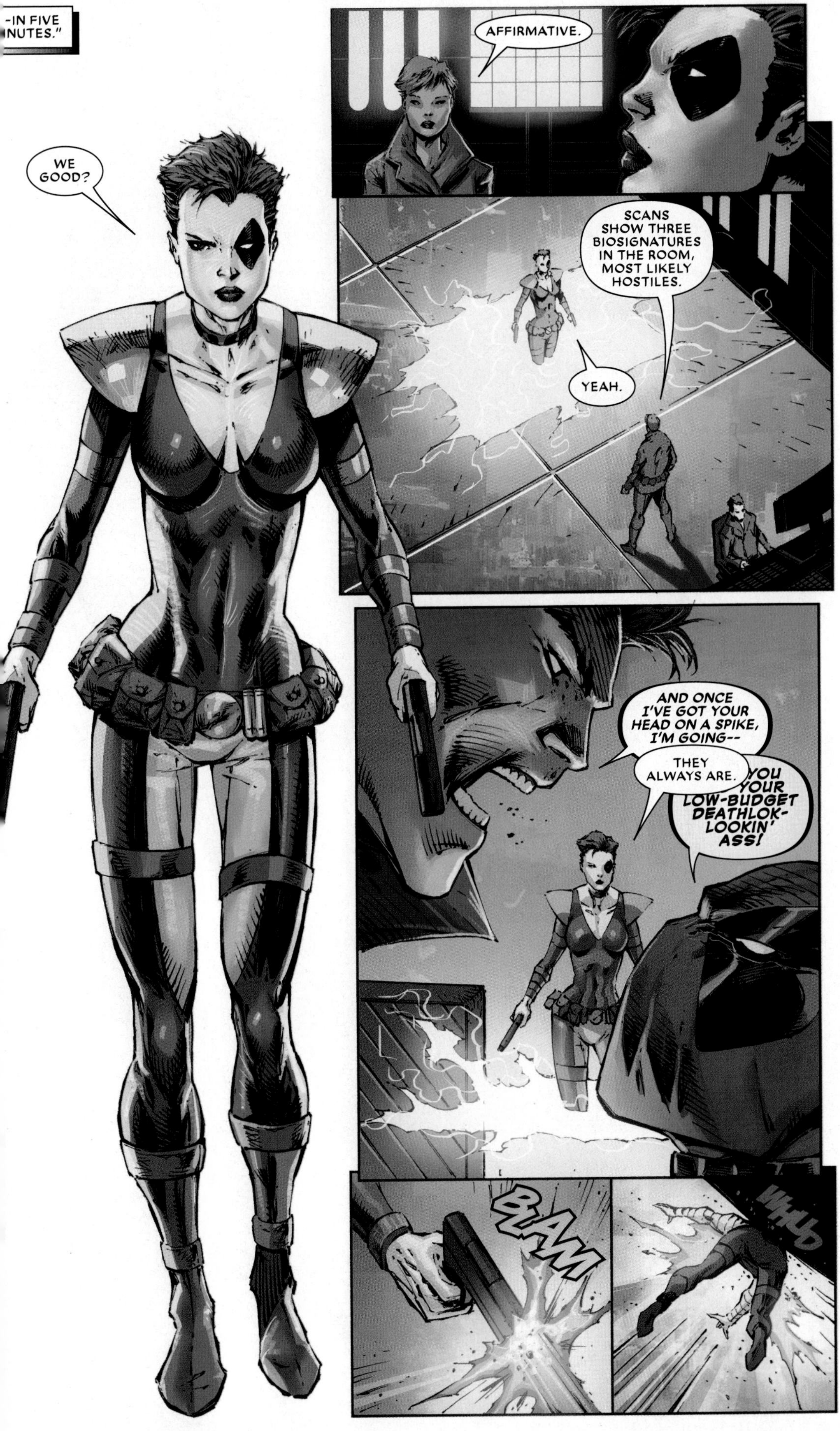
-IN FIVE NUTES."
WE GOOD?
AFFIRMATIVE.
SCANS SHOW THREE BIOSIGNATURES IN THE ROOM, MOST LIKELY HOSTILES.
YEAH.
AND ONCE I'VE GOT YOUR HEAD ON A SPIKE, I'M GOING--
THEY ALWAYS ARE.
YOU YOUR LOW-BUDGET DEATHLOK-LOOKIN' ASS!
BLAM
WHUD

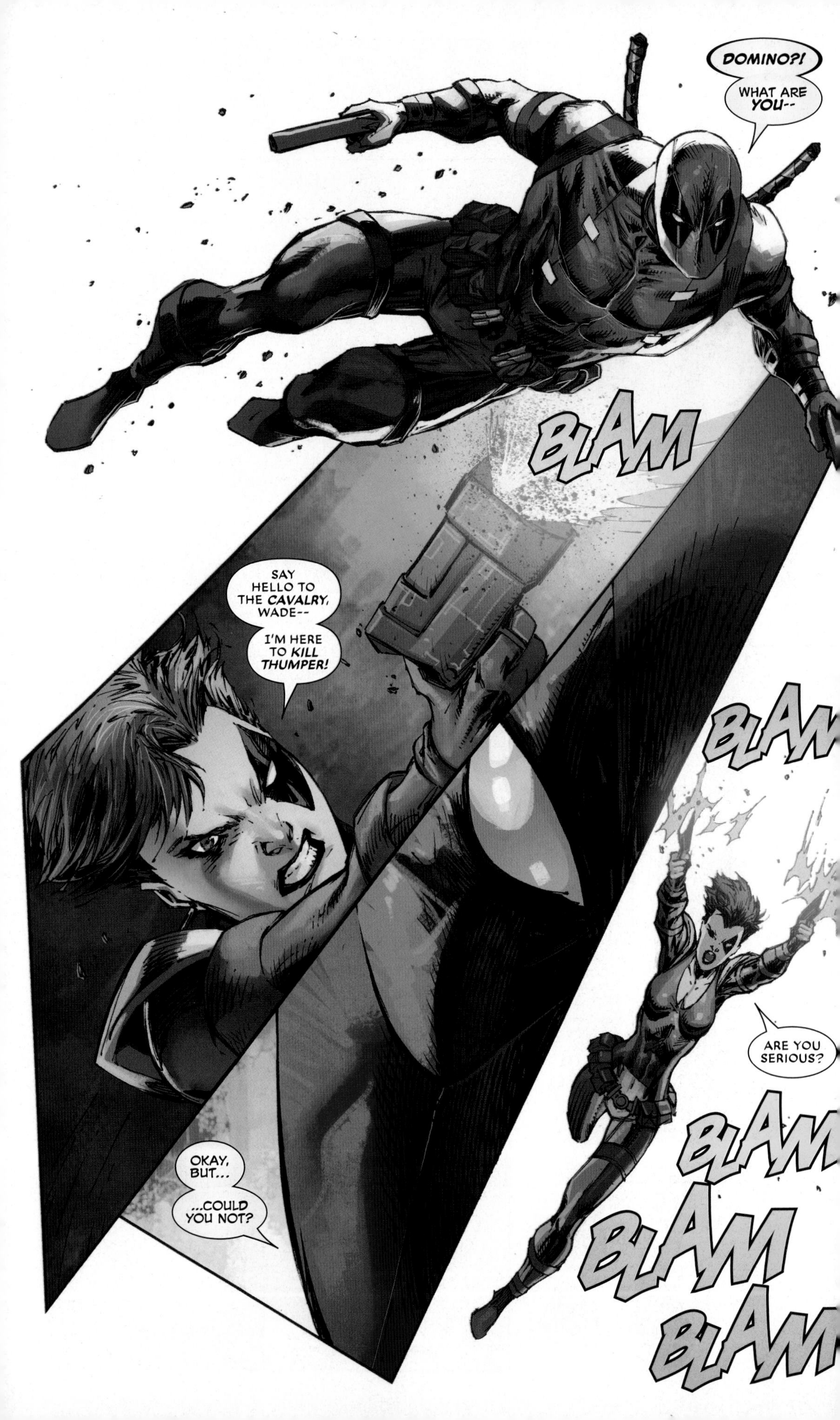
DOMINO?!
WHAT ARE YOU--
BLAM
SAY HELLO TO THE CAVALRY, WADE--
I'M HERE TO KILL THUMPER!
BLAM
ARE YOU SERIOUS?
OKAY, BUT...
...COULD YOU NOT?
BLAM
BLAM
BLAM

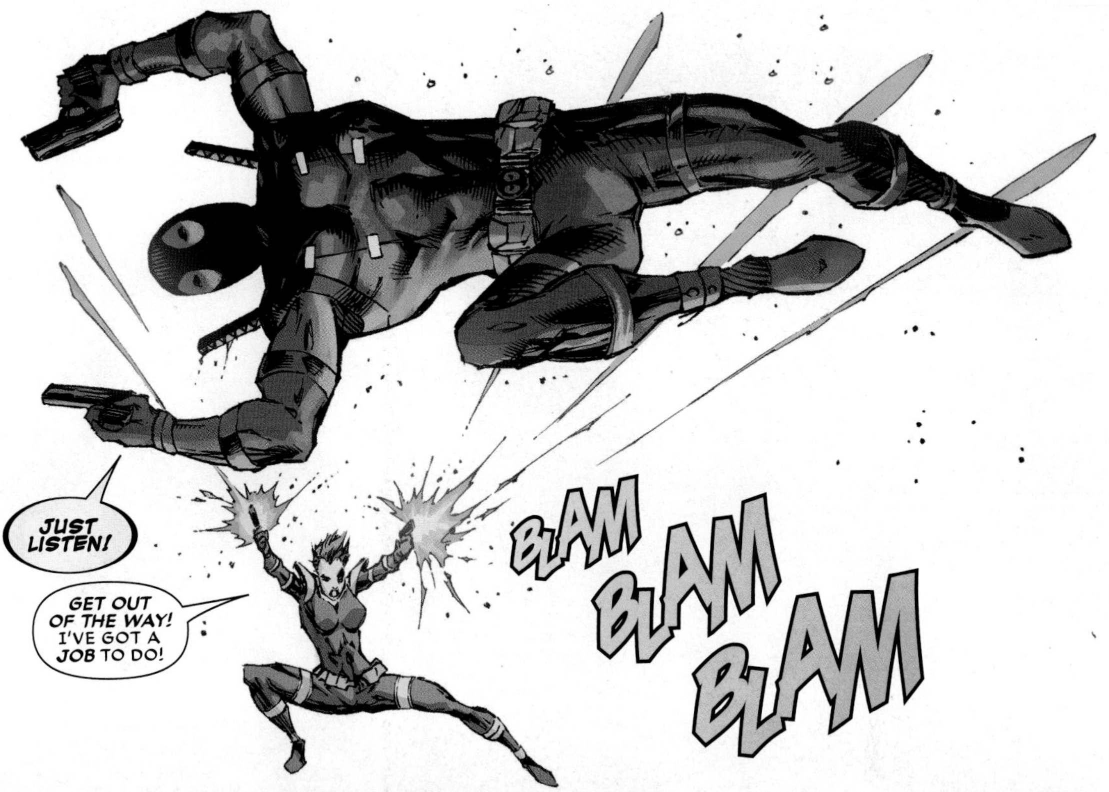
JUST LISTEN!
GET OUT OF THE WAY! I'VE GOT A JOB TO DO!
BLAM
BLAM
BLAM

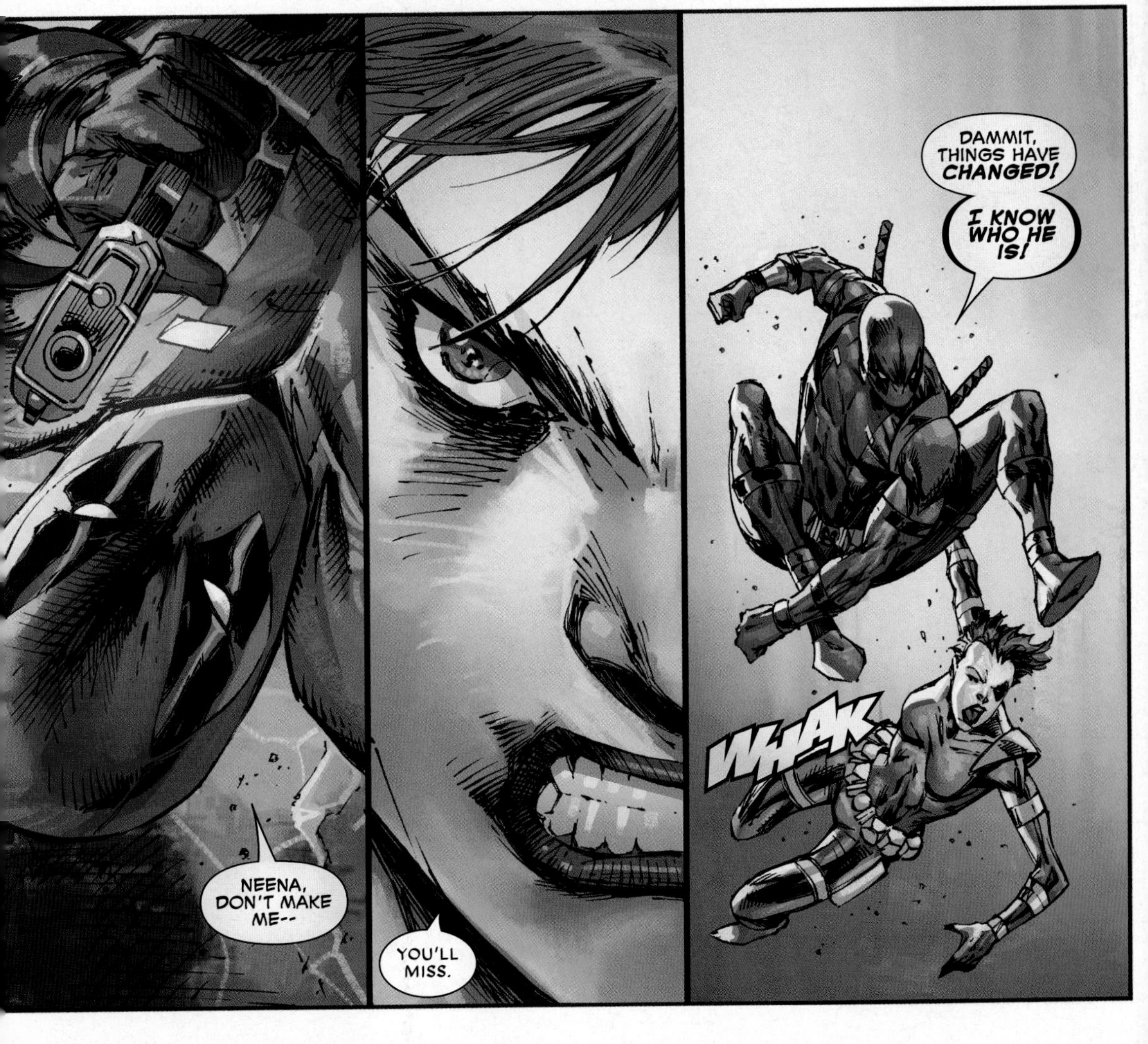
NEENA, DON'T MAKE ME--
YOU'LL MISS.
DAMMIT, THINGS HAVE CHANGED!
I KNOW WHO HE IS!
WHAK

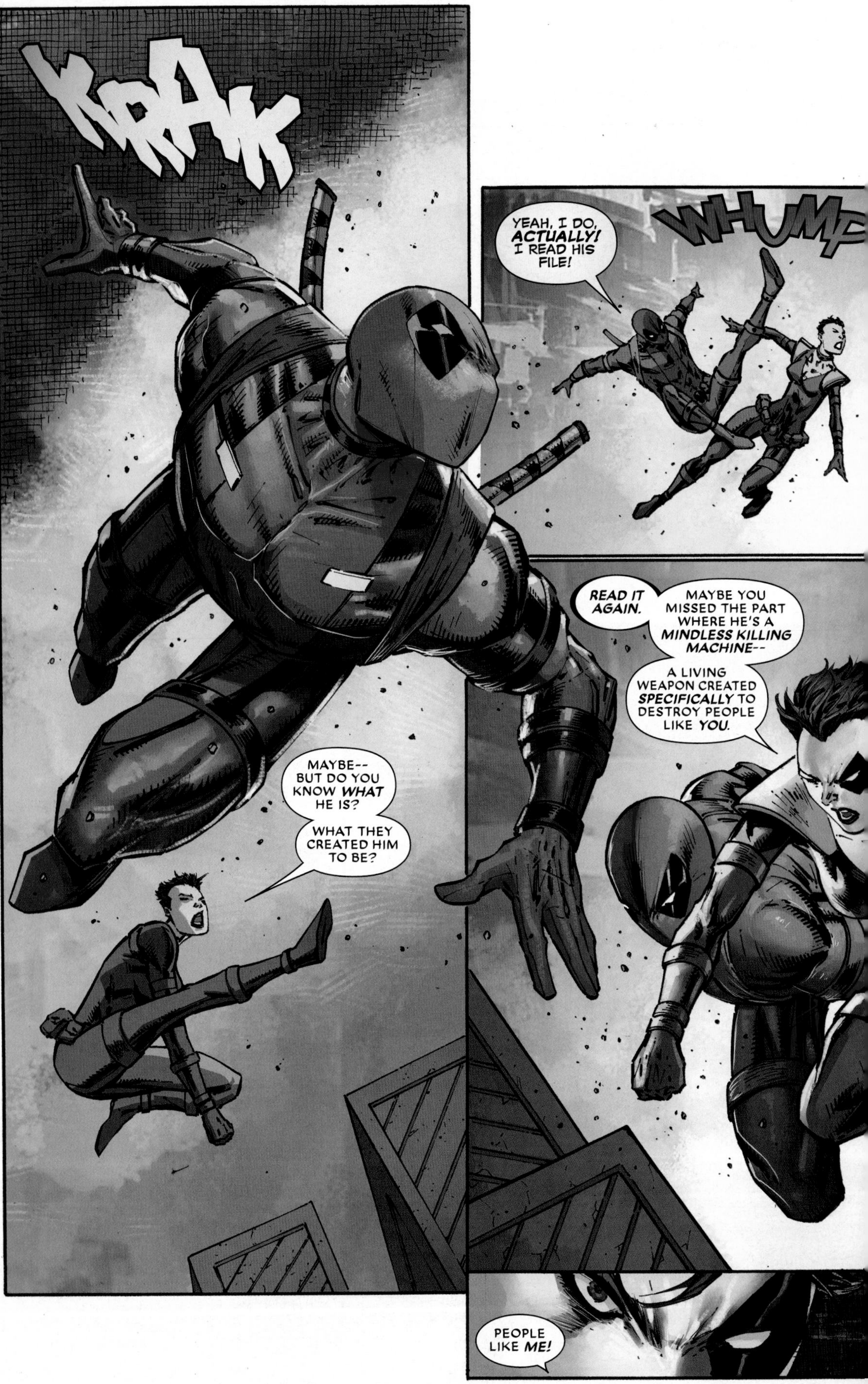

KRAK
MAYBE-- BUT DO YOU KNOW WHAT HE IS?
WHAT THEY CREATED HIM TO BE?
WHUMP
YEAH, I DO, ACTUALLY! I READ HIS FILE!
READ IT AGAIN.
MAYBE YOU MISSED THE PART WHERE HE'S A MINDLESS KILLING MACHINE--
A LIVING WEAPON CREATED SPECIFICALLY TO DESTROY PEOPLE LIKE YOU.
PEOPLE LIKE ME!

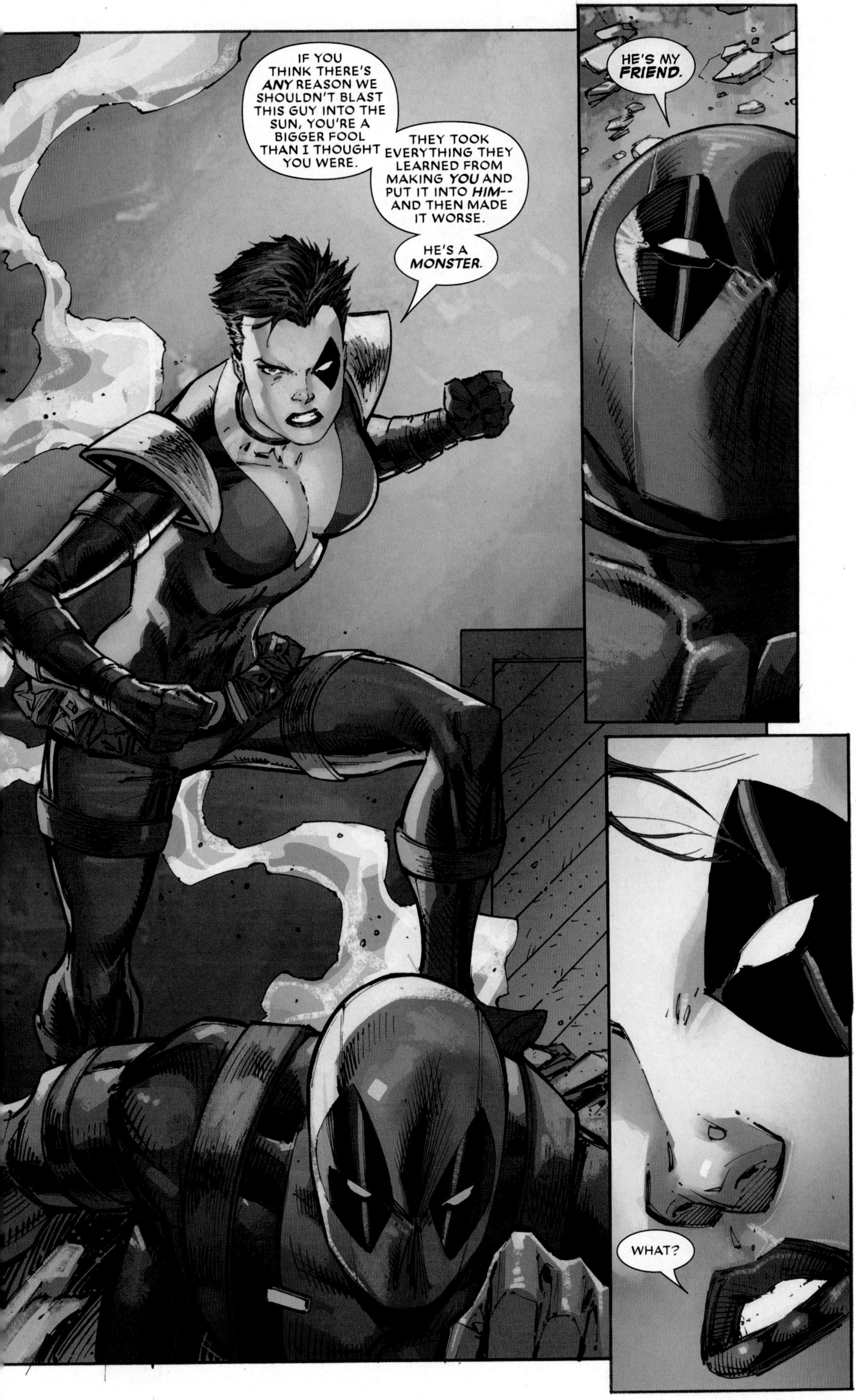
IF YOU THINK THERE'S ANY REASON WE SHOULDN'T BLAST THIS GUY INTO THE SUN, YOU'RE A BIGGER FOOL THAN I THOUGHT YOU WERE.
THEY TOOK EVERYTHING THEY LEARNED FROM MAKING YOU AND PUT IT INTO HIM--AND THEN MADE IT WORSE.
HE'S A MONSTER.
HE'S MY FRIEND.
WHAT?

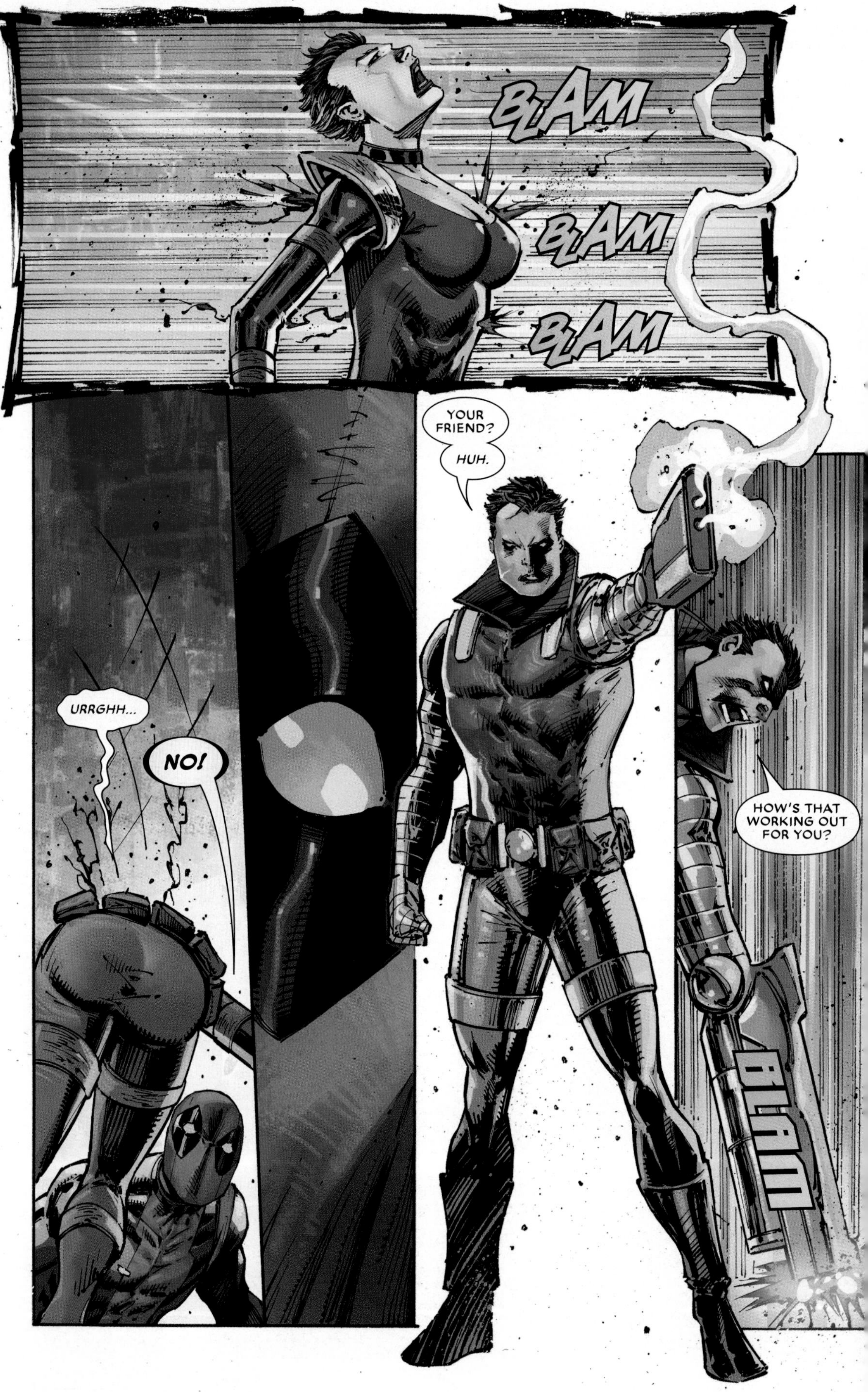
BLAM
BLAM
BLAM
URRGHH...
NO!
YOUR FRIEND?
HUH.
HOW'S THAT WORKING OUT FOR YOU?
BLAM

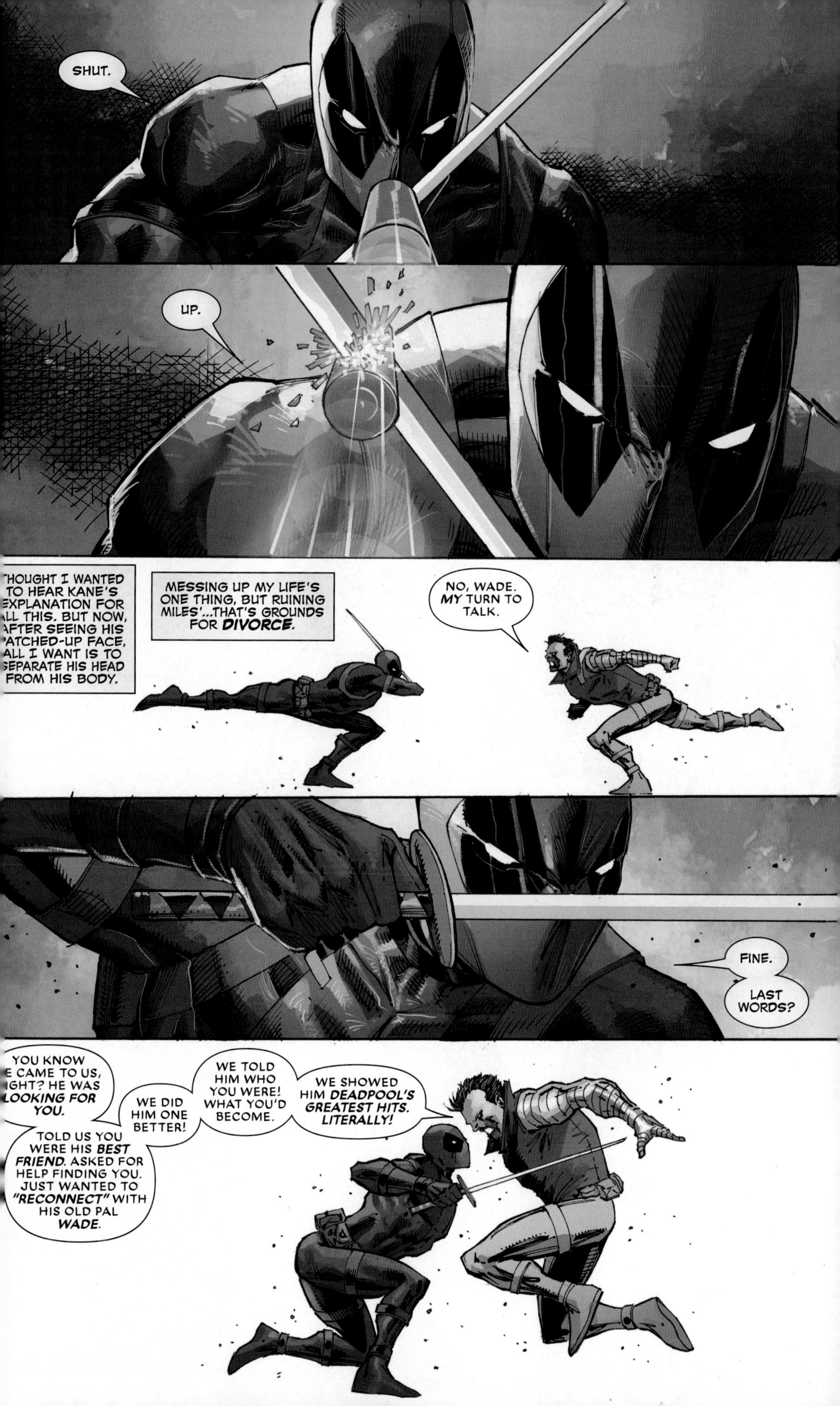
SHUT.
UP.
THOUGHT I WANTED TO HEAR KANE'S EXPLANATION FOR ALL THIS. BUT NOW, AFTER SEEING HIS PATCHED-UP FACE, ALL I WANT IS TO SEPARATE HIS HEAD FROM HIS BODY.
MESSING UP MY LIFE'S ONE THING, BUT RUINING MILES'...THAT'S GROUNDS FOR DIVORCE.
NO, WADE. MY TURN TO TALK.
FINE.
LAST WORDS?
YOU KNOW HE CAME TO US, RIGHT? HE WAS LOOKING FOR YOU.
TOLD US YOU WERE HIS BEST FRIEND. ASKED FOR HELP FINDING YOU. JUST WANTED TO "RECONNECT" WITH HIS OLD PAL WADE.
WE DID HIM ONE BETTER!
WE TOLD HIM WHO YOU WERE! WHAT YOU'D BECOME.
WE SHOWED HIM DEADPOOL'S GREATEST HITS. LITERALLY!

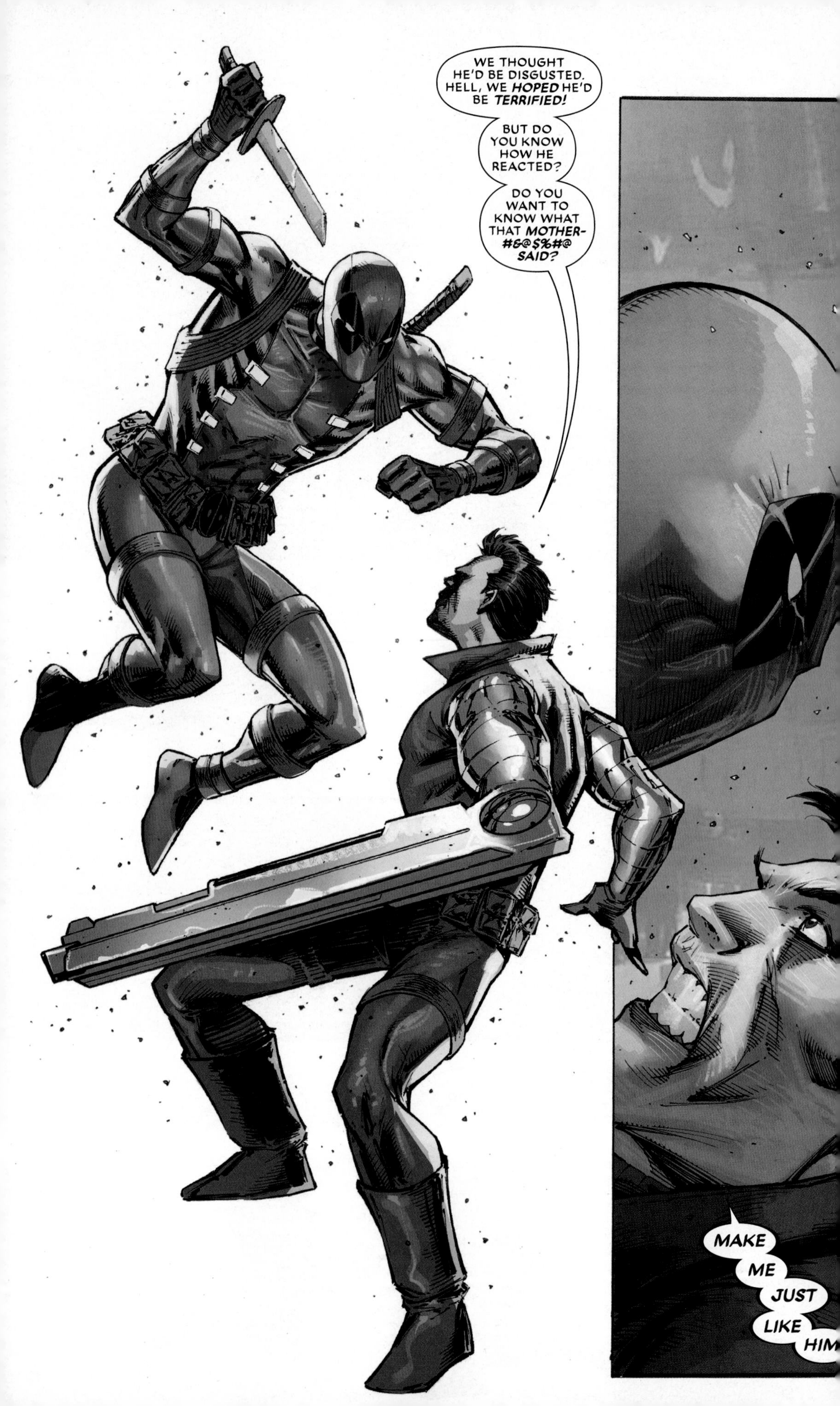

WE THOUGHT HE'D BE DISGUSTED. HELL, WE HOPED HE'D BE TERRIFIED!
BUT DO YOU KNOW HOW HE REACTED?
DO YOU WANT TO KNOW WHAT THAT MOTHER-#&@$%#@ SAID?
MAKE ME JUST LIKE HIM

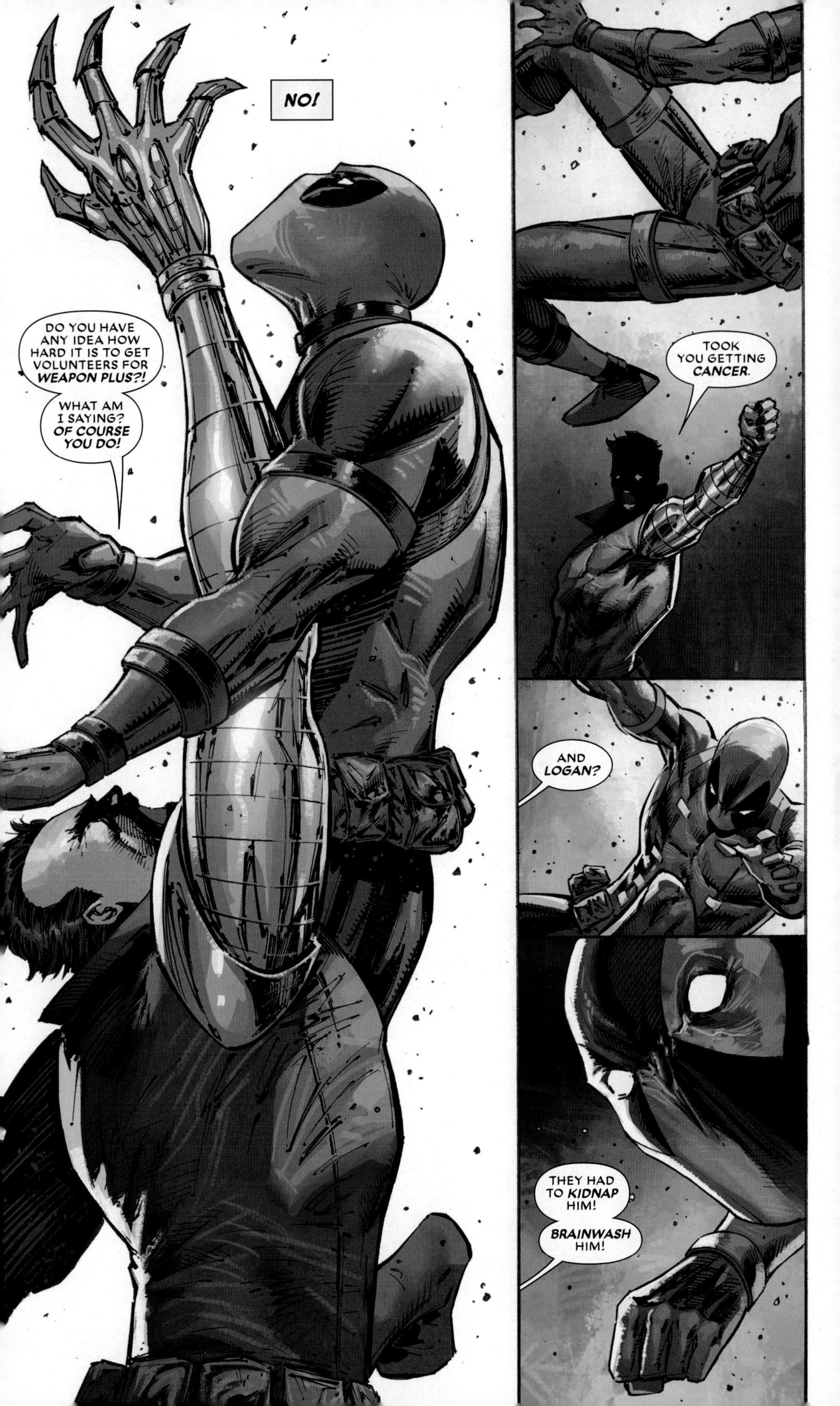
NO!
DO YOU HAVE ANY IDEA HOW HARD IT IS TO GET VOLUNTEERS FOR WEAPON PLUS?!
WHAT AM I SAYING? OF COURSE YOU DO!
TOOK YOU GETTING CANCER.
AND LOGAN?
THEY HAD TO KIDNAP HIM!
BRAINWASH HIM!

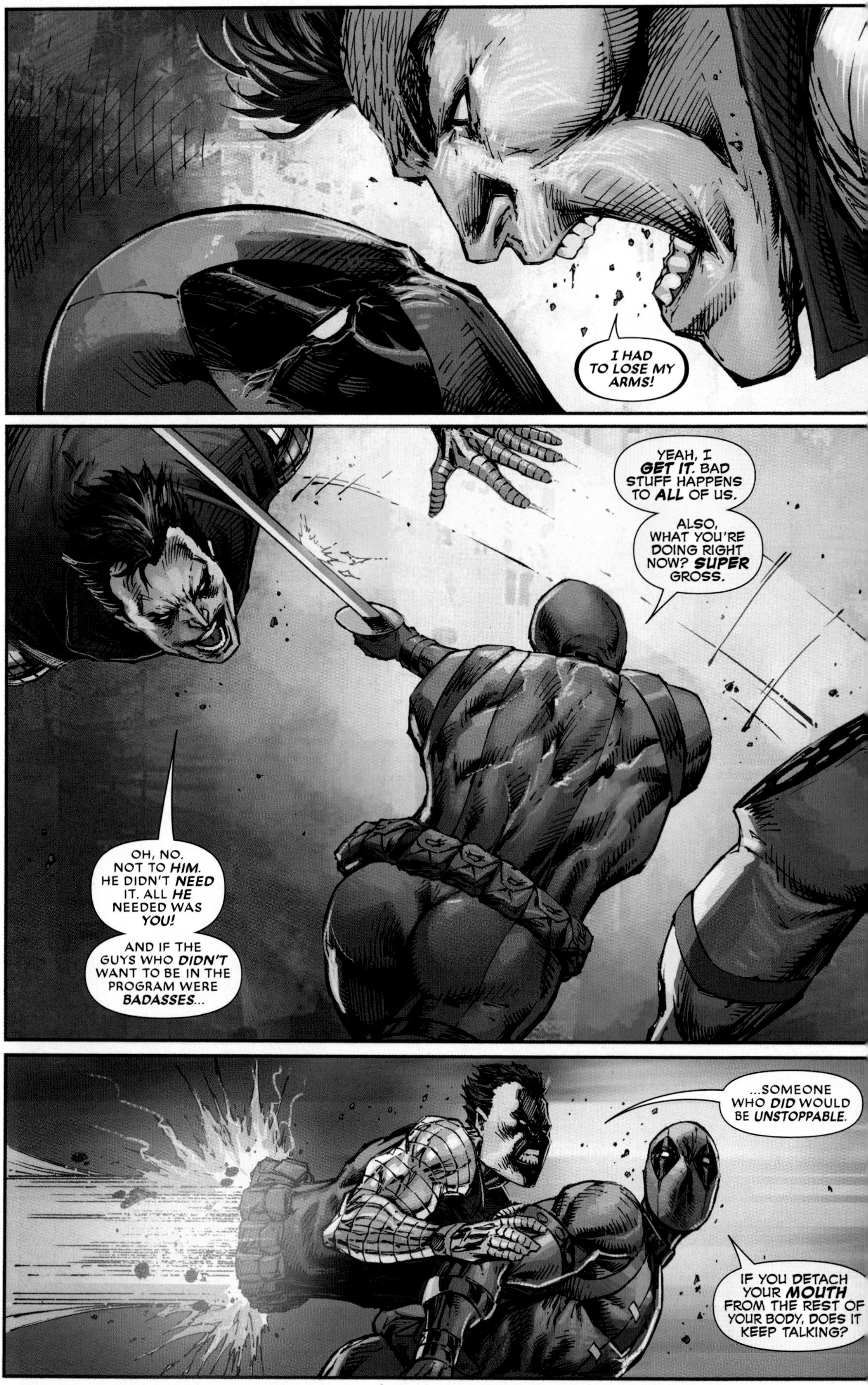
I HAD TO LOSE MY ARMS!
YEAH, I GET IT. BAD STUFF HAPPENS TO ALL OF US.
ALSO, WHAT YOU'RE DOING RIGHT NOW? SUPER GROSS.
OH, NO. NOT TO HIM. HE DIDN'T NEED IT. ALL HE NEEDED WAS YOU!
AND IF THE GUYS WHO DIDN'T WANT TO BE IN THE PROGRAM WERE BADASSES...
...SOMEONE WHO DID WOULD BE UNSTOPPABLE.
IF YOU DETACH YOUR MOUTH FROM THE REST OF YOUR BODY, DOES IT KEEP TALKING?

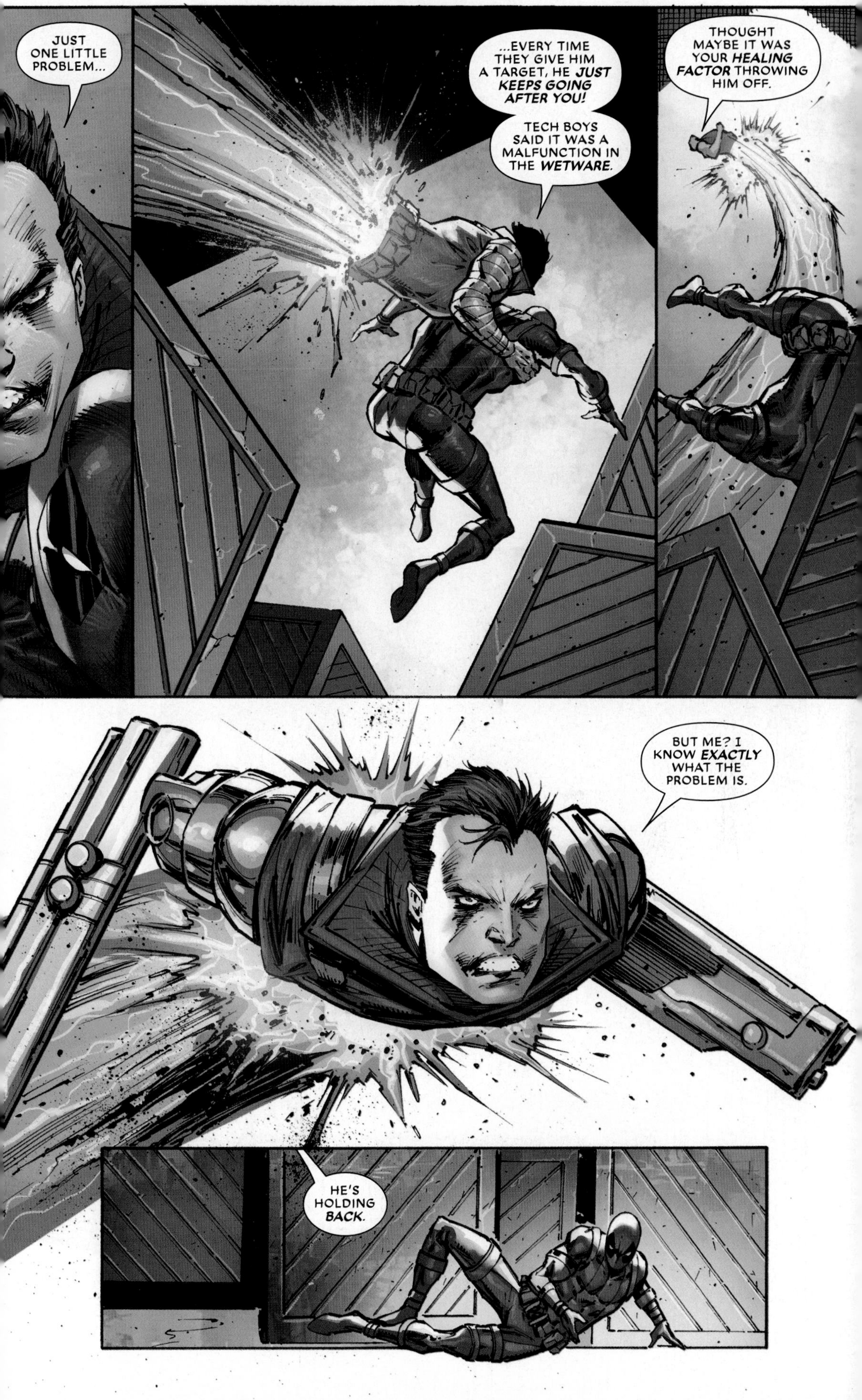
JUST ONE LITTLE PROBLEM...
...EVERY TIME THEY GIVE HIM A TARGET, HE **JUST KEEPS GOING AFTER YOU!**
TECH BOYS SAID IT WAS A MALFUNCTION IN THE **WETWARE.**
THOUGHT MAYBE IT WAS YOUR **HEALING FACTOR** THROWING HIM OFF.
BUT ME? I KNOW **EXACTLY** WHAT THE PROBLEM IS.
HE'S HOLDING **BACK.**

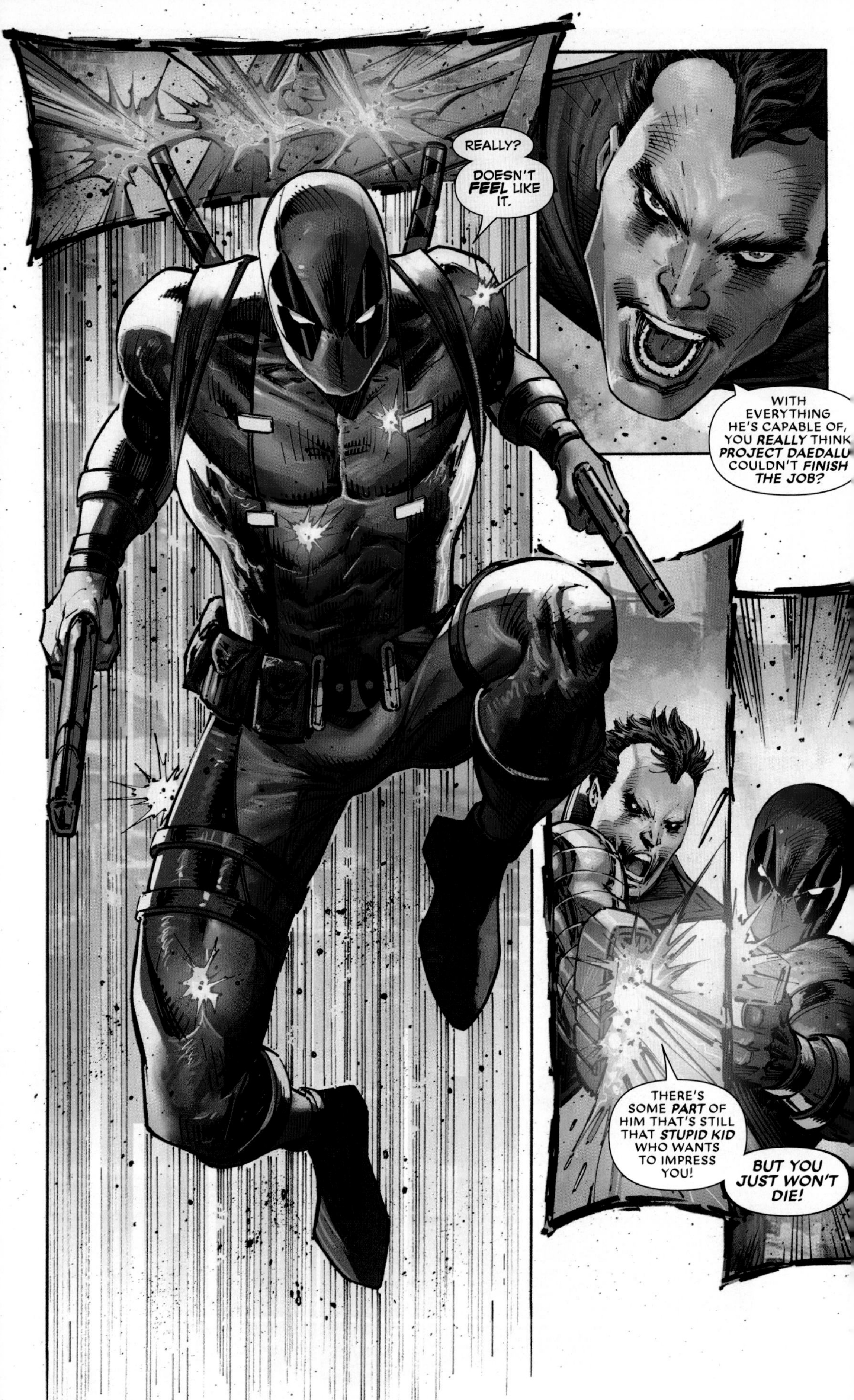
REALLY?
DOESN'T FEEL LIKE IT.
WITH EVERYTHING HE'S CAPABLE OF, YOU REALLY THINK PROJECT DAEDALU COULDN'T FINISH THE JOB?
THERE'S SOME PART OF HIM THAT'S STILL THAT STUPID KID WHO WANTS TO IMPRESS YOU!
BUT YOU JUST WON'T DIE!

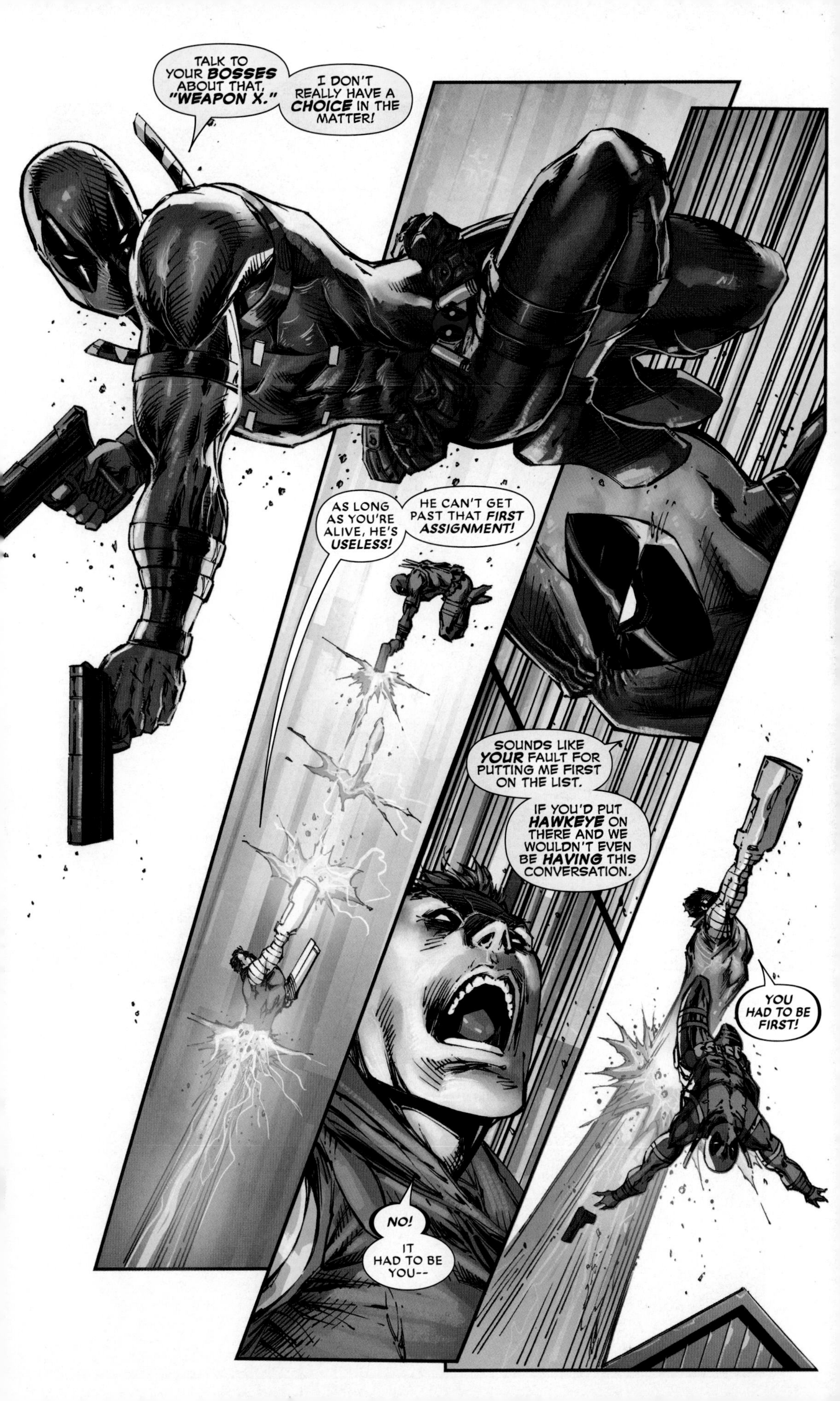

TALK TO YOUR BOSSES ABOUT THAT, "WEAPON X."
I DON'T REALLY HAVE A CHOICE IN THE MATTER!
AS LONG AS YOU'RE ALIVE, HE'S USELESS!
HE CAN'T GET PAST THAT FIRST ASSIGNMENT!
SOUNDS LIKE YOUR FAULT FOR PUTTING ME FIRST ON THE LIST.
IF YOU'D PUT HAWKEYE ON THERE AND WE WOULDN'T EVEN BE HAVING THIS CONVERSATION.
NO!
IT HAD TO BE YOU--
YOU HAD TO BE FIRST!

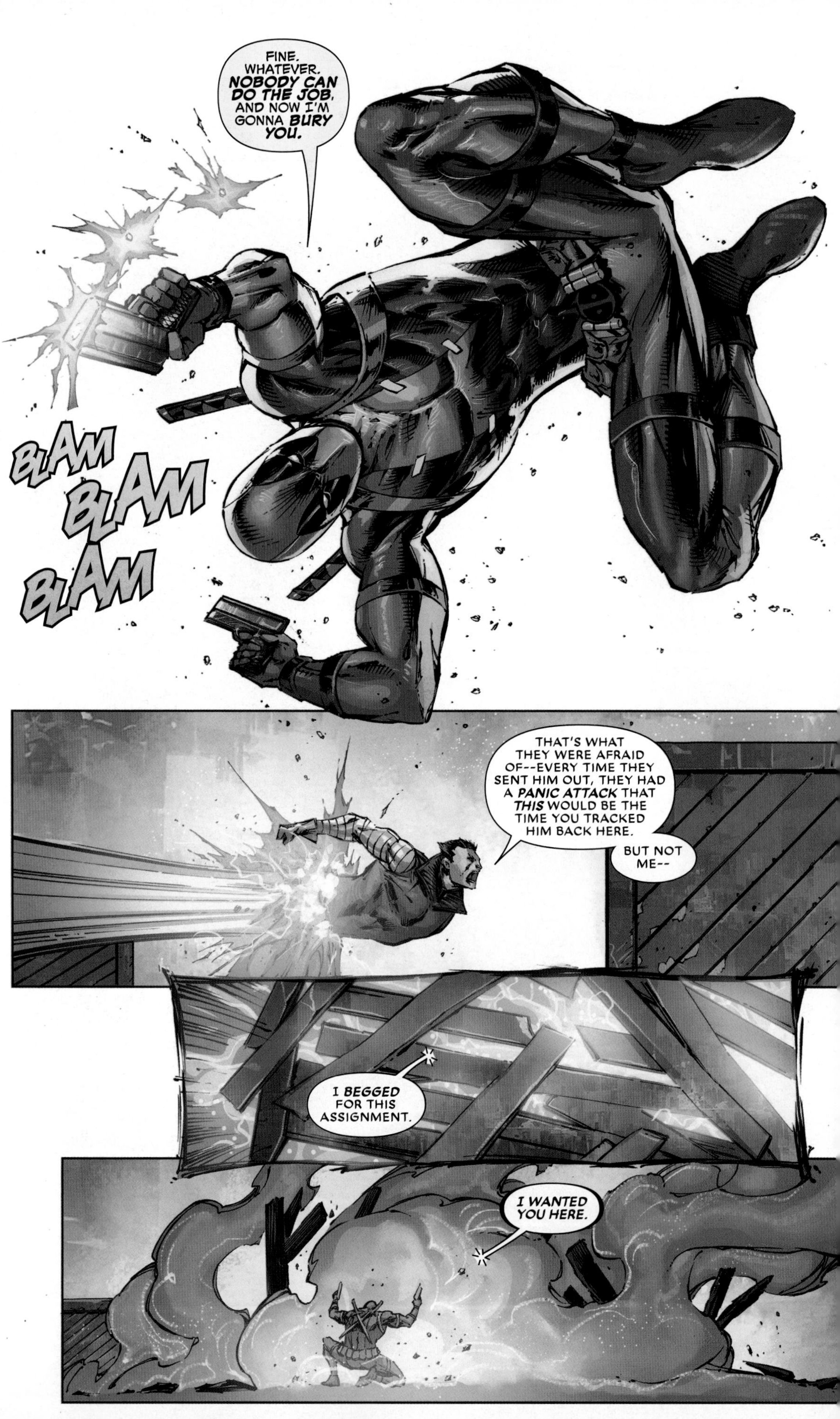
FINE. WHATEVER. NOBODY CAN DO THE JOB, AND NOW I'M GONNA BURY YOU.
BLAM
BLAM
BLAM
THAT'S WHAT THEY WERE AFRAID OF--EVERY TIME THEY SENT HIM OUT, THEY HAD A PANIC ATTACK THAT THIS WOULD BE THE TIME YOU TRACKED HIM BACK HERE.
BUT NOT ME--
I BEGGED FOR THIS ASSIGNMENT.
I WANTED YOU HERE.

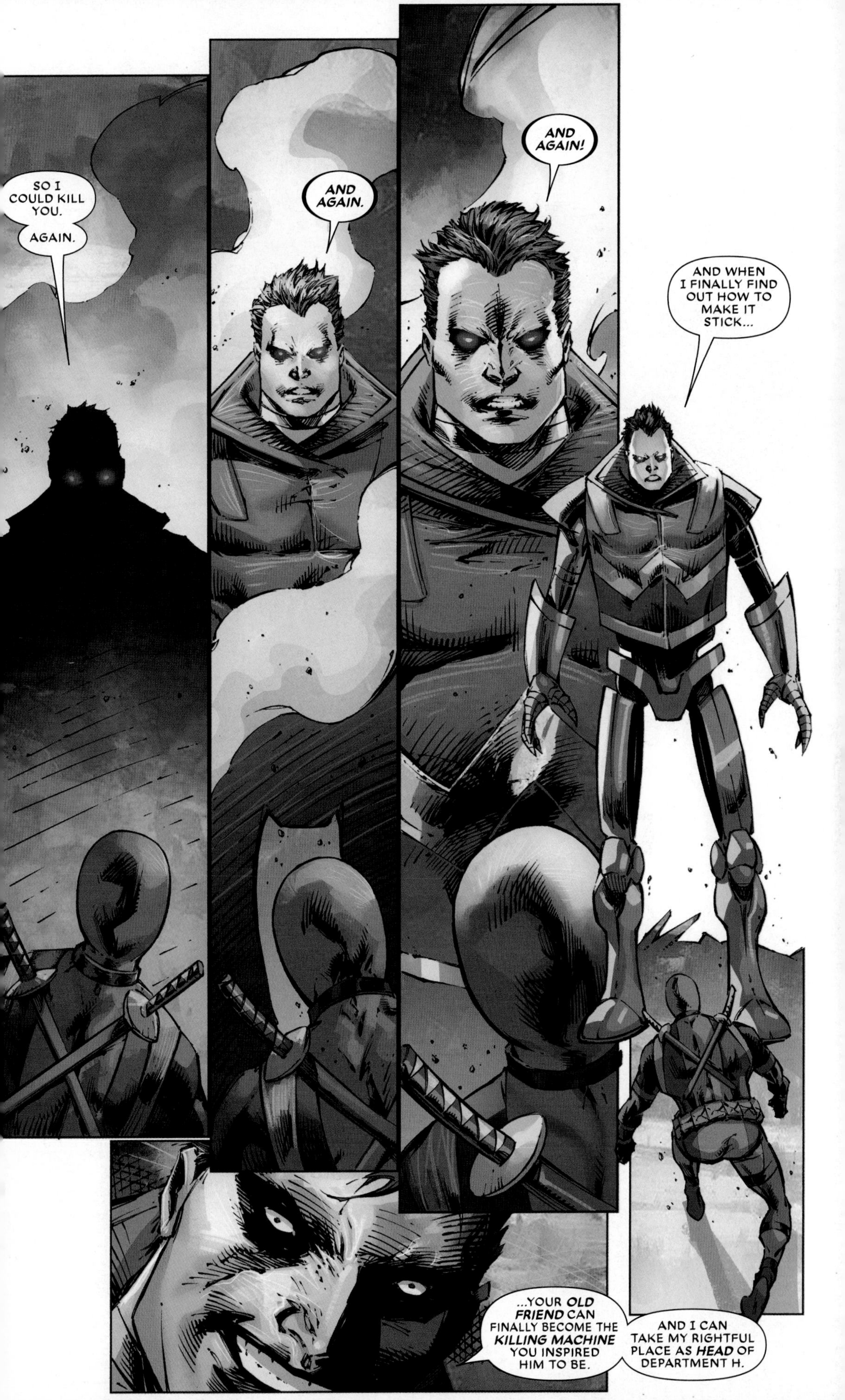
SO I COULD KILL YOU.
AGAIN.
AND AGAIN.
AND AGAIN!
AND WHEN I FINALLY FIND OUT HOW TO MAKE IT STICK...
...YOUR OLD FRIEND CAN FINALLY BECOME THE KILLING MACHINE YOU INSPIRED HIM TO BE.
AND I CAN TAKE MY RIGHTFUL PLACE AS HEAD OF DEPARTMENT H.

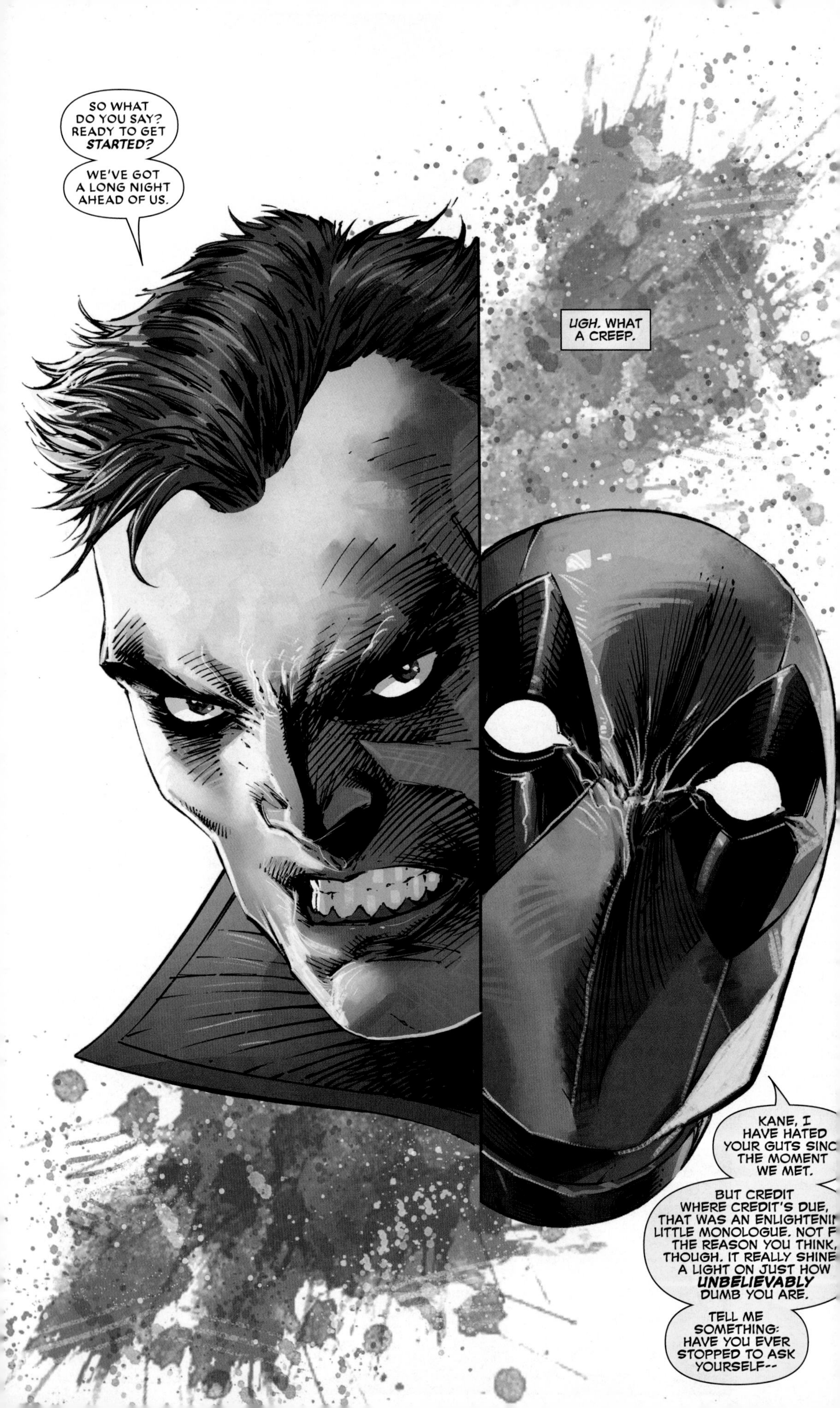
SO WHAT DO YOU SAY? READY TO GET *STARTED?*
WE'VE GOT A LONG NIGHT AHEAD OF US.
UGH. WHAT A CREEP.
KANE, I HAVE HATED YOUR GUTS SINC THE MOMENT WE MET.
BUT CREDIT WHERE CREDIT'S DUE, THAT WAS AN ENLIGHTENI LITTLE MONOLOGUE. NOT F THE REASON YOU THINK, THOUGH. IT REALLY SHINE A LIGHT ON JUST HOW ***UNBELIEVABLY*** DUMB YOU ARE.
TELL ME SOMETHING: HAVE YOU EVER STOPPED TO ASK YOURSELF--

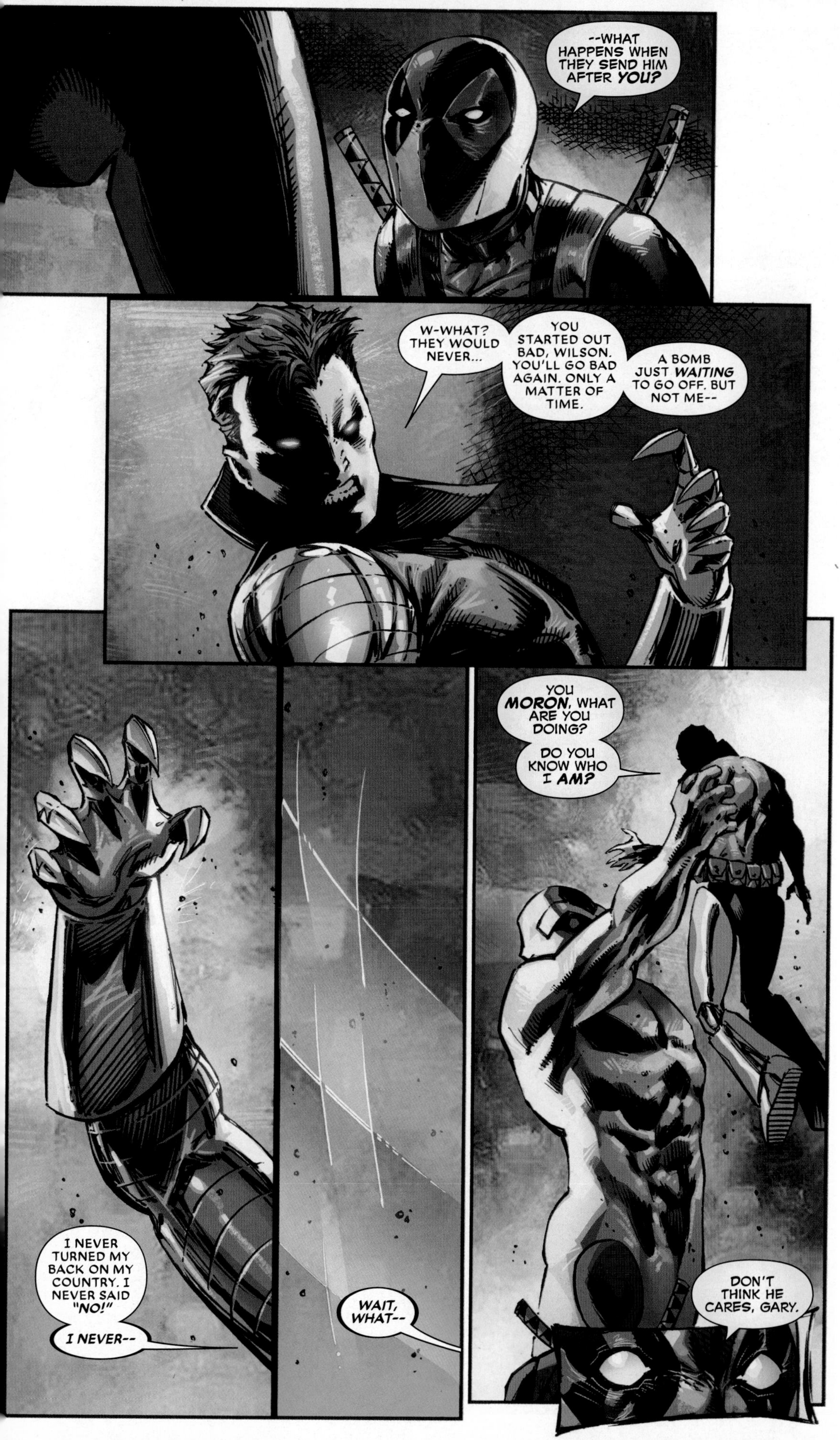
--WHAT HAPPENS WHEN THEY SEND HIM AFTER YOU?
W-WHAT? THEY WOULD NEVER...
YOU STARTED OUT BAD, WILSON. YOU'LL GO BAD AGAIN. ONLY A MATTER OF TIME.
A BOMB JUST WAITING TO GO OFF. BUT NOT ME--
I NEVER TURNED MY BACK ON MY COUNTRY. I NEVER SAID "NO!"
I NEVER--
WAIT, WHAT--
YOU MORON, WHAT ARE YOU DOING?
DO YOU KNOW WHO I AM?
DON'T THINK HE CARES, GARY.

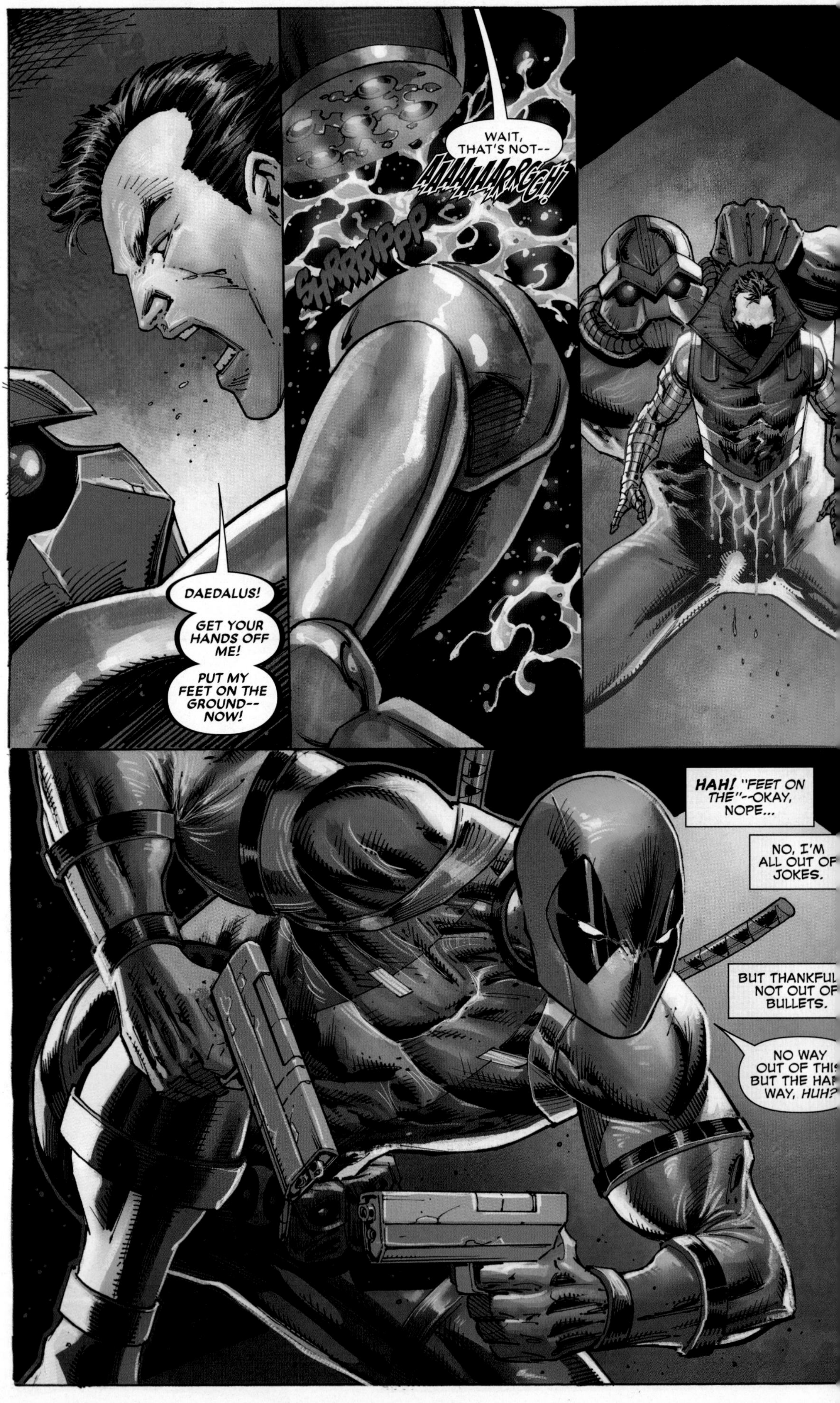

DAEDALUS!
GET YOUR HANDS OFF ME!
PUT MY FEET ON THE GROUND--NOW!
WAIT, THAT'S NOT--
AAAAAAARRGGH!
SHRRRIPPP
HAH! "FEET ON THE"--OKAY, NOPE...
NO, I'M ALL OUT OF JOKES.
BUT THANKFUL NOT OUT OF BULLETS.
NO WAY OUT OF THIS BUT THE HAR WAY, HUH?

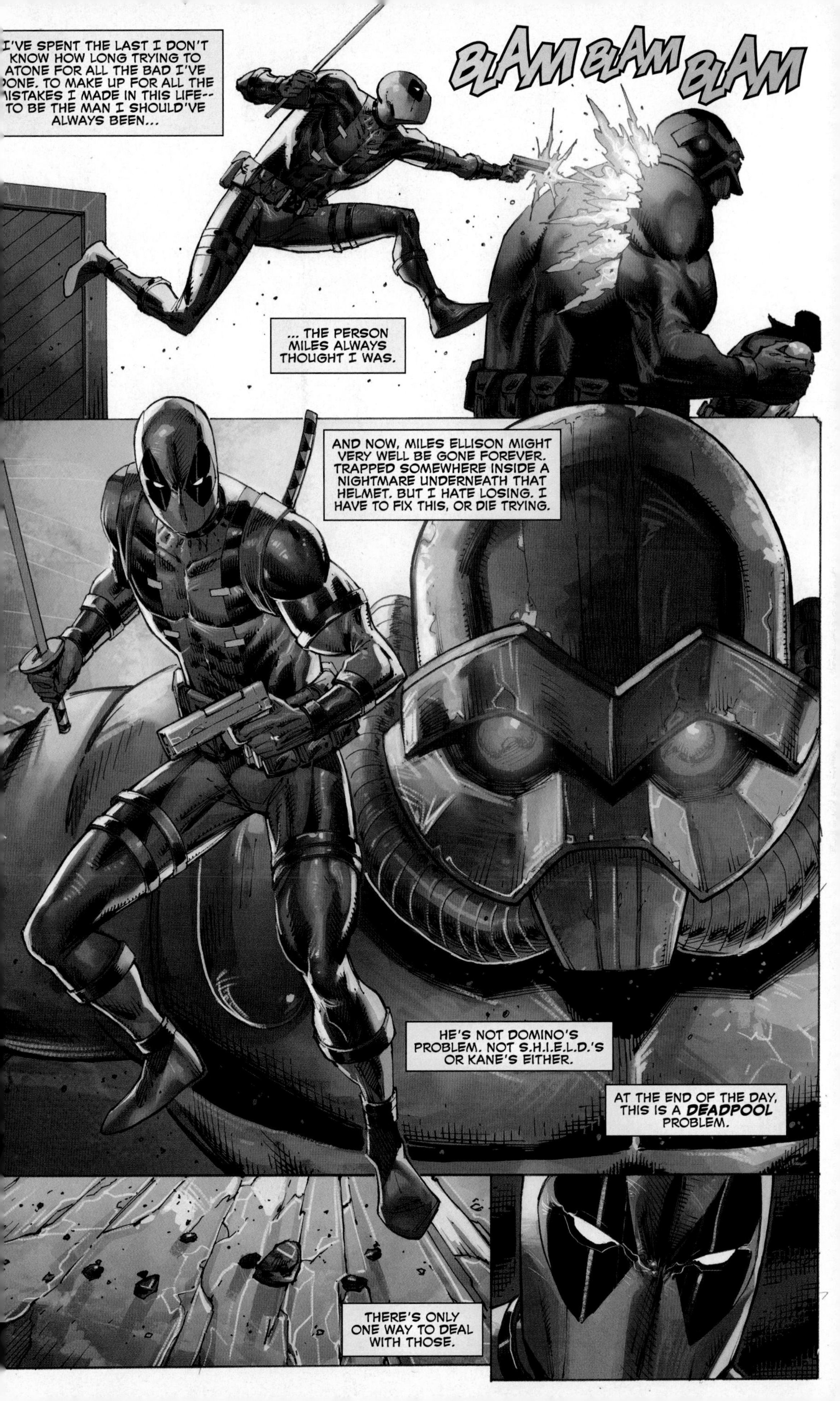

I'VE SPENT THE LAST I DON'T KNOW HOW LONG TRYING TO ATONE FOR ALL THE BAD I'VE DONE. TO MAKE UP FOR ALL THE MISTAKES I MADE IN THIS LIFE-- TO BE THE MAN I SHOULD'VE ALWAYS BEEN...
BLAM BLAM BLAM
... THE PERSON MILES ALWAYS THOUGHT I WAS.
AND NOW, MILES ELLISON MIGHT VERY WELL BE GONE FOREVER. TRAPPED SOMEWHERE INSIDE A NIGHTMARE UNDERNEATH THAT HELMET. BUT I HATE LOSING. I HAVE TO FIX THIS, OR DIE TRYING.
HE'S NOT DOMINO'S PROBLEM. NOT S.H.I.E.L.D.'S OR KANE'S EITHER.
AT THE END OF THE DAY, THIS IS A DEADPOOL PROBLEM.
THERE'S ONLY ONE WAY TO DEAL WITH THOSE.

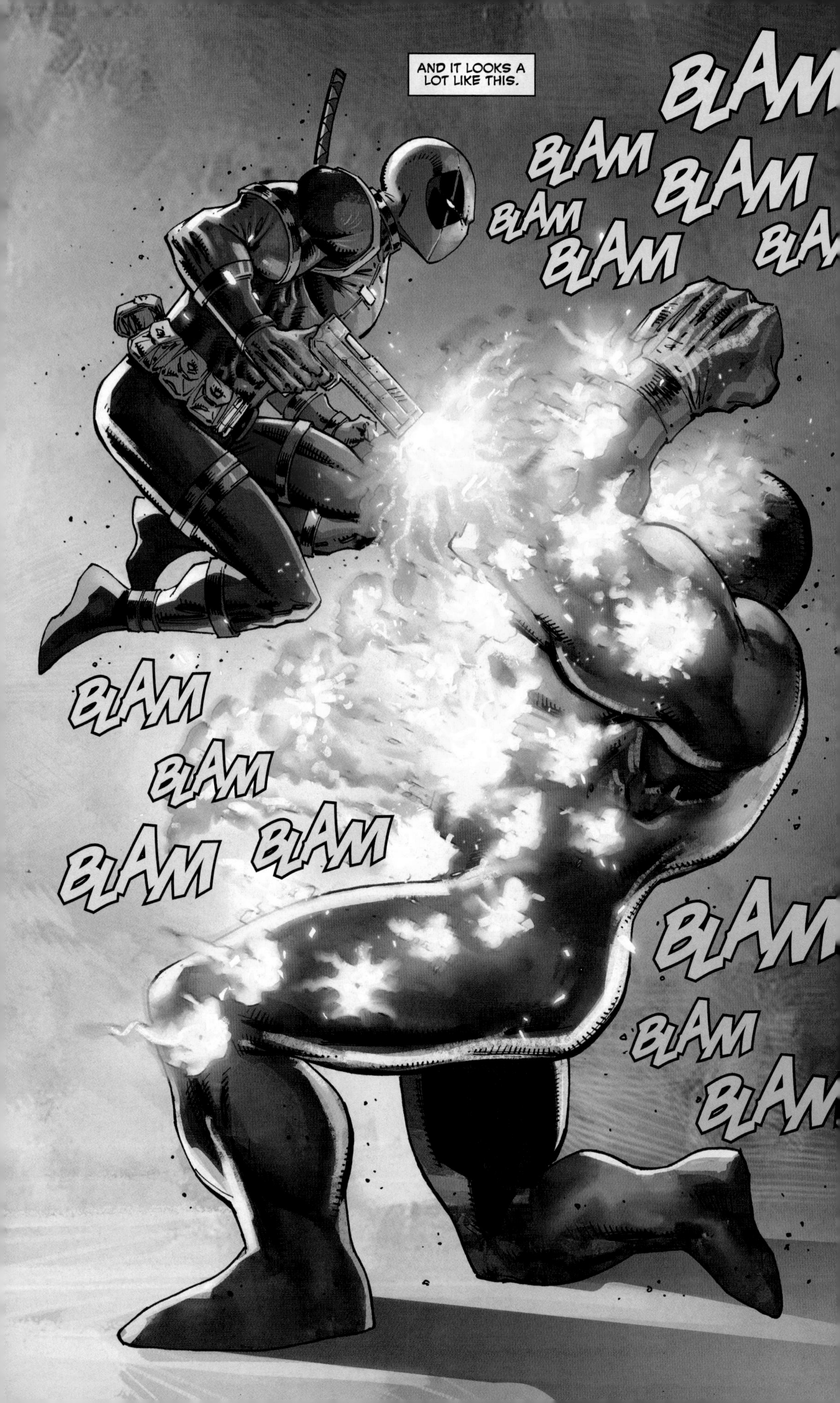
AND IT LOOKS A LOT LIKE THIS.
BLAM
BLAM
BLAM
BLAM
BLAM
BLAM
BLAM
BLAM
BLAM
BLAM
BLAM
BLAM
BLAM
BLAM

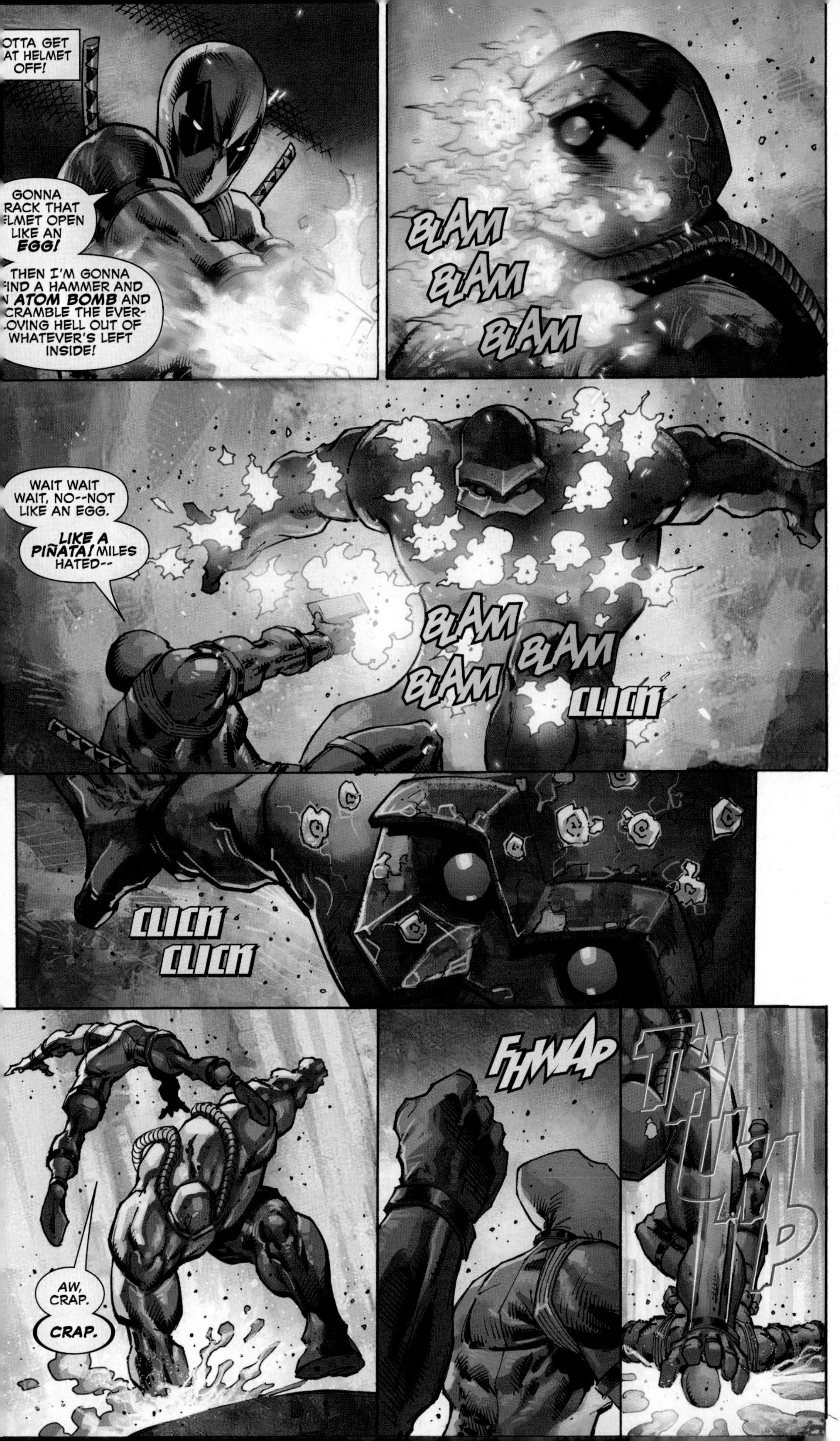

OTTA GET
AT HELMET
OFF!
GONNA
RACK THAT
ELMET OPEN
LIKE AN
EGG!
THEN I'M GONNA
FIND A HAMMER AND
N ATOM BOMB AND
CRAMBLE THE EVER-
LOVING HELL OUT OF
WHATEVER'S LEFT
INSIDE!
BLAM
BLAM
BLAM
WAIT WAIT
WAIT, NO--NOT
LIKE AN EGG.
LIKE A
PIÑATA! MILES
HATED--
BLAM
BLAM
BLAM
CLICK
CLICK
CLICK
AW,
CRAP.
CRAP.
FHWAP
THUD

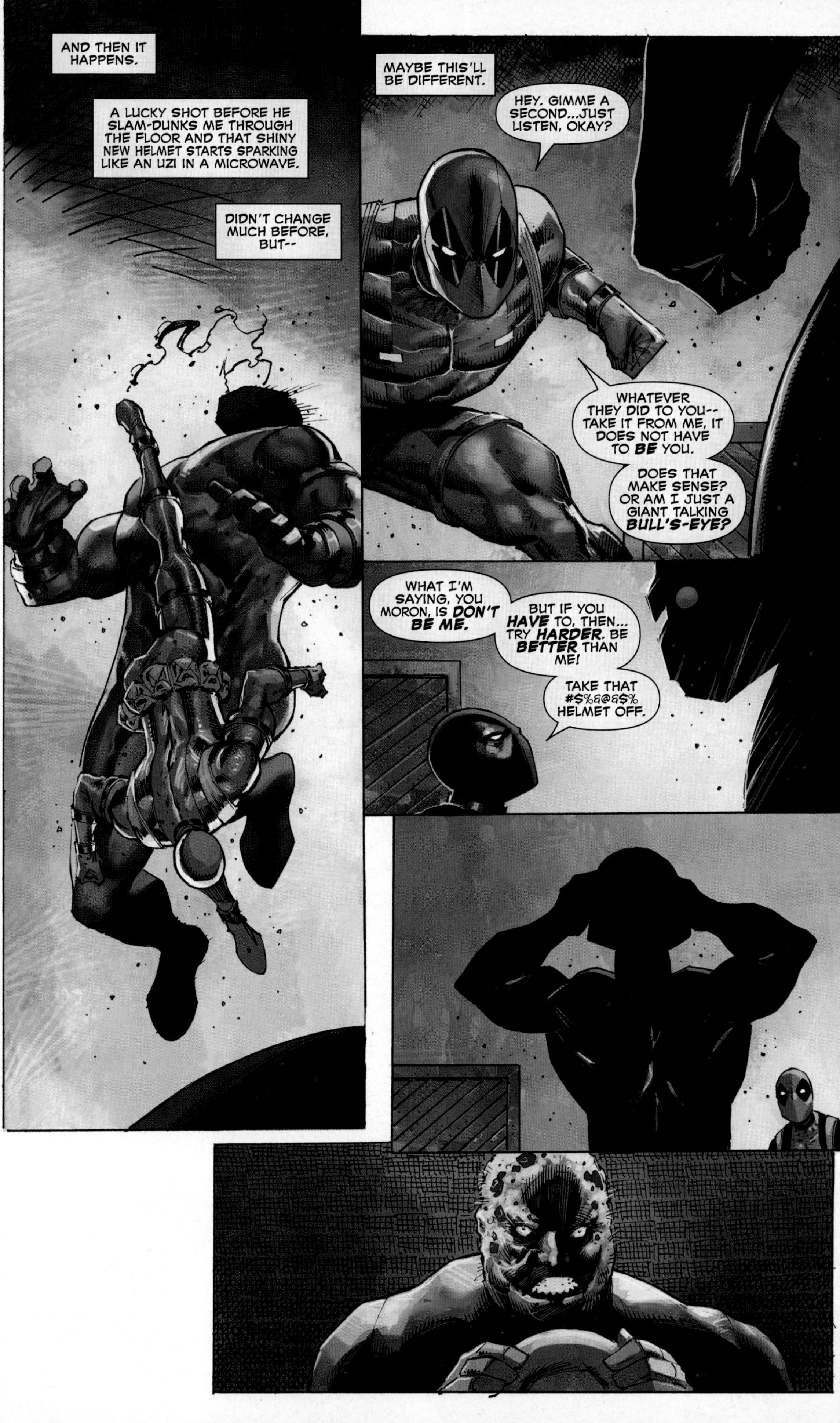
AND THEN IT HAPPENS.
A LUCKY SHOT BEFORE HE SLAM-DUNKS ME THROUGH THE FLOOR AND THAT SHINY NEW HELMET STARTS SPARKING LIKE AN UZI IN A MICROWAVE.
DIDN'T CHANGE MUCH BEFORE, BUT--
MAYBE THIS'LL BE DIFFERENT.
HEY. GIMME A SECOND...JUST LISTEN, OKAY?
WHATEVER THEY DID TO YOU-- TAKE IT FROM ME, IT DOES NOT HAVE TO BE YOU.
DOES THAT MAKE SENSE? OR AM I JUST A GIANT TALKING BULL'S-EYE?
WHAT I'M SAYING, YOU MORON, IS DON'T BE ME.
BUT IF YOU HAVE TO, THEN... TRY HARDER. BE BETTER THAN ME!
TAKE THAT #$%&@&$% HELMET OFF.

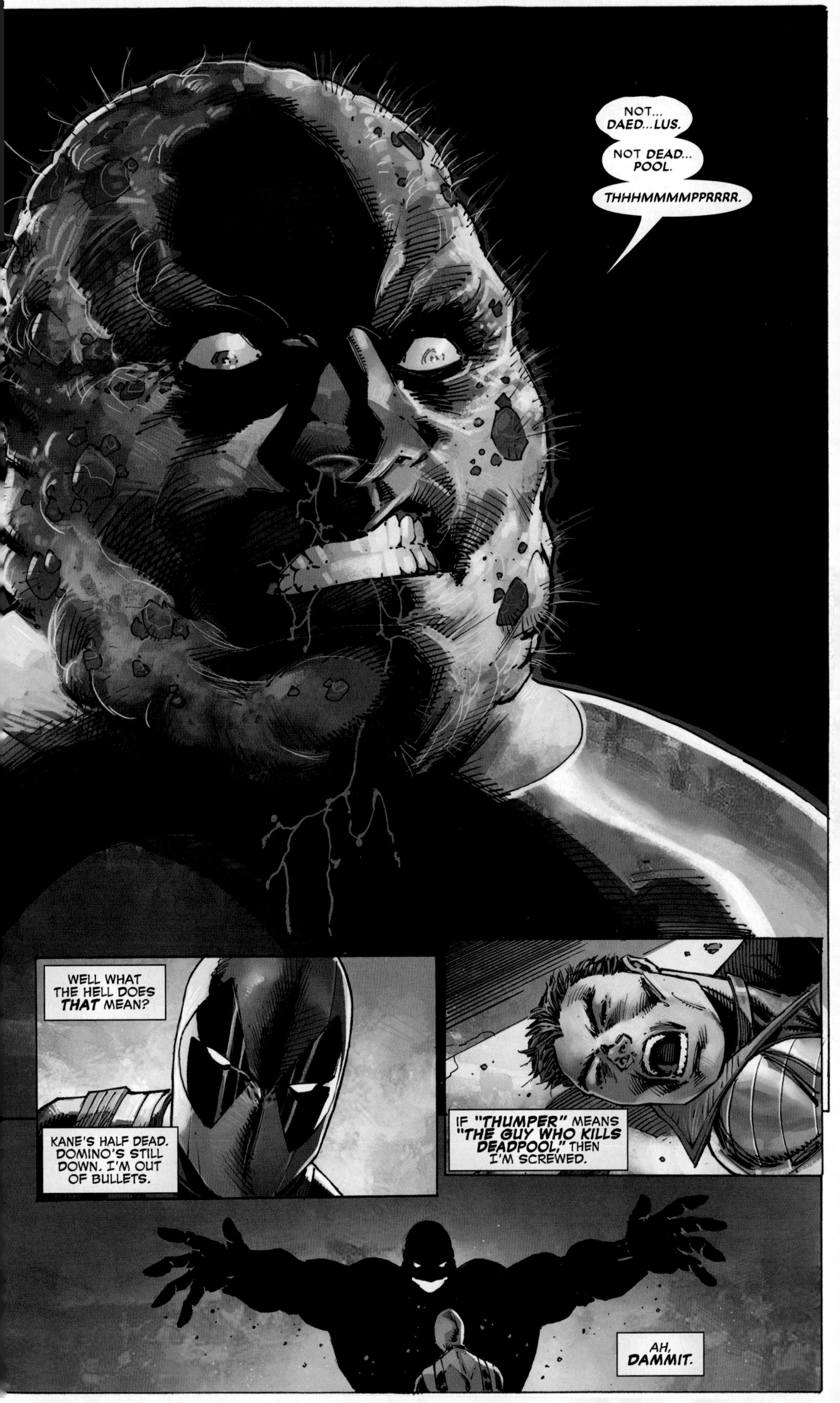
NOT... DAED...LUS.
NOT DEAD... POOL.
THHHMMMMPPRRRR.
WELL WHAT THE HELL DOES *THAT* MEAN?
KANE'S HALF DEAD. DOMINO'S STILL DOWN. I'M OUT OF BULLETS.
IF *"THUMPER"* MEANS *"THE GUY WHO KILLS DEADPOOL,"* THEN I'M SCREWED.
AH, *DAMMIT.*

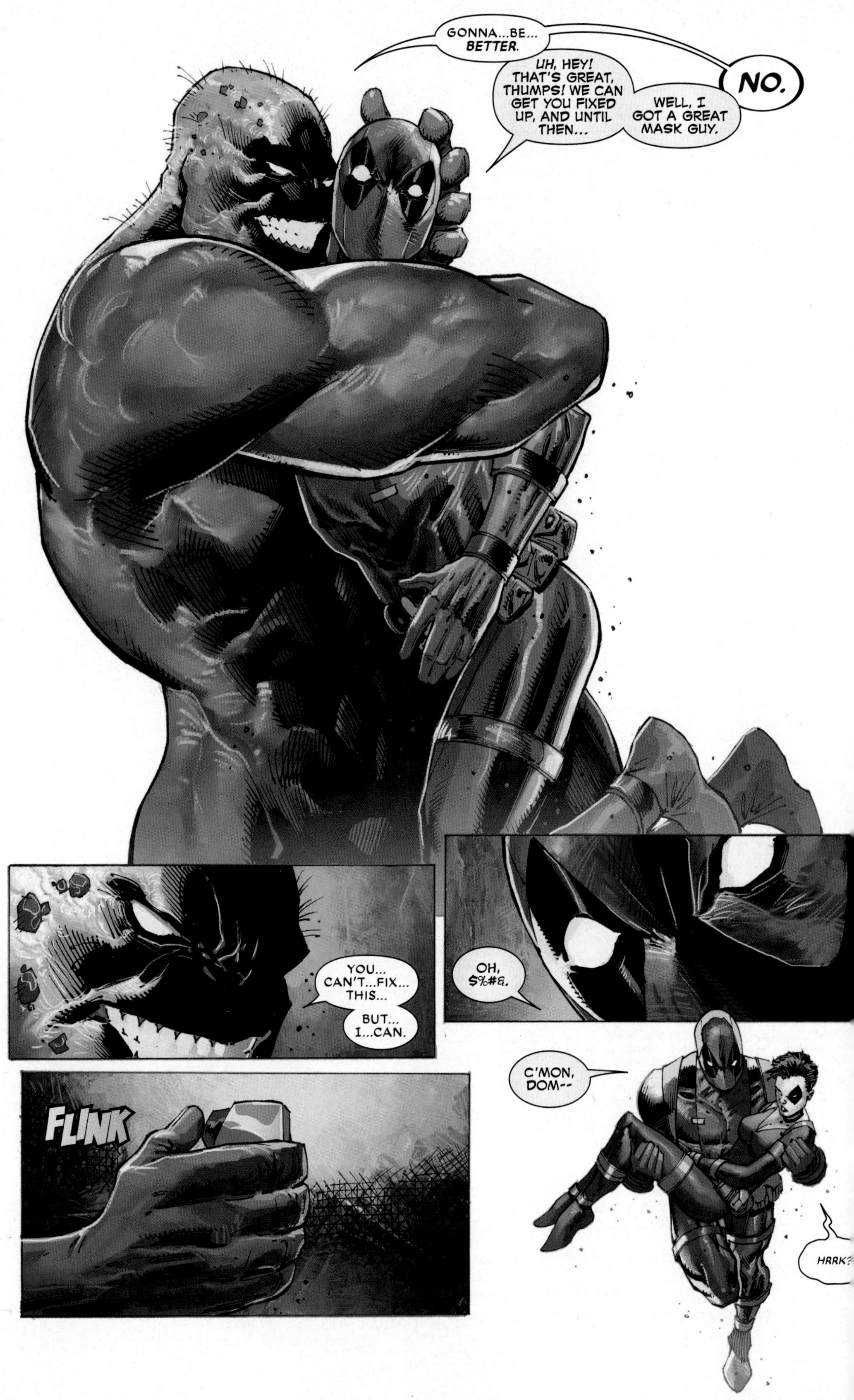
GONNA...BE... BETTER.
UH, HEY! THAT'S GREAT, THUMPS! WE CAN GET YOU FIXED UP, AND UNTIL THEN...
NO.
WELL, I GOT A GREAT MASK GUY.
YOU... CAN'T...FIX... THIS...
BUT... I...CAN.
OH, $%#&.
FLINK
C'MON, DOM--
HRRK?

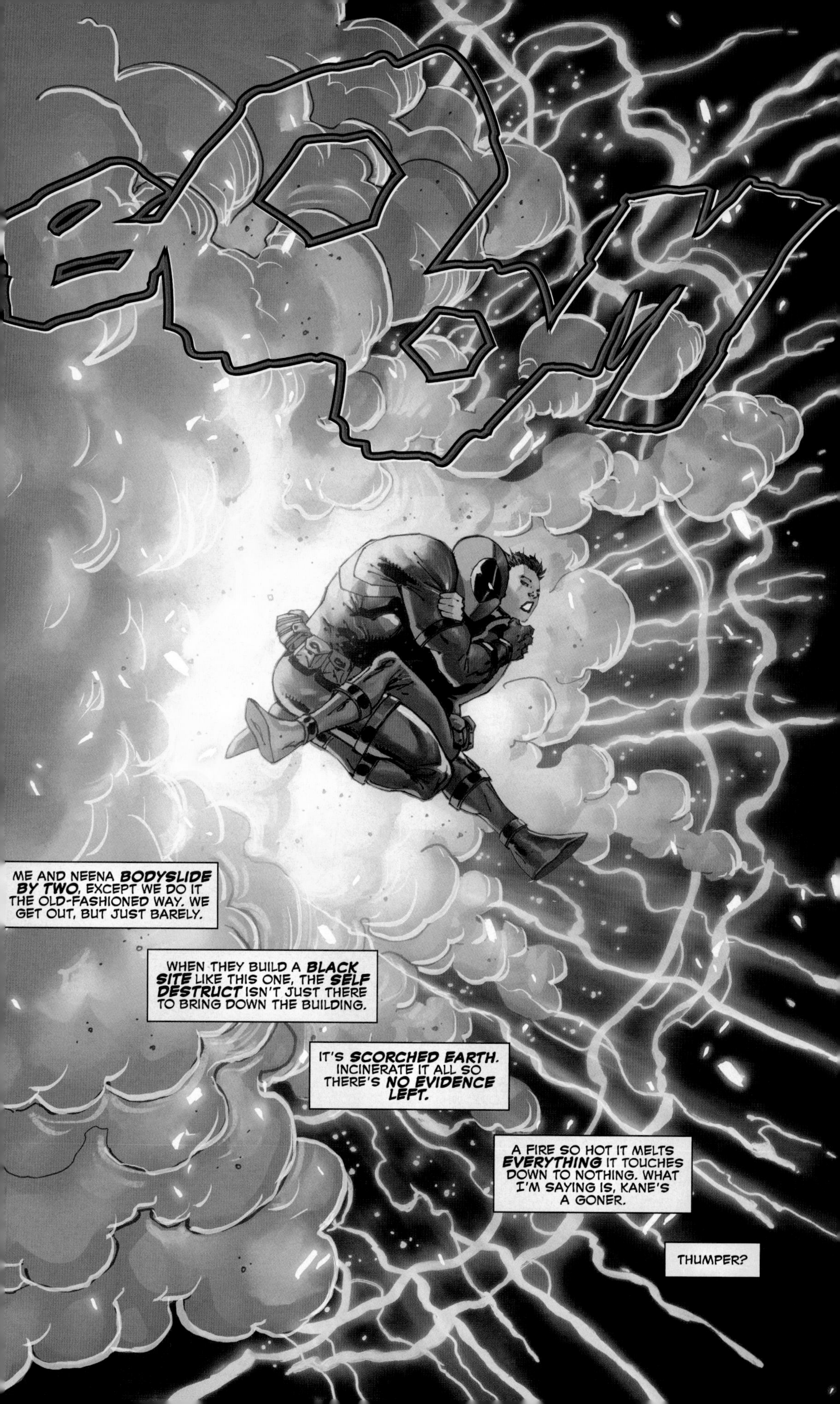
BOOOM
ME AND NEENA BODYSLIDE BY TWO, EXCEPT WE DO IT THE OLD-FASHIONED WAY. WE GET OUT, BUT JUST BARELY.
WHEN THEY BUILD A BLACK SITE LIKE THIS ONE, THE SELF DESTRUCT ISN'T JUST THERE TO BRING DOWN THE BUILDING.
IT'S SCORCHED EARTH. INCINERATE IT ALL SO THERE'S NO EVIDENCE LEFT.
A FIRE SO HOT IT MELTS EVERYTHING IT TOUCHES DOWN TO NOTHING. WHAT I'M SAYING IS, KANE'S A GONER.
THUMPER?

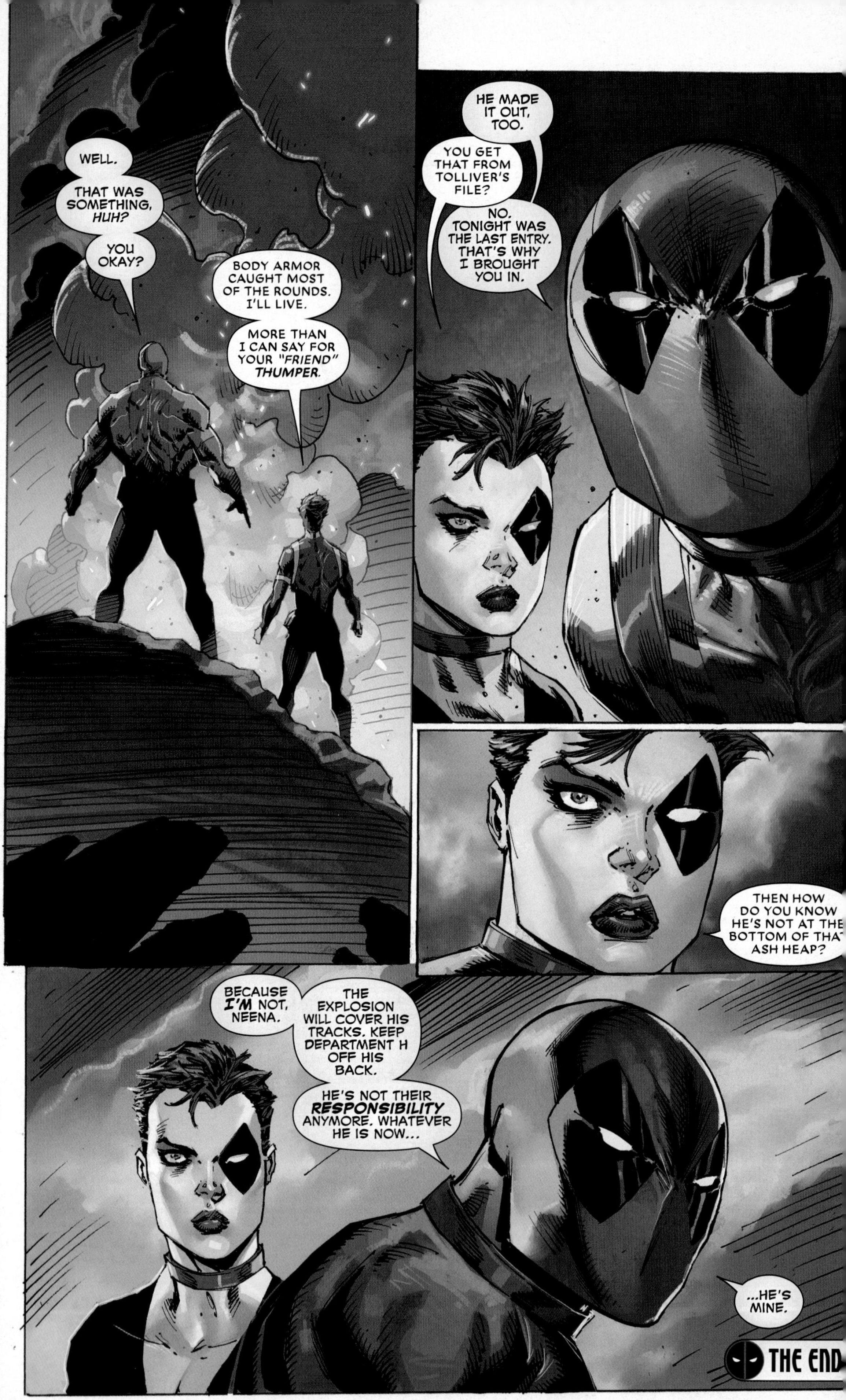

WELL.
THAT WAS SOMETHING, *HUH?*
YOU OKAY?
BODY ARMOR CAUGHT MOST OF THE ROUNDS. I'LL LIVE.
MORE THAN I CAN SAY FOR YOUR *"FRIEND"* ***THUMPER***.
HE MADE IT OUT, TOO.
YOU GET THAT FROM TOLLIVER'S FILE?
NO. TONIGHT WAS THE LAST ENTRY. THAT'S WHY I BROUGHT YOU IN.
THEN HOW DO YOU KNOW HE'S NOT AT THE BOTTOM OF THAT ASH HEAP?
BECAUSE ***I'M*** NOT, NEENA.
THE EXPLOSION WILL COVER HIS TRACKS. KEEP DEPARTMENT H OFF HIS BACK.
HE'S NOT THEIR ***RESPONSIBILITY*** ANYMORE. WHATEVER HE IS NOW...
...HE'S MINE.
THE END

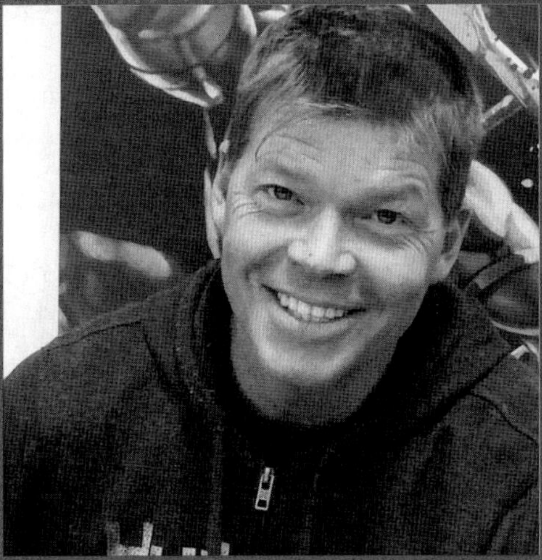

Reimagining *New Mutants* into *X-Force* was only the start for industry maverick **ROB LIEFELD**, one of the forefathers of the 1990s comics revolution. After introducing both Cable and Deadpool, he launched an even bigger collaboration as one of the founders of Image Comics with his original property *Youngblood*. In 1996, he participated in Marvel's controversial multi-title "Heroes Reborn" event. After collaborating with Alan Moore on revamped Image creations, Liefeld reunited with co-writer Fabian Nicieza on an X-Force miniseries, and then revisited "Heroes Reborn" in *Onslaught Reborn* with writer Jeph Loeb. Liefeld returned to his most famous co-creation with the graphic novel *Deadpool: Bad Blood*.

CHRIS SIMS is a writer who lives in North Carolina. With Chad Bowers, he has co-written *X-Men '92* and *Down Set Fight*, and has also written *Dracula the Unconquered* and *Radical Guardian Skater X*. His favorite color is blue.

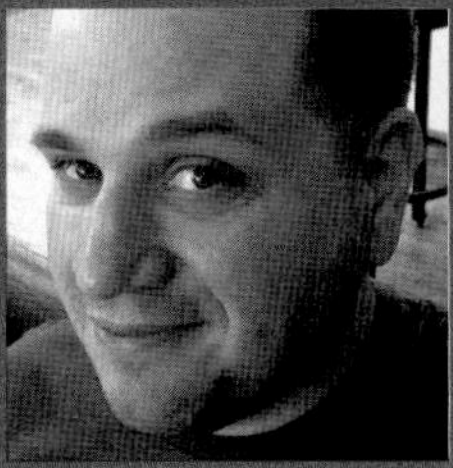

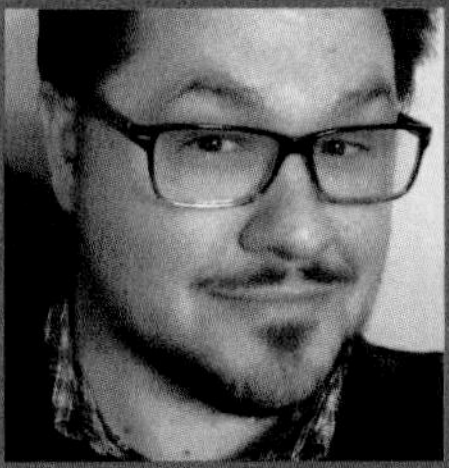

CHAD BOWERS is a comics writer from South Carolina. With Chris Sims, his credits include the fan-favorite Marvel Comics series *X-Men '92*, *Guardians of the Galaxy: Monsters Unleashed*, and *Civil War II: Choosing Sides*. He's worked for Oni Press, Dynamite Entertainment, BOOM! Studios, and currently writes *Youngblood* at Image Comics.

ROMULO FAJARDO JR. is a Filipino comic book colorist. For more than ten years he's worked for publishers like Marvel, DC Comics, Valiant and IDW, and has colored fan-favorite characters including Batman, Wonder Woman, Deadpool, X-Men, Captain America, Transformers, G.I. Joe and much more.

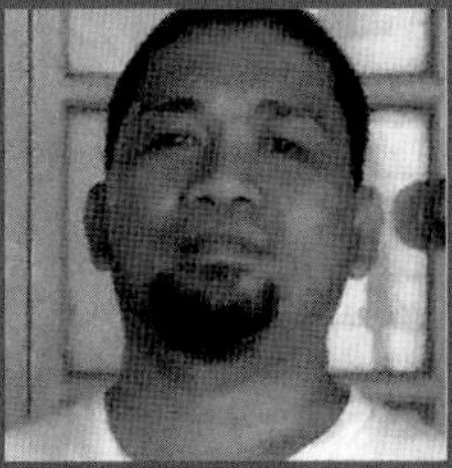

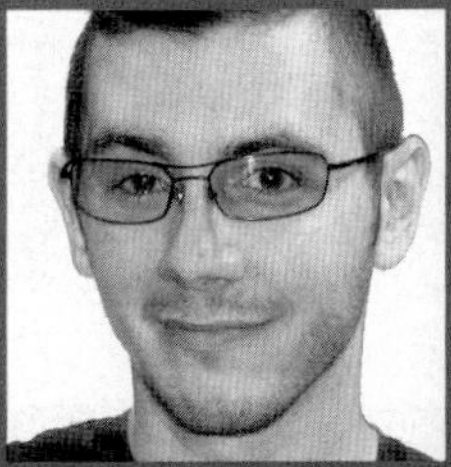

JOE SABINO started his career at Marvel by helping to launch their digital comics project straight out of college in 2007. He then shifted into the Bullpen for a year doing production and compositing on the current titles before joining VC as a letterer. He's been the letterer for *Thor*, *Deadpool*, *The Dark Tower* and many other series since then.

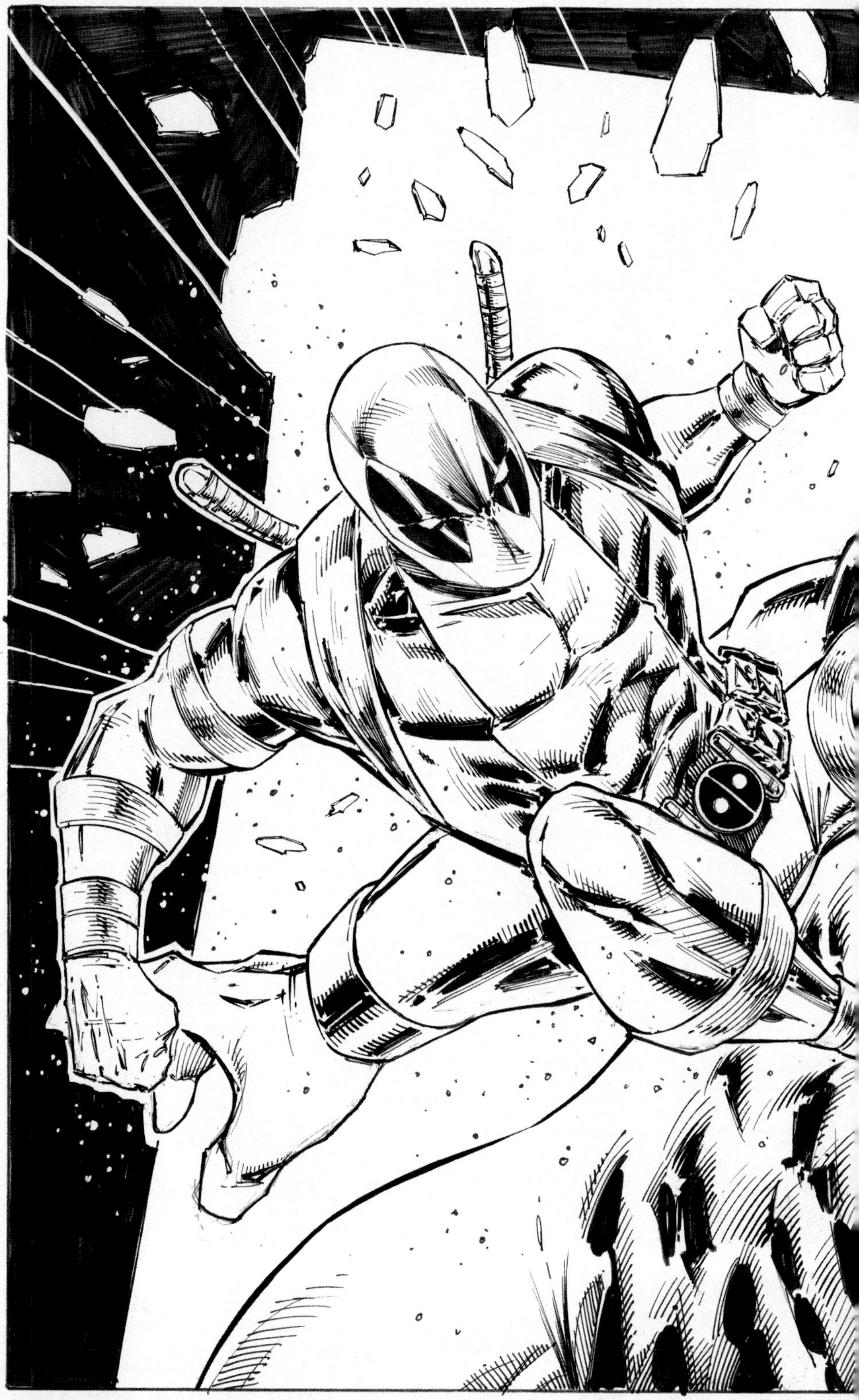

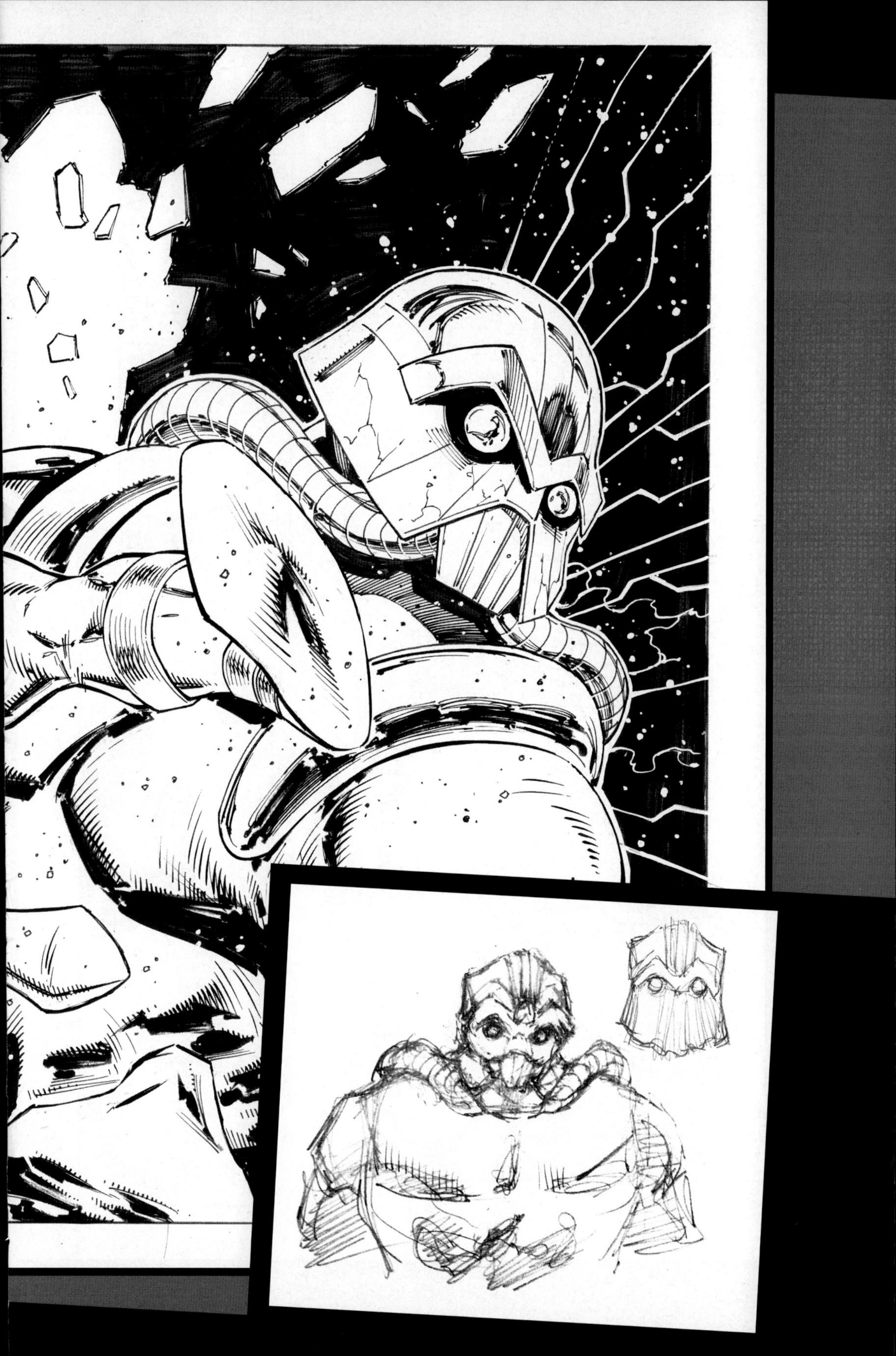

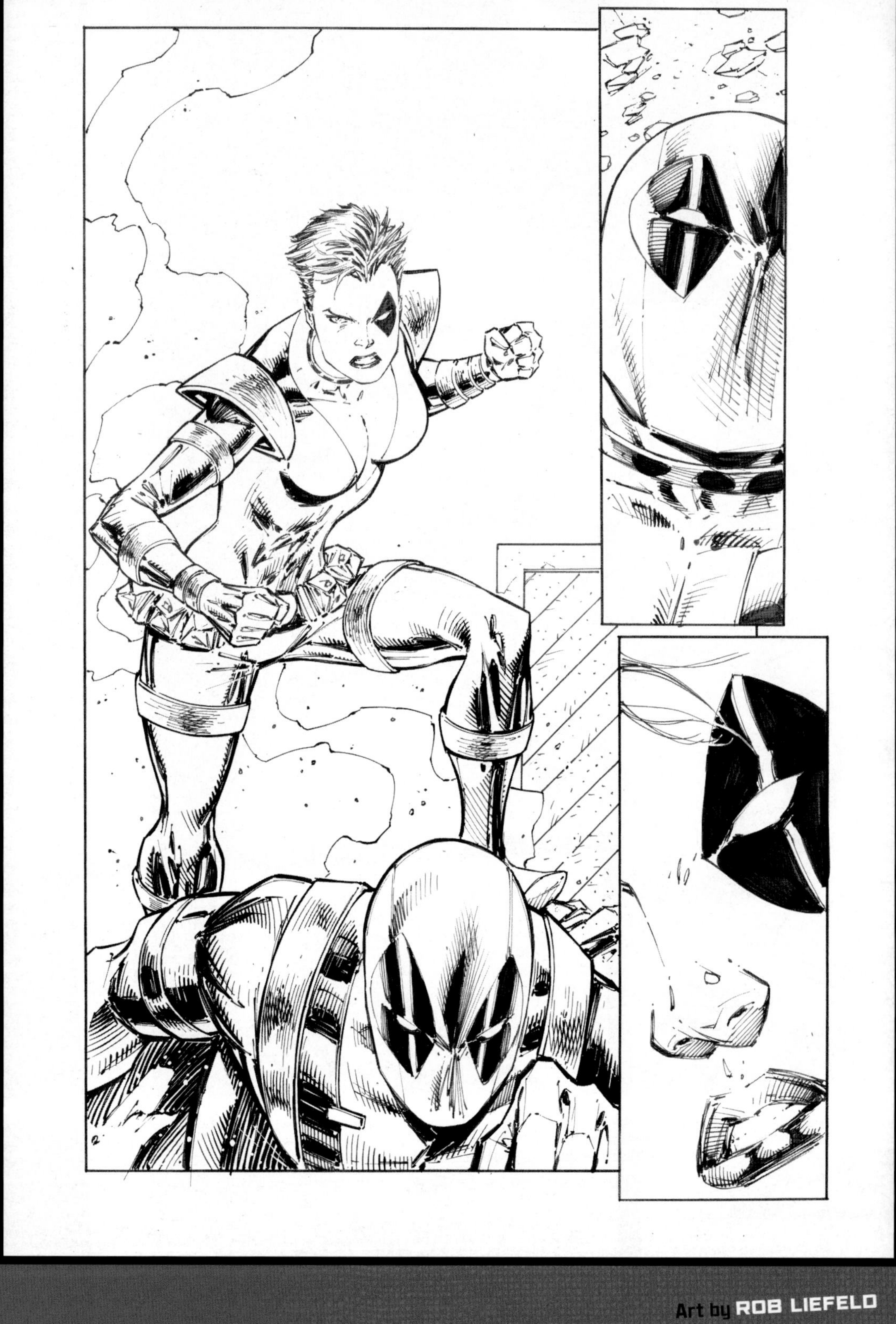

Art by **ROB LIEFELD**

WANT TO KNOW THE BEST WAY TO EXPLORE THE MARVEL UNIVERSE? THIS GUIDE WILL SHOW YOU WHERE TO BEGIN!

FOLLOW THE ADVENTURES OF

DEAD-POOL

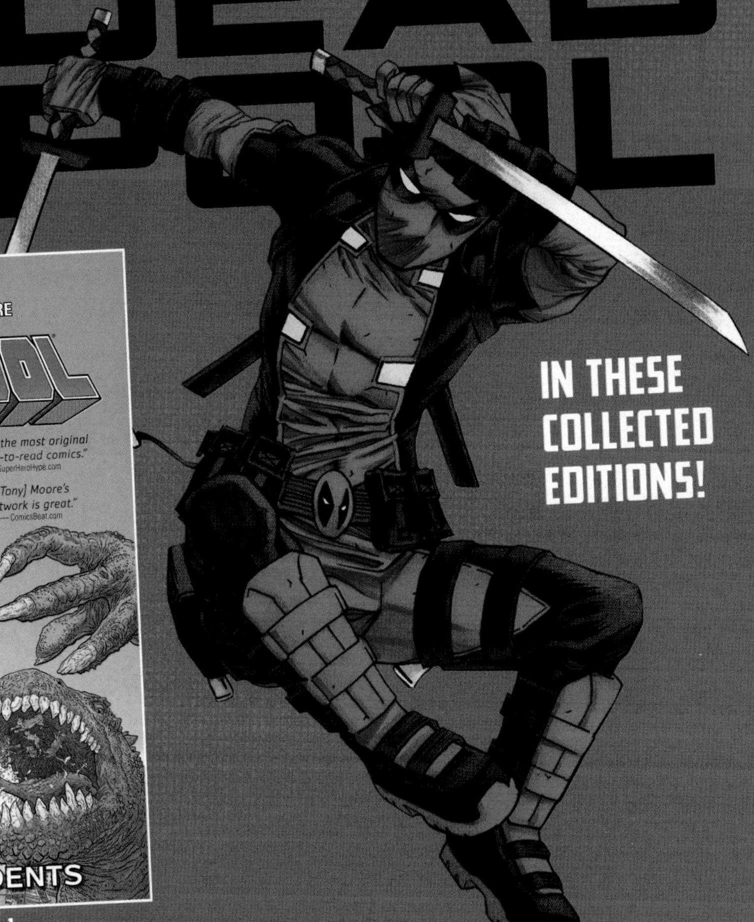

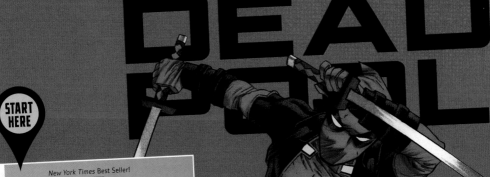

IN THESE COLLECTED EDITIONS!

START HERE

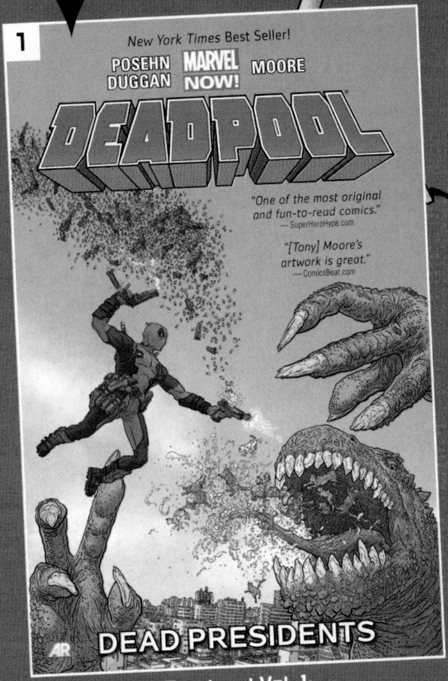
1
New York Times Best Seller!
POSEHN
DUGGAN
MARVEL NOW!
MOORE
DEADPOOL
"One of the most original and fun-to-read comics."
— SuperHeroHype.com
"[Tony] Moore's artwork is great."
— ComicsBeat.com
DEAD PRESIDENTS

Deadpool Vol. 1:
Dead Presidents

ISBN 978-0-7851-6680-1

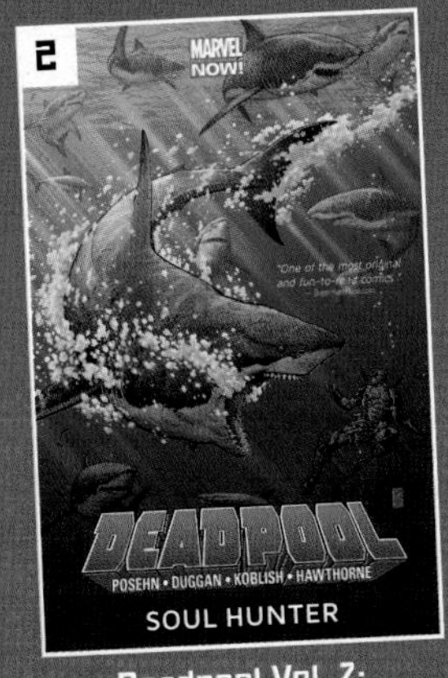
2
MARVEL NOW!
DEADPOOL
POSEHN • DUGGAN • KOBLISH • HAWTHORNE
SOUL HUNTER

Deadpool Vol. 2:
Soul Hunter

ISBN 978-0-7851-6681-8

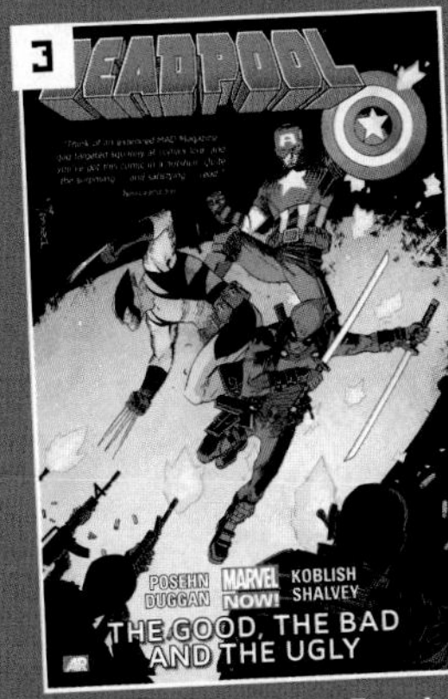
3
DEADPOOL
POSEHN
DUGGAN
MARVEL NOW!
KOBLISH
SHALVEY
THE GOOD, THE BAD AND THE UGLY

Deadpool Vol. 3: The Good, the Bad and the Ugly

ISBN 978-0-7851-6682-5

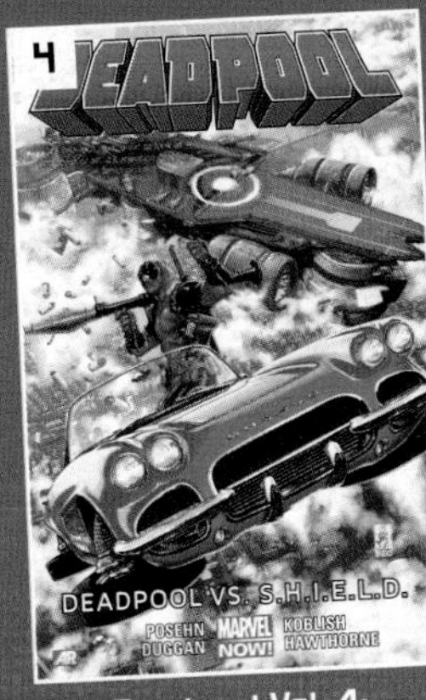
4
DEADPOOL
DEADPOOL VS. S.H.I.E.L.D.
POSEHN
DUGGAN
MARVEL NOW!
KOBLISH
HAWTHORNE

Deadpool Vol. 4:
Deadpool vs. S.H.I.E.L.D.

ISBN 978-0-7851-8932-9

CONTINUED ON NEXT PAGE ▶

CONTINUED FROM PREVIOUS PAGE

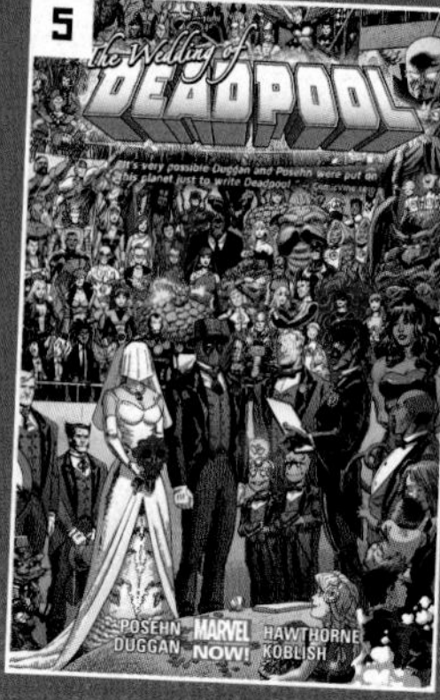
5
the Wedding of
DEADPOOL
POSEHN
DUGGAN
MARVEL NOW!
HAWTHORNE
KOBLISH

Deadpool Vol. 5:
The Wedding of Deadpool

ISBN 978-0-7851-8933-6

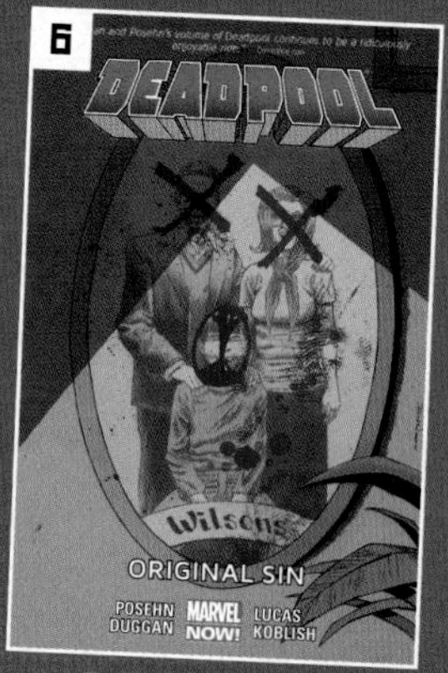
6
DEADPOOL
Wilsons
ORIGINAL SIN
POSEHN
DUGGAN
MARVEL NOW!
LUCAS
KOBLISH

Deadpool Vol. 6:
Original Sin

ISBN 978-0-7851-8934-3

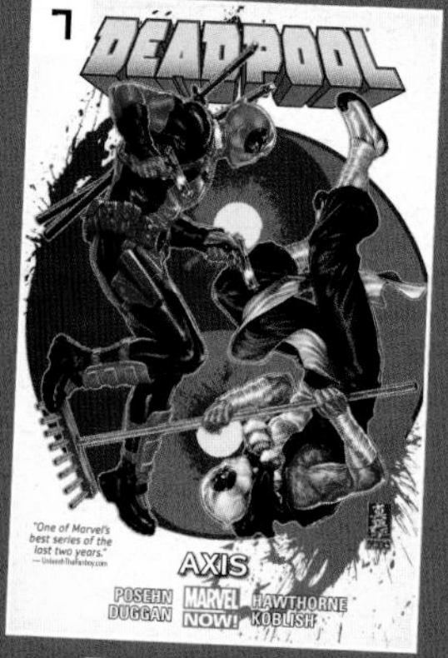
7
DEADPOOL
"One of Marvel's best series of the last two years."
AXIS
POSEHN
DUGGAN
MARVEL NOW!
HAWTHORNE
KOBLISH

Deadpool Vol. 7:
Axis

ISBN 978-0-7851-9243-5

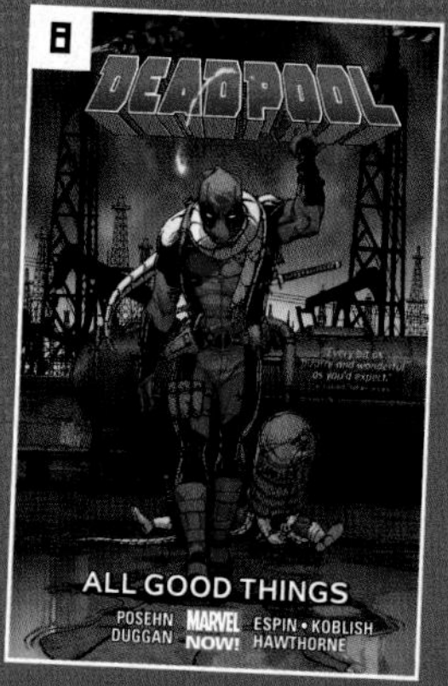
8
DEADPOOL
ALL GOOD THINGS
POSEHN
DUGGAN
MARVEL NOW!
ESPIN • KOBLISH
HAWTHORNE

Deadpool Vol. 8:
All Good Things

ISBN 978-0-7851-9244-2

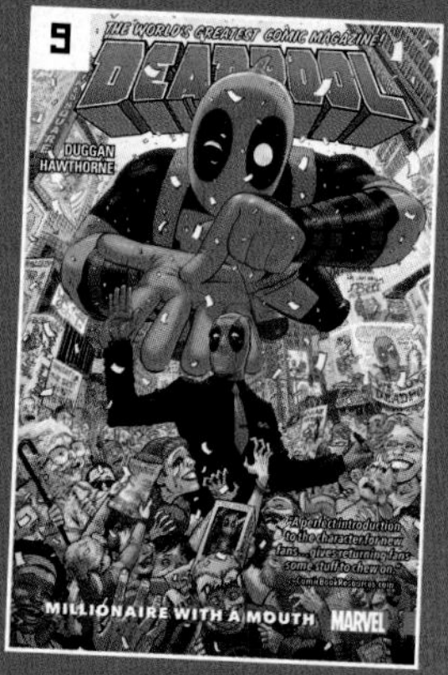
9
THE WORLD'S GREATEST COMIC MAGAZINE!
DEADPOOL
DUGGAN
HAWTHORNE
MILLIONAIRE WITH A MOUTH
MARVEL

Deadpool: World's Greatest
Vol. 1 - Millionaire with a Mouth

ISBN 978-0-7851-9617-4

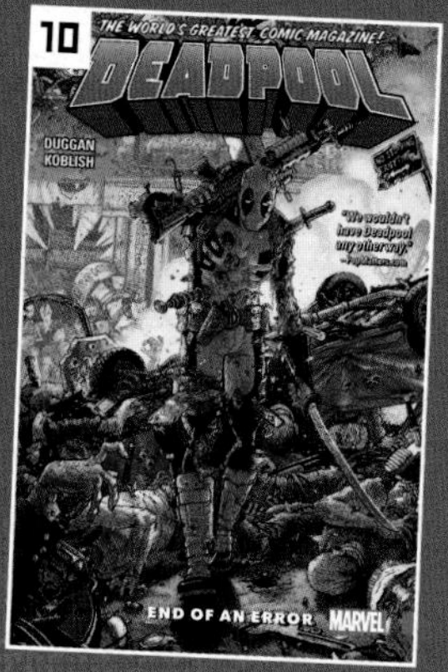
10
THE WORLD'S GREATEST COMIC MAGAZINE!
DEADPOOL
DUGGAN
KOBLISH
END OF AN ERROR
MARVEL

Deadpool: World's Greatest
Vol. 2 - End of an Error

ISBN 978-0-7851-9618-1

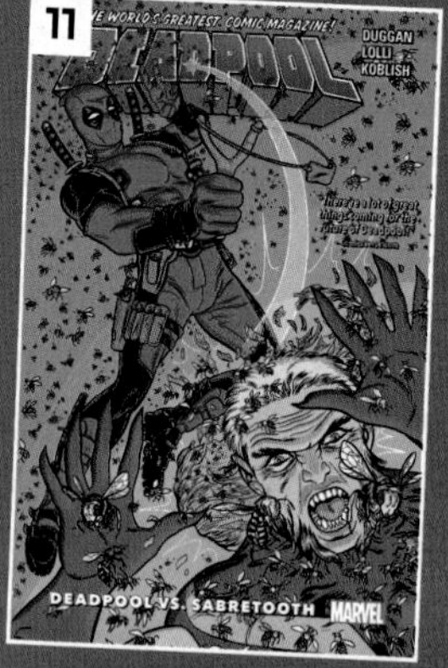
11
THE WORLD'S GREATEST COMIC MAGAZINE!
DEADPOOL
DUGGAN
LOLLI
KOBLISH
DEADPOOL VS. SABRETOOTH
MARVEL

Deadpool: World's Greatest
Vol. 3 - Deadpool Vs. Sabretooth

ISBN 978-0-7851-9619-8

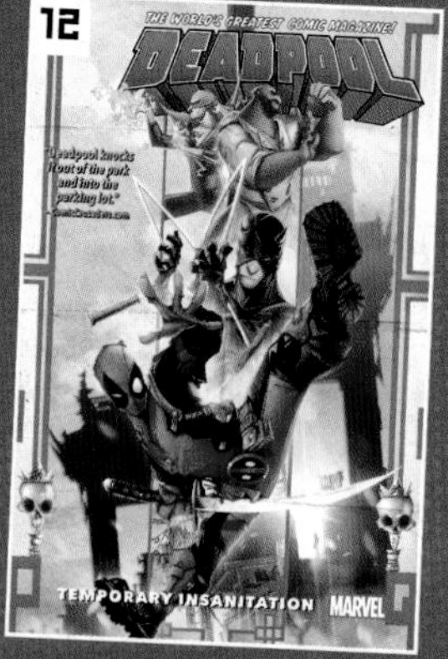
12
THE WORLD'S GREATEST COMIC MAGAZINE!
DEADPOOL
TEMPORARY INSANITATION
MARVEL

Deadpool: World's Greatest
Vol. 4 - Temporary Insanitation

ISBN 978-1-302-90091-5

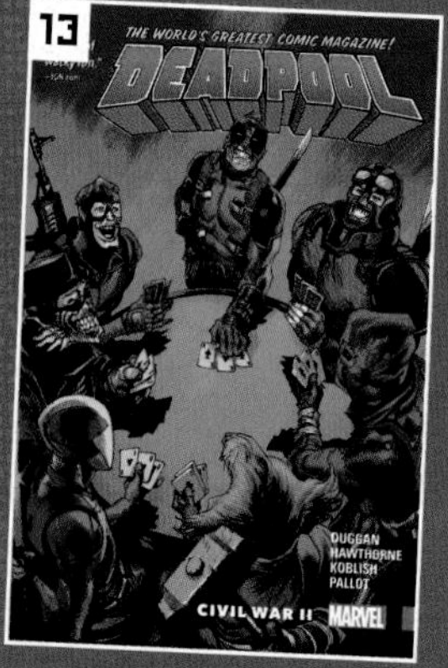
13
THE WORLD'S GREATEST COMIC MAGAZINE!
DEADPOOL
DUGGAN
HAWTHORNE
KOBLISH
PALLOT
CIVIL WAR II
MARVEL

Deadpool: World's Greatest
Vol. 5 - Civil War II

ISBN 978-1-302-90148-6

MARVEL COLLECTED EDITIONS

DEADPOOL
V GAMBIT
"Dynamic art and hilarious writing."
–ComicsVerse.com
ACKER
BLACKER
BEYRUTH
PETER
THE "V" IS FOR "VS."
MARVEL

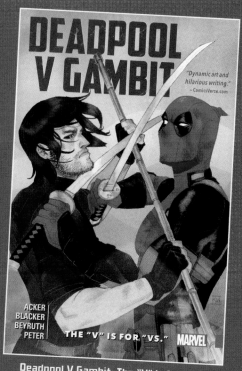

Deadpool V Gambit: The "V" is for "Vs."

ISBN 978-1-302-90179-0

MARVEL
DEADPOOL VS CARNAGE
BUNN • ESPIN • JACINTO

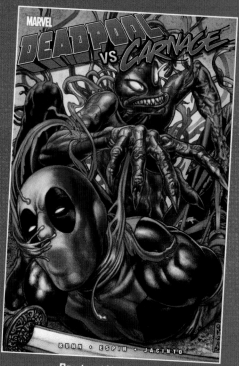

Deadpool Vs. Carnage

ISBN 978-0-7851-9015-8

DEADPOOL
VS THANOS
IT WAS A JOKE, MARVEL!
I WAS JOKING WHEN I SAID I WANTED TO FIGHT THANOS!
"SEELEY'S WRITING PERFECTLY FITS DEADPOOL'S SIGNATURE 'MERC WITH A MOUTH' STYLE."
SEELEY
MARVEL
BONDOC

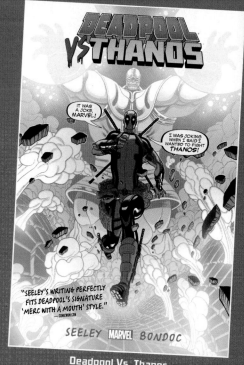

Deadpool Vs. Thanos

ISBN 978-0-7851-9703-4

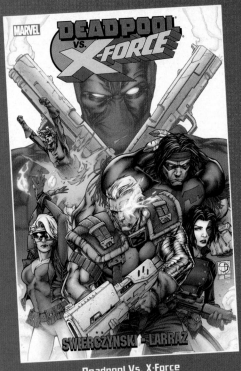

Deadpool Vs. X-Force
ISBN 978-0-7851-5437-2

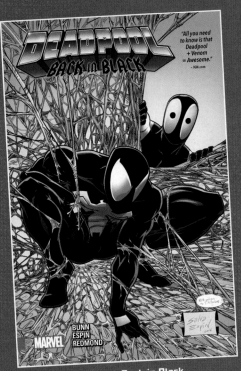

Deadpool: Back in Black
ISBN 978-1-302-90188-2

Hawkeye Vs. Deadpool
ISBN 978-0-7851-9310-4